Small Venues

Small Venues

Precarity, Vibrancy and Live Music

Sam Whiting

BLOOMSBURY ACADEMIC
NEW YORK • LONDON • OXFORD • NEW DELHI • SYDNEY

BLOOMSBURY ACADEMIC
Bloomsbury Publishing Inc
1385 Broadway, New York, NY 10018, USA
50 Bedford Square, London, WC1B 3DP, UK
29 Earlsfort Terrace, Dublin 2, Ireland

BLOOMSBURY, BLOOMSBURY ACADEMIC and the Diana logo
are trademarks of Bloomsbury Publishing Plc

First published in the United States of America 2023
This paperback edition published 2025

Copyright © Sam Whiting, 2023

For legal purposes the Acknowledgements on p. vii constitute
an extension of this copyright page.

Cover Illustration by Sianne van Abkoude

All rights reserved. No part of this publication may be reproduced or transmitted in any form or by any means, electronic or mechanical, including photocopying, recording, or any information storage or retrieval system, without prior permission in writing from the publishers.

Bloomsbury Publishing Inc does not have any control over, or responsibility for, any third-party websites referred to or in this book. All internet addresses given in this book were correct at the time of going to press. The author and publisher regret any inconvenience caused if addresses have changed or sites have ceased to exist, but can accept no responsibility for any such changes.

Whilst every effort has been made to locate copyright holders the publishers would be grateful to hear from any person(s) not here acknowledged.

Library of Congress Cataloguing-in-Publication Data
Names: Whiting, Sam (Musicologist), author.
Title: Small venues : precarity, vibrancy and live music / Sam Whiting.
Description: [1st.] | New York : Bloomsbury Academic, 2023. |
Includes bibliographical references and index. |
Summary: "Considers the social and cultural value of small live music venues"– Provided by publisher.
Identifiers: LCCN 2023002741 (print) | LCCN 2023002742 (ebook) | ISBN 9781501379888 (hardback) | ISBN 9781501379895 (paperback) | ISBN 9781501379925 (ebook) | ISBN 9781501379918 (pdf) | ISBN 9781501379901 (ebook other)
Subjects: LCSH: Popular music–Social aspects–Australia–History. | Music-halls–Australia–History. | Bars (Drinking establishments)–Australia–History. | Nightclubs–Australia–History. | Music and architecture–Australia.
Classification: LCC ML3918.P67 .W48 2023 (print) | LCC ML3918.P67 (ebook) | DDC 725/.810994–dc23/eng/20230206
LC record available at https://lccn.loc.gov/2023002741
LC ebook record available at https://lccn.loc.gov/2023002742

ISBN:	HB:	978-1-5013-7988-8
	PB:	978-1-5013-7989-5
	ePDF:	978-1-5013-7991-8
	eBook:	978-1-5013-7992-5

Typeset by Integra Software Services Pvt. Ltd.

To find out more about our authors and books visit www.bloomsbury.com
and sign up for our newsletters.

Contents

List of figures	vi
Acknowledgements	vii

Part One   Live music and small venues

Introduction	3
1 Theorizing live music: 'Scenes', 'subcultures' and the 'live music ecology'	23

Part Two   Vibrancy

2 Live music and the city	57
3 Place, space and small venues	109

Part Three   Precarity

4 Capital, value and cultural intermediaries	163
Conclusion	183
References	201
Index	225

Figures

1	The Grace Emily Hotel, Adelaide (Source: Author provided)	84
2	Format (Source: Ianto Ware)	92–93
3	Map of inner Fitzroy and Collingwood featuring the Old Bar and the Tote (Source: Jacob L'Huillier Lunt)	110
4	The Tote: downstairs floor plan featuring main band room and front bar (Source: The Tote)	126
5	The Old Bar: downstairs floor plan featuring front bar (bar servery), band room and stage (Source: The Old Bar)	127
6	The Old Bar (Source: Sianne van Abkoude)	129

Acknowledgements

This book draws on the accounts and knowledge of many live music workers and musicians who were kind enough to give up their time to share their experiences, and I would like to acknowledge those workers and artists first and foremost.

I would also like to thank the various colleagues, collaborators and mentors that contributed to the drafting of this book or helped shape it in some way, namely Ian Rogers, Catherine Strong, Shelley Brunt, Catherine Hoad, Ben Morgan, Rosie Roberts, Paige Klimentou, Adrian Franklin, Jon Stratton, Ianto Ware, Tami Gadir, Kyle Devine, Kat Nelligan, Pat O'Grady, Steve Threadgold, Caitlin McGrane, Marissa Willcox, Susan Luckman, Justin O'Connor, Will Straw and many others who reviewed drafts or provided advice along the way. Scholarly work is collective labour, and I stand on the shoulders of all my comrades inside and outside of the academy in producing this book.

Finally, I would like to thank my partner Sarah for her patience, kindness and support over a very strange and busy few years while writing this book. I'm not sure I could have done it without her.

Excerpts from Chapter 4 were originally published in 'The live gig', in G Stahl & JM Percival (eds), *The Bloomsbury Handbook of Popular Music, Space and Place*, Bloomsbury Academic, New York, pp. 241–54. Excerpts from Chapter 5 were originally published in 'The value of small live music venues: alternative forms of capital and niche spaces of cultural production', *Cultural Sociology*, vol. 15, no. 4 (2021), pp. 558–78.

Part One

Live music and small venues

Introduction

Icebreaker questions are a fraught business. They can either open up a conversation with a potential friend or alienate an entire room. Asking the right one is a delicate task, and a certain degree of intuition and insight into your audience is always helpful. As someone who has spent a lot of time socializing with people who perform and engage with popular music regularly, particularly music performed in socially charged environments such as bars, pubs and festivals, 'What was your first gig?' is a common icebreaker whenever there is a lull in conversation (although it is often asked with the concealed intention of outdoing someone). Answers range from (a) prideful, in witnessing a seminal band in their prime, to (b) embarrassment, at revealing what is now considered to be a youthful or teenage guilty pleasure, or (c) being dragged to a concert with your parents, which might have been a foundational moment in terms of bonding or a boring night out, depending on your perspective.

Perhaps a better question, and one that might reveal more, is 'What was your favourite gig?' Among popular music fans, this is often met with a serious expression and a statement of 'How can I pick just one?' However, quickly, two very different types of memories begin to be described, both specific to their settings or sense of place. Festivals or large stadium concerts are perhaps the most common 'favourite gigs' among music lovers. Strong memories might include the spectacle, the lighting, the set list, the costumes, the people they were with, the drugs they took, the set pieces, where they stayed, how they got there, the misadventures, the anticipation, the highlights, the jokes, the anecdotes, the moments shared – in short, *the event*. As multi-sensory extravaganzas of light, sound and substances, festivals and large stadium concerts leave a lasting impression on popular music lovers. Settings, both social and physical, along with weather, landscape, state of mind, performance and audience, all play a role in creating a world removed from the mundanity of everyday life. Such an escape creates a timelessness that is impossible to recreate and a liminal zone of temporal space that can only be accessed at the next rendition of 'the event', although never fully re-entered again, as such events are ephemeral and unique. They are therefore heavily informed by place, but do not necessarily contribute to place as an ongoing narrative. Memories of these types of 'events' sit in stark relief when juxtaposed against other, more 'everyday' experiences of live music.

The other common answer to the question 'What was your favourite gig?' reveals a very different live music experience. This is the local gig, the secret show, the house party, the small bar, the happy accident, the intimate performance, the 'inside word'. When describing these, people often recount the space itself, how they moved through it, its capacity, the volume of the crowd, the energy of the performance, the banter, the bump-ins, the dancing, the sweat, the booze, sometimes the blood, the atmosphere, the sensation: *the vibe*. These experiences are the everyday interactions with live music that leave a lingering feeling of connection, of contribution, of belonging.

Unlike the stadium concert, the small venue – the bricks-and-mortar spaces in which these everyday experiences of live music take place – plays an active and decided role in shaping and curating 'the vibe'. And unlike festivals, small venues play an ongoing role in the social and cultural life of music scenes, contributing to the cultural life of cities, suburbs and towns. These are spaces where musicians, music lovers and other music scene participants regularly meet not only to engage in performance and appreciation of live music but often to socialize, to share a drink, a yarn, a dance, a memory. Such small venues have often occupied a space between precarity and vibrancy, as new residential and business developments, noise restrictions, gentrification, rent spikes and other factors have made their operations increasingly tenuous. Yet, without these spaces, the complex infrastructure that local music scenes rely on for their proliferation – the 'ecosystem',[1] so to speak – would be deeply lacking.

The small venue

Throughout the history of popular music, the careers of many culturally significant artists and groups began on the small stages of local bars, clubs, pubs and discotheques. When stories of the Beatles, Jimi Hendrix, and the New York punk,

---

[1] The systems through which local music-making practices are organized have been referred to by a diversity of terms, all with their own specific definitions and histories within the scholarly study of live music. These are explored, defined and discussed further in Chapter 1, as is my use of 'ecosystem' as a relevant term here.

hardcore and post-punk scenes are told, iconic venues such as the Cavern, the Marquee and CBGB serve as the settings of their early chapters. Small live music venues such as these are pivotal in the narratives and history of popular music. They were the testing grounds, the hangouts, the place to be. However, very few of them survive. The marginal nature of niche spaces of cultural production – such as small live music venues – often oriented towards supporting a community or providing a platform for emerging artists at the expense of greater profit seeking, as well as operating as independent establishments removed from franchises that might secure their economic stability, has meant that these spaces are exposed to risk more regularly than larger, more corporate live music spaces. The problem for small live music venues then is walking the line between financial sustainability and their role as spaces of niche cultural production.

Small live music venues are essential to a vibrant live music culture. In cities around the world, small venues facilitate the sociality and grassroots culture that make local music scenes exciting hotbeds of talent and creativity. Such scenes are often flashpoints in the history of popular music, 'moments' in a time and place where several elements coalesce to give rise to an exciting new sound or cohort of artists that change the course of popular music. Scholars and historians of popular music often identify cities and eras with these moments – Manchester in the 1980s, Seattle in the 1990s, New York in the 2000s and so on – yet the small live music venues that were the sites of sociality and performance that embodied these scenes are typically relegated to footnotes in their histories, with few still operating today. Further to their significance, small live music venues are entry-level performance spaces for up-and-coming musicians, providing important opportunities for emerging bands, as well as important sites of socialization for music scene participants. These niche cultural spaces are often precarious business operations walking the line between financial viability and leading-edge creativity. Such small venues are fundamental to the sustainability of local music scenes, yet their social and cultural value has often been overlooked throughout scholarly and academic studies of these scenes. This book will focus on the triumphs and struggles of the small live music venue as a distinct phenomenon, demonstrating its significance as a space of cultural production that serves a wide range of emerging music scenes and performers while also striving to make ends meet. The book will explore this tension, as well as the other important roles small live music venues play, as incubators for emerging talent, social hubs for music scene participants, niche hospitality venues and demarcated cultural spaces that serve to both include and exclude specific communities.

The problems inherent in small venues' position as decidedly *niche* spaces, symbolically coded to align with specific scenes and therefore products of gatekeeping often limited to a community of practice, will be teased out in the following chapters. Such tensions will be explored through the lens of cultural sociology and in reference to the academic study of popular music, as well as the study of cultural spaces more broadly. Although there are already several excellent monographs exploring live music venues as cultural and social phenomena (e.g. Cohen 2007; Finnegan 2007; Holt 2020; Kronenburg 2019; Shank 1994), an in-depth scholarly discussion of small live music venues as distinct spaces of social interaction and cultural production such as this book is a novel contribution to the literature on live popular music spaces. Such venues are grassroots spaces of cultural labour and production that often struggle with issues of financial precarity yet are fundamental to the musical culture of a city or town, acting both as platforms for emerging performers and spaces of sociality for local music scenes. Small venues sit at the intersection of several fields of study, which all contribute to an understanding of their unique function. Below, I outline some of these intersections, framing small venues as a specific type of cultural space.

Small venues and popular music

The history of popular music is strongly associated with the history of small venues. As the amalgamation of a diverse range of genres and musical traditions specific to cultural, ethnic, migrant and working-class groups, what we today refer to as 'popular music' had its beginnings in small live music venues. For example, in his excellent architectural history of popular music performance venues, Robert Kronenburg notes:

> The story of vaudeville [in the United States] is primarily one of influence from Europe via Music Hall and variety; however, the story of honky-tonks and juke joints is clearly the reverse, for in the years before and after the First World War, it was in these small, informal, sometimes barely legal venues that the principal strands of global popular music performance would be forged – blues, country, jazz, and rock 'n' roll.
>
> (2019, pp. 37–8)

Also, before these brassed-up (and later amped-up) proto popular music genres hit the stage, folk and other acoustic forms of music required the intimacy of small spaces for purposes of magnification and volume.

Prior to the invention of electronic sound reproduction technologies, such as microphones, speakers and other amplification devices, the physical space of small venues played a significant role in allowing musicians to be heard over the din of a rowdy audience or a dance floor. Certain instruments were designed to cut through the noise of the crowd, but others struggled to be heard, and the placement of instruments in a room, or more importantly the room's size and volume, were fundamental to the mix. A result of this sonic dilemma was that many stages and performance spaces in smaller venues were placed in a corner or at the end of a long room, so that the sound could be projected out. Although this issue of projecting acoustic music is no longer such a problem, the precedent of placing the stage in a corner or at the short-end of a long room continues. Indeed, many small venues are still designed as long rectangles or oblongs with low ceilings featuring the stage at one end, replicating early popular music performance spaces. Such design features inherently influence the vibe of small venues, emphasizing qualities of intimacy and sociality.

In discussions of how small venues influence what is specific to the diverse genres of popular music, we must consider that popular music often begins as niche or emerging and as strongly associated with youth, class and local music traditions (Bennett 2001). In the modern era, different forms and genres of popular music may become mainstream very quickly, moving to bigger and brighter stages within a matter of months. However, many forms of popular music are nurtured within small venues before they conquer the stadiums of the world. Indeed, even those artists or popular music forms that seem to take the world by storm overnight have often been working at their craft under a different guise or moniker in front of local audiences in the intimate settings of a city or town's small venues for months or often years before their meteoric rise.

Further, popular music has long been defined in terms of a perceived cultural hierarchy and is historically determined in said hierarchy as being beneath 'high' culture (i.e. art music). However, this distinction has been considerably undermined over the last twenty to thirty years (Middleton 1990; Middleton & Manuel 2010; Regev 2013; Shuker 2013, 2022), with scholars turning their attention towards the way in which audiences engage with and define experiences of popular music (Brabazon 2011, p. 2). In addition to these definitions, I define popular music not only in terms of its audience but also regarding the spaces in which it is performed. These spaces are familiar and welcoming for those that regularly attend and are also broadly lacking in a sense of formality. They are not only performance spaces but meeting places, built for socialization, celebration and the forming of identities, both individual and collective. Popular music, in this sense, is not chamber, theatre or concert music, nor is it the sound art of contemporary galleries. It is the musical practices that take place in more informal, casual and ordinary settings, such as the local pub, club or bar.

Small venues and place making

Small venues are specific to and informed by the places in which they are embedded. As spaces that have often been adapted from previous uses, small venues are heavily informed by their built environment. This can be seen in the character of the spaces themselves, often haphazard or otherwise subject to ongoing processes of 'making do' in less-than-ideal circumstances. These processes can be invisible, that is, negotiating with landlords, neighbours and other co-located businesses to secure and re-secure tenure, a process influenced by place-based factors such as rent, overheads, gentrification and the interdependence and 'competitive-collaboration' specific to highly networked and densely tenanted cultural hubs (O'Connor 2007). However, it is often more blatantly visible, as many small venues are engaged in a constant process of renovation, maintenance and upkeep, regardless of whether they are newly built. Such venues might be in a fluctuating state of 'finding what works' or housed in older buildings that are either reluctantly or purposefully kept in a state of 'falling down, breaking down, falling apart' (venue manager, fieldwork interview, 2015) as a deliberate point of aesthetic distinction.

Place-based factors also influence the social and cultural content of these spaces, their role in the neighbourhoods, streets, cities and towns in which they are housed. As bricks-and-mortar spaces that 'do not just exist in people's minds' (Behr et al. 2016b, p. 19), small venues are strongly influenced by spatial, social, liminal and time-of-day sensitivities that are interdependent and shape their perceived identities (Gibson et al. 2017, pp. 40–2). A basement inner-city rock and roll venue such as Cherry Bar in the CBD of Melbourne, Australia, might trade heavily on its grungy, dark and dingy dive-bar aesthetic, but it also benefits from the after-work crowd of corporate lawyers filing in from the adjacent skyscrapers (such as 101 Collins Street), looking for somewhere edgy to get a cheap pint. In contrast, the dedicated performance spaces (i.e. band rooms) of venues like Howler in the northern

Melbourne suburb of Brunswick may frequently host some of the hippest emerging musical acts, specifically catering to scenesters living nearby, but its open-air front bar/beer garden attracts a diverse crowd of young people from every corner of greater Melbourne's vast suburban sprawl. Such sociospatial factors contribute nuance to the identities of small venue spaces, complicating the narratives of these spaces to make them distinct from what they and their curators claim them to be.

Although many small venues are purpose built, many are housed in adapted or adopted spaces (Kronenburg 2011, 2013) often originally designed for socializing as a priority, among other previous uses. These might include old public houses (i.e. pubs), restaurants, community halls, cafes, pool halls and other spaces built for gathering, celebration or the sharing of food, drink and entertainment. Sociality is often then already established as a historical precedent in these spaces by measure of their prior use and physical layout. However, through their curation and commitment to various music scenes (explored further in Chapters 3 and 4), small venues remake these spaces as new and ongoing spaces of sociality specific to live music cultures, which are themselves subject to change.

To adequately understand the importance of small live music venues, the intersection between ideas of place, memory and belonging must be considered. This adds to an appreciation of the nuances of venue spaces, the sociality and materiality of which are fundamental to their status in music scenes and the live music ecosystem:

> The pub as a local live music venue is therefore much more than merely an undervalued site of creativity – it is a central place in life histories, a place of emotional investment, transition, and transient community, of coming of age.
> (Gallan & Gibson 2013, p. 176)

This notion positions small live music venues in a broader cultural narrative of belonging and social cohesion.

Small venues and sociality

Small venues are meeting places for music scene participants, as well as other cultural workers. They are points of connection, of intersection and interaction. Other music industries–adjacent spaces such as bars, nightclubs, rehearsal rooms, recording studios, record stores, conservatories, universities and the broader night-time economy also serve as spaces of sociality, as do the share houses, the house parties, the squats. What makes small venues distinct as spaces of sociality is their role as dedicated spaces for the simultaneous production and consumption of live music within an intimate, familiar and everyday setting.

However, viewing small venues as social hubs implies notions of both inclusion and exclusion. Participants who are more socially entrenched in these spaces reap the benefits of participation, as the scene tends to favour those with a distinct habitus.[2] Although this is problematic, it is not to say that these venues are not tolerant, inclusive spaces, but more that a niche sense of habitus facilitates access more readily to those that are ensconced in the scene and its social field/space (Butler 1999). Such limitations and tensions will be explored further in Chapters 3 and 4.

The nexus between a small venue's dual roles of encouraging social interaction and facilitating emerging musical activity means that the experiences that take place in these spaces are vital to a city's greater cultural life. In determining the social and cultural value of small live music venues it has been demonstrated that these venues serve as the grassroots foundation of a city's live music ecosystem or 'ecology' (Behr et al. 2016b). Indeed, the social interactions that occur in small live music venues are integral to the live music culture of a city, as it is within and between these interactions that local music scenes are articulated, acting as the bedrock upon which a broader live music ecosystem is built.[3] These interactions need material environments in which to occur and be articulated, something that the concept of scene does not fully account for, and which studies of music scenes have previously not considered at length. Further, small venues allow for the intimacy of social experience that local music scenes require to thrive, and therefore serve as ideal case studies for studying intersections between music scenes and the live music ecosystem. Without these spaces, local music scenes would not be able to flourish, as larger venues only host acts that are already established. Further, larger concert venues do not allow for the same kinds of

---

[2] 'Habitus' is a broad term that encompasses the dispositions and experiences that make up an individual's understanding of the world and their place in it. Habitus is defined as that which generates the horizons of personal expectations that guide what feels 'natural' to some and alienating to others (Kahn-Harris 2007, pp. 70–3): the 'schemata or structures of perception, conception and action' (Bourdieu 2002, p. 27). See Chapters 3 and 4 for further discussion.
[3] Such an ecosystem can be defined as the combination of material infrastructures, policy settings, built environment and disparate yet independent social actors (and their multiple 'agencies') that facilitate and contribute to a city or town's live music culture. See Chapter 1 for further discussion.

intimate sociality that small live music venues afford (Holt 2014, p. 24). It is for these reasons that small venues are important staging grounds for emerging talent and the scenes that nurture them.

Small venues, emerging talent and cultural production

The role of small venues as spaces for the ongoing production of 'culture'[4] – emerging, niche, underground, up and coming – often places them both at the cutting edge of new global trends in popular music and in the service of local musical communities whose participants have, may or will never be aspirational in their musical careers. As niche spaces of cultural production, small venues play host to the rising stars, but also the hobbyists, the amateurs, the 'life-stylers'. Many of these hobbyists are interested mainly in the social and cultural nourishment they receive from engaging with local music scenes and communities (Rogers 2008), rather than long-term careers in the music industries. However, the melting pot of styles, the commitment to new musical futures and the willingness to provide emerging acts with a platform position small venues as some of the only spaces in which new and aspirant acts can cut their teeth. They are therefore also training grounds for individual musicians who may not have found their calling yet but are in the process of establishing themselves as contenders, as well as bands navigating the early stages of their careers with aspirations for bigger stages. This is an important and distinct function of small venues, as few other performance spaces take the same kinds of risks on new and emerging musical acts that small venues do.

The groundwork of establishing a career in the music industries is often carried out in small venue spaces. This involves not only winning over audiences with engaging, entertaining or interesting performances but the socializing and networking that happens before and after the show. Like many of the creative industries, careers in the music industries are built on informal connections and intangible resources. Social capital supports and invigorates interaction between participants, and the role of 'alternative forms of capital' (Scott 2012) will be discussed further in Chapter 4.

---

[4] I refer here to Raymond Williams' iconic three definitions of culture, specifically his third – 'independent and abstract noun which describes the works and practices of intellectual and especially artistic activity' (1976, p. 90) – although all three are relevant to the types of culture produced and facilitated within small live music venues.

As an industry that relies heavily on face-to-face networking and personal relationships (Crewe & Beaverstock 1998), the music industries are driven by individuals whose social currency is significant and to whom social capital is extremely important. The informal nature of the music industries 'blurs the business–social divide' (Watson 2008, p. 18), giving social and business relationships a similar standing. This is relevant in the context of local music scenes and the early stages of musical careers – where financial gain is relatively limited – and is also consistent with the experience of cultural and creative industries workers in general, as the long hours spent socializing with others and the overlap between work and play generates a strong and affective community (Pratt 2000, p. 431), wherein social capital plays a dominant role.

The exchanges and interactions that make up a music scene are demonstrations of social capital at work, and the role of small venues in facilitating these exchanges and interactions is key. They facilitate personal encounters between strangers, encouraging socializing and informal networking more readily than larger venues due to their intimate setting and lack of anonymity (Holt 2014, p. 24). Small venues are therefore not only launching pads for emerging musical acts to use as platforms towards greater opportunities but are also social spaces wherein the initial discussions and sharing of interests that are foundational to the formation of bands and strengthening of creative bonds occur.

Small venue spaces accommodate local music scenes – made up of scene participants (musicians, hospitality staff, cultural workers, audience members and more) – providing these scenes with social space and the means to articulate themselves as collective forms of identity. The sense of belonging, familiarity and consistency found in small live music venues are what makes them beloved spaces of community practice, but also explains why they are attractive to emerging musicians and scene participants looking for a place to call their own. Their value as social hubs for music scenes and as niche spaces of cultural production – important 'stepping-stone' performance sites for budding musicians – contributes to the crucial and essential role that small live music venues perform as the grassroots foundation of a city's live music ecosystem.

Small venues and financial precarity

As capitalist ventures, small venues make for curious case studies. Not all are run for profit, and many are community-managed spaces, either staffed by volunteers or managed as not-for-profits (often with charitable goals, albeit not always successful ones[5]). Others, such as many of those in continental Europe, are owned and managed by the state (either federal, local or municipal governments).[6] However, small venues in the Anglosphere of the UK, Canada, Australia, the United States and New Zealand are commonly run as for-profit small businesses, and it is within these spaces that an interesting tension lies between the pursuit of capital and the role of small venues as niche spaces of cultural production and sociality.

In prioritizing presenting a platform for emerging and not-yet-established local and touring acts, as well as providing performance spaces for cutting-edge (often avant-garde), but also conventional and niche musical forms, small venues are inherently limited in their ability to appeal to the cultural mainstream. Although many small venues counter this limitation through considered curation of the space to appeal to a dedicated and loyal local audience, as well as the consistent hosting of popular acts capable of attracting sizeable audiences, the physical capacity and niche nature of these spaces means that these approaches can only achieve so much. Further, many small venue owners and booking agents are resistant to appealing directly to the cultural mainstream, as a sense of exclusivity and hipness is often what gives these spaces their distinct charm. Indeed, gatekeeping is core business for some small live music venues (Gallan 2012), as efforts to make these spaces accessible to all – including dominant or hegemonic cultural forms, but also marginalized communities[7] – would tarnish their brand as niche spaces specific to emerging, local, underground or experimental musical practices. Such gatekeeping might not be an issue if small venues were not also beholden to substantial overheads, wage costs, taxation and rent. However, to cover these costs of production while maintaining their niche appeal, small venues must walk a fine line between the pursuit of capital and the pursuit of culture.

This tension between remaining financially viable and playing host to new musical cultures and the risks associated with such cultures is what positions small venues as distinct from other ventures within the live music industry. Certainly, throughout the broader cultural economy we can find similar examples of risk specific to entry-level cultural spaces, such as new theatre and

---

[5] Shebeen was a prominent small live music venue in inner-city Melbourne that operated as a not-for-profit committed to donating 100 per cent of its profits to social enterprises and other charitable causes. However, when the venue's closure was announced, it was also disclosed that very little profit had been made and therefore passed on to these causes (Dow 2016; Moskovitch 2016; Rychter 2016).

[6] Many French venues are supported by public authorities. These are known as *Scenes de Musiques Actuelles* (Popular Music Stages) and are dedicated to concert promotion and hosting local acts (Guibert 2011).

[7] A significant side effect of many small venues' efforts to maintain a niche appeal is that they often end up excluding marginalized communities and other cultural identities.

dance companies, start-up game studios and other design studios, and even independent record labels. However, the context for each of these case studies is substantially different. For example, local theatre and dance companies often have established connections with state and community patronage that serve as a historical precedent (Poon & Lai 2008). Start-ups are more coldly subjected to the rules of the market and are also driven by high-risk/high-reward venture capital, paradoxically rendering them often more risk-averse than the average small live music venue, as small venues are low reward and therefore regarded as lower stakes. Finally, the remaining independent record labels that are not subsidiaries of major labels or have otherwise been swallowed by larger companies are often run as either hobbies or break-even enterprises (Galuszka & Wyrzykowska 2016, 2018; Kaitajärvi-Tiekso 2018). Further, due to their fixed physical nature as bricks-and-mortar spaces, small venues do not have access to the same economies of scale and international markets that independent record labels do via the internet, online distribution and international shipping channels. However, a comparison between independent record labels and small live music venues is still the most consistent and relevant, as both appeal to a niche audience while attempting to turn a profit. It is this tension between facilitating distinct modes of cultural production not necessarily amenable to a large consumer base or strong returns while remaining financially viable that makes small live music venues a particularly fascinating area of research. Much of this tension is a result of the historical precedent set by 'popular music' and its impact on the venues dedicated to its performance.

Popular music has been viewed as a largely market-driven venture from its inception and therefore has not been provided with the same level of access to state or community support that other cultural forms have enjoyed. Although many European and particularly non-Anglophone countries have a history of state support for popular music and the venues that house it (Guibert 2011; Street 1993), it has only been since the COVID-19 pandemic that significant and direct monetary assistance has been made available to the popular music industries at scale and across countries that previously resisted such interventions. In Australia, for example, the JobKeeper wage and salary subsidy scheme deployed by the federal government to offset potential mass unemployment meant that many small venues and other music industries firms received direct government support for the first time. Such direct support raises new questions and discussions for how the popular music industries – industries usually ineligible for substantial government funding and investment – might be able to access further support in the future. However, until such questions are answered, small live music venues will continue to serve as ideal case studies through which to explore issues of culture versus commerce.

Small venues and the cultural economy

The 'cultural economy', as the melange of economic activity concerned with cultural production and activities (Pratt 2009), intersects with small live music venues at a variety of points and vectors. So too does the notion of 'cultural' economy: the cultural and/or social dimensions of economic activity. These may include the marketing of a product, service or event, or the networks of tangible and intangible labour and capital that are drawn towards the organization of cultural production.

There are multiple ways that small venues contribute to the 'cultural economy' or 'cultural' economy. These may include:

1. Live music as an 'event', which employs the labour of multiple actors, both onstage and off. These include the artist's promoter, booker or manager; the venue booking agent; publicists, both for the musicians, the venue or just the event; sound engineers, both side of stage and front of house; musicians, of course; audience members; bar staff; venue management; door staff; and a variety of other technicians and management who are either peripherally or directly involved with the facilitation of the 'live music event'. This event is usually either ticketed (or subsidized in another way) to generate capital that is redistributed to relevant parties. Other capital is also generated by bar and merchandise sales, and certain firms and actors engaged in facilitating the live music event benefit from these transactions to varying degrees.
2. Second, there is the refinement and reproduction of intellectual property (IP), but also often the real-time *production* of IP. This is the musical performance itself; more specifically the music being performed, which is intertwined with the 'live music event' but explicitly concerned with its musical content. In most small live music venues, popular music or other contemporary forms of music are reproduced in a way that mirrors or reflects their previously rehearsed or recorded forms, but never exactly. This is the reproduction of intellectual property, and this reproduction often leads to the refinement of the song, the performance or the musical idea over time. However, many improvisatory musical forms, such as jazz, are concerned

with the real-time production of new work (and thus, new 'intellectual property') as an ephemeral performance specific to the live music event. Providing a stage and a venue for the interrelationship between the live music 'event', the reproduction of previously composed or recorded musical work, and the real-time production of creative work as raw labour is another contribution that small live music venues make to the cultural economy.

3. Third, beyond what happens in the venue on the night and the labour and capital that must align for this to occur, a kaleidoscope of other forms of cultural production beyond musical activity is involved. These include graphic design work for promotional material such as banner ads, posters and flyers, the coordination of this material, press and other media designed to publicize the event (radio advertisements, interviews, social media advertising etc.), street signage and other visual material relevant to the venue itself (e.g. chalkboards, multimedia displays), and the design and production of merchandise to be sold in association with the performance (T-shirts, records, CDs, stickers, other clothing and accessories), which may be sold at the performance or bundled with the initial ticket purchase. This cultural production is the result of skilled labour that encompasses many corners of the modern cultural and creative industries and alludes to an ecosystem of creative labour and production that aligns with the live music industries, but also takes in a variety of disparate and varied sectors.

4. Finally, there are various 'alternative forms of capital' (Scott 2012; Whiting 2021), of which cultural capital is a primary example and one that is specific to small venues, as explored further in Chapter 4. Such non-material value forms (e.g. social and cultural capital) are fundamental to the transactions and exchanges that small live music venues engage in as a sort of 'core business' beyond business.

Outline of this book

The aim of this book is to make salient the kinds of cultural work that small live music venues do and the forms of sociality that they encourage. Further, beyond its unique focus on small live music venues, this book proposes two major theoretical interventions. These are:

1. An alignment between the well-researched concept of music 'scenes' (Bennett & Rogers 2016b; Rogers 2008; Straw 1991, 2001) and the more recently established concept of a 'live music ecology' (Behr, Brennan & Cloonan 2014; Behr et al. 2016b). Although distinct, these two concepts overlap in significant ways to uncover a deeper understanding of how the live music sector functions. Small live music venues serve as ideal case studies to study this intersection as demonstrated throughout the book, and Chapter 1 focuses on this specifically.
2. A discussion of the relevance and significance of alternative forms of capital – cultural, social, symbolic etc. (Bourdieu 1984, 1986, 1997, 2002) – within small venue spaces and across the live music sector, a sector that is often defined by informality and power structures that stem from casual social arrangements and embodied forms of status (Hesmondhalgh 2006; Thornton 1996; Threadgold 2015; Threadgold & Nilan 2009). This is explored throughout the book, although Chapter 4 is dedicated to a discussion of capital, value and cultural intermediaries.

Beyond these two theoretical interventions, this book considers small live music venues in general, gauging their value as sites of social exchange and the generation of multiple forms of labour, capital and value. This book builds on the literature on music scenes and draws on ethnographies of small live music venues to demonstrate the substantial impact small venues have on local music scenes and live music ecosystems, their greater social and cultural value, and their significance as spaces of cultural production and labour. This is particularly timely considering the stress that the live music sector has been placed under during the COVID-19 pandemic, the confidence in the sector that will be required to revive it and ongoing concerns such as the pressing climate emergency, its growing impact on policy and the highly itinerant and increasingly unstable globally networked live performance industry.

This introduction has provided an overview of the topic of small venues and live music, outlining the significance of this research. It defined small live music venues as niche spaces of cultural production and discussed their position in the history of popular music as valuable sites of place making, sociality and incubators for emerging talent. Here, small live music venues are contextualized as significant case studies symbolic of the precarious nature of the cultural sector at large. This introduction has framed the project within the broader context of live music research, mapping out the reasoning behind and rationale for this book. It emphasized the significance of this research amidst discussions concerning the value of the creative and cultural industries. Here I will also outline the three parts of this book – Part One: 'Live Music and Small Venues', Part Two: 'Vibrancy', and Part Three: 'Precarity' – and provide a summary of their individual chapters below.

Chapter 1 contains an overview of current and previous writing on music scenes, subcultures and the live music ecology (defined herein as the 'live music ecosystem'), and their relevance as descriptors of socio-musical practice. It serves as a review of the history, usage and definitions of various descriptors of socio-musical practice, offering a critique of each. Chapter 1 marries the concepts of 'scene' and the 'live music ecology', and rejects 'subculture' as a descriptor of modern cultural consumption and music-making practices. This is an important theoretical distinction in the context of small live music venues, as it opens discussion regarding small venues as points of convergence between informal, fluid and 'horizontal' forms of sociality (such as music scenes) and more concrete, rigid and 'vertical' power structures (i.e. live music ecosystems). This distinction will also better serve to distinguish small venues as niche spaces of cultural production and illustrate the cultural work that they do alongside the sociality they facilitate, demonstrated through historical case studies and recent ethnographic research in *Part Two: Vibrancy* (Chapters 2 and 3).

Chapter 2 discusses the significance of several prominent 'music cities', and their live music scenes, including examples both historic and contemporary, well-known and typical, with a focus on the small venues that have facilitated these scenes. The first half of the chapter provides an overview of the concept of the 'music city' and its prominence within policy and planning discourse, including a critique of the manner in which the concept has been applied as an urban-regeneration strategy similar to that of the 'creative city'. This discussion and critique provide context and background to the role of small venues within modern cities, and the ways in which they have been both leveraged and ignored within urban development discourses. It will also provide an Australian context, setting up the chapter's two case study cities.

The second half of Chapter 2 comprises two sections that each focus on the small venues of regionally distinct contemporary Australian cities, comparing their local music scenes, policy settings and social, cultural and economic specificities, and discussing their translocal connections. Drawing on ethnography and recent research, each section focuses on the typicality of the small venues of these cities and the relations between them as they occupy different strata within each city's live music ecosystem. These sections focus on the small venues and live music ecosystems of (a) Brisbane, Australia, and (b) Adelaide, Australia. A brief discussion of the role of small venues in regional, rural and remote settings follows. Using commonplace examples, Chapter 2 highlights the significance of small live music venues within the context of cities and emphasizes their role as spaces of cultural production and sociality for music scenes, offering a 're-imagining' of the music city upon its conclusion.

Drawing on in-depth ethnographies of two case study venues in Melbourne, Australia, Chapter 3 will discuss the role of small venues as social hubs for music scenes, and as the foundation of a broader network of spaces within the city. Small venues are ideal case studies for a demonstration of how music scenes and the live music ecosystem intersect. Using this theoretical framework and centring on data gained from fieldwork interviews with active scene participants, I make an argument for small venues as niche spaces of cultural production; important spaces without which both music scenes and live music ecosystems would collapse, or at least cease to function in recognizable terms.

Melbourne is renowned internationally as a particularly vibrant 'music city', and its small venues serve as ideal case studies for this kind of research. However, although the ethnographic research that informs this project is specific to Melbourne, my findings and theoretical interventions are relevant internationally. Chapter 3 therefore has wider implications for small venues and live music beyond the local context of Melbourne, Australia, demonstrating the social and cultural value(s) of small venues generally. Chapter 3 makes an argument for the intimacy of small live music venues, not only as spaces for emerging performers to engage with audiences but also as hotbeds of social interaction that contribute to the formation of music scenes and the foundation of a broader ecosystem. This value chain is grounded in the social interactions and chance encounters found in niche spaces of cultural production, such as small venues.

Chapter 4 will discuss how various cultural intermediaries, such as venue booking agents, mobilize alternative forms of capital (social, cultural, symbolic etc.) and exchange these for revenue. This is significant, as such processes serve both to legitimate the status of small venues in local music scenes and to attract the revenue and economic capital that allows niche spaces of cultural production to remain financially sustainable. Chapter 4 draws on the work of prominent sociologist Pierre Bourdieu, his acolytes and his critics to outline, define and critique concepts such as cultural, social and symbolic capital, habitus and field, discussing their impact on small venue spaces and their significance in discussions of small venues as sites of social and cultural value. Through a discussion of Bourdieusian notions of capital, I posit that booking agents and other cultural intermediaries convert venues' intrinsic value into instrumental value, while emphasizing that it is this intrinsic value that is their true source of revenue, capital and value, economic or otherwise. This conversion is exercised through booking agents' curation of the venue space, their relationships with musicians and artist managers and their ability to promote an air of sociality in and around small venue spaces. The primary argument of this penultimate chapter is that small venues contribute to live music cultures in nuanced, informal ways that remain vital despite their elusiveness. Chapter 4 also determines that financial precarity is endemic within the small venue sector, but that such precarity is a by-product of niche, cultural-capital-oriented spaces that view economic capital as a dull necessity for sustaining cultural production (Scott 2017).

Finally, the book's concluding chapter, summarizing its two key theoretical interventions and the case studies presented in each of its chapters, bringing them together to inform a final discussion of small venues as unique cultural institutions. The conclusion calls for a reconsideration – in both policy and research contexts – of the significant social and cultural work that small venues do, as well as their role as social hubs for local music scenes and the foundation of a live music ecology that spans the value chain of the live music sector, from the pub to the stadium (Behr et al. 2014). The conclusion will present a summary of the main findings of the book and will also offer suggestions for further research on small live music venues.

A discussion of the intrinsic value of small live music venues comes at a pertinent time given the duress suffered by the cultural and creative industries following the COVID-19 pandemic. Small venues are significant not only because of their generative impact on local economies but because they are spaces of belonging, community, sociality and cultural exchange. This book provides an original account of an institution that is integral to the history of popular music yet is often framed as the backdrop rather than the foreground of this history. It identifies the intrinsic forms of value to be found in the cultural production and sociality facilitated by small venues while also demonstrating how these intrinsic values are leveraged to attract revenue. The book provides breadth by considering the small live music venue generally, drawing on contemporary research from the United States, UK and Europe, while also providing depth through a set of lively ethnographic case studies.

The findings of this book reflect broader trends across the live music sector (Behr et al. 2014; Homan 2014; New South Wales Parliament 2018; Newton & Coyle-Hayward 2018; Shaw 2013), echoing previous empirical work on live music venues and scenes (Bennett & Rogers 2016a, 2016b; Cohen 2013a, 2013b; Finnegan 2007; Gallan 2012; Gallan & Gibson 2013; Rogers 2008; Shank 1994; Straw 1991), which indicate that small live music venues are often 'passion projects' that walk the line between precarity and vibrancy. However, the significance of small live music venues as spaces of social and cultural value is not often discussed in ways that consider their precarity. This book considers the financial hardships that small venue owners have often willingly chosen to face through the nature of their business models, promoting their small venues as niche spaces of cultural production over and above profit-making opportunities. Teetering on the edge of viability yet essential for a major cultural industry, the small live music venue makes for a compelling and fascinating topic for further discussion.

1

Theorizing live music: 'Scenes', 'subcultures' and the 'live music ecology'

Since popular music arose as a serious scholarly pursuit from the 1970s onwards (e.g. Frith 1978; Hall & Jefferson 1976; Hebdige 1979), several terms have gained prevalence within academic discourse as descriptors of popular music cultures and, by extension, those music-making practices and live music cultures synonymous with music venues. These terms have emerged from various disciplines within the social sciences, such as cultural studies (e.g. scenes, subcultures), sociology (fields of cultural production, art worlds etc.) and popular music studies itself (e.g. the so-called live music ecology), which draws on methods and concepts from multiple disciplines. Each of these terms is informed by discipline-specific definitions and understandings of culture and cultural forms, how participants engage with culture, and what this means for the places and spaces in which cultural events take place. In relation to small live music venues, which are already heavily influenced by factors of space, place, identity and materiality, scenes, subcultures and the live music ecology are all relevant as descriptors of socio-musical practice. However, other conceptual understandings of live music's production and consumption – such as art worlds (Becker 1982; Martin 2006) and social network analysis (Crossley, McAndrew & Widdop 2014) – have also been useful in shaping understandings of live music's impact,[1] and the role of small venues in facilitating this.

A wealth of literature dedicated to live music studies now exists, drawing on a variety of methods and conceptual frameworks (Behr et al. 2016b; Bennett 1999b; Bennett & Peterson 2004; Gough 2021; Guerra 2020; Hesmondhalgh 2005; Holt 2010, 2012, 2014, 2020; Homan 2002, 2008, 2010, 2011a, 2011b; Straw 1991, 2001; van der Hoeven & Hitters 2019, 2020). The most dominant,

---

[1] For a comprehensive analysis, comparison and critical review of established concepts of live music's production and consumption, see van der Hoeven et al. (2020).

popular and significant of these frameworks have been scenes, subcultures and recent ecological approaches, which remain influential across much of the current research on live music and venues (Behr et al. 2016b; Bennett & Rogers 2016b; Haenfler 2014). Therefore, within the theory of live music applied here, I wish to focus on these concepts and articulate their relevance to small live music venues specifically. To this end, this chapter contains an overview of current and previous work on music scenes, subcultures and the live music ecology, and the relevance of these concepts as descriptors of socio-musical practice, as models of cultural production and consumption, infrastructures, collectives, and as spaces of assembly, mediation, and transgression. Foremost it serves as a review of the history, usage and definitions of these descriptors, offering a critique of each and a repositioning in terms of their relevance to small venues.

Historical developments

During the 1970s, many academics, music writers and journalists were striving to understand the link between political movements, contemporary consumer culture, popular music and the so-called cultural revolution of the late 1960s (Howard 1969; Marwick 2011; Rex 1975), alongside similar but distinct youth and music cultures that had emerged throughout the 1970s (Hall & Jefferson 1976; Hebdige 1979; Willis 1978). Initially a descriptor of the various hippie, 'beatnik' and other youth cultures prevalent throughout the West in the 1950s and 1960s, 'counterculture' had been posited as a term for the numerous youth movements advocating lifestyles distinct or otherwise removed from hegemonic or 'mainstream' culture (Braunstein & Doyle 2013; Gair 2007). These movements gained popularity at a point of time in which the live popular music performance – the 'live event' – was becoming a powerful and influential way of engaging with popular music. Although the most iconic, historicized and contested of these events were often outdoor music festivals – Woodstock, the Isle of Wight, Glastonbury, Myponga, Sunbury and so on (Bennett 2017; Buckland 2021; Holt 2020; Price 2021) – small venues also had a substantial role to play in the development of popular music culture generally (Kronenburg 2019) and were fundamental to many of the Western rock canon's key developments and 'moments' (Holt 2020).

Due to their niche appeal and scale, small venues have been important performance spaces for emerging forms of popular music yet to gain a wide audience. Rather than a cabaret or nightclub style event, with seated or dining audiences followed by dancing, the 1960s and early 1970s saw the rise of original popular music groups regularly performing in small, intimate spaces for standing (and drinking) audiences. Such spaces helped to articulate what the 'counterculture' looked like, how it was experienced and where those that were considered a part of it went to gather.

Despite its revolutionary pretensions, the idea of a counterculture was quickly subsumed within broader structures of power, as mainstream popular music icons came to embody it and quickly popularized it within dominant culture. By the mid-1970s there was little that was 'counter' about those youth and musical movements previously associated with the 'counterculture', as they quickly became the common signifiers of the Western rock and pop music canons. Despite this canonization and the erstwhile homogenization of popular culture that accompanied globalization, the 1970s wrought new music styles, often emerging from the small venues of major cities and towns. Many of these were former industrial centres rapidly moving away from traditional industries, such as manufacturing. The small venues of these cities were spaces where acts could experiment without the need for the polish that larger stages demanded and in front of audiences desperate for musical forms that reflected their lived realities. Accompanying the proliferation of small urban venues, deindustrialization in the West throughout the 1970s and 1980s saw a generation of working-class youth looking for new avenues of cultural expression.

Punk, dub, ska, heavy metal, reggae and other genres specific to small venues in the 1970s – genres that at the time had not yet gained the commercial appeal or mainstream acceptance of 'pop' and 'rock' but were emerging as new and exciting forms of popular music – began to accumulate fans who embodied and embraced a range of identifiers that were seen as distinct and specific to these musical forms. Scholars, particularly those of the Birmingham Centre for Contemporary Cultural Studies (BCCCS), described these identifiers and their 'fit' with the adherents' lifestyles, values and musical preferences as a homology[2] (Shuker 2022, pp. 187–8). In an effort to typify and categorize these youth and fan cultures and the sense of homology that defined them, scholars and popular music writers established the ontological framework known as 'subcultures'.

---

[2] Homology is defined as the consistency of style between a subculture and its symbolic objects – dress, appearance, language, music – 'objects in which [the subculture] could see their central values held and reflected' (Clarke et al. 1976, p. 56).

While there are multiple definitions of subcultures, they can be broadly defined as social groups organized around shared interests and practices (Gelder & Thornton 1997). However, importantly, subcultures were also defined by the types of cultural forms they were resistant to, positioned against or in subversion of, usually a parent culture or another form of hegemonic power (Shuker 2022, p. 348). Prior to the 1990s, 'subcultures' were the dominant means and framework through which youth cultures, musical cultures and other identifiable sociocultural activities relating to popular music were conceptualized and discussed. As such groups often used live music events as a means of socializing and organizing, subcultures also became synonymous with certain genres and subgenres of popular music and associated live performances. Indeed, popular music was integral to most subcultural identities and their articulation as discernible cultural formations. Understanding subcultures and the places that they congregated – often small live music venues – was therefore integral to a general theory of live popular music throughout this period of scholarship. However, following the publication of Will Straw's oft-cited journal article 'Systems of articulation, logics of change: communities and scenes in popular music' (1991), the broader concept of music 'scenes' began to replace subcultures as the dominant framework through which both the cultural and sociological study of live and popular music was approached. The 'post-subcultural' turn which followed (Bennett 2011) was also accompanied by a concerted critique of subcultures and associated value forms – that is, 'subcultural capital' (Jensen 2006; Weinzierl & Muggleton 2003), discussed further in Chapter 4 – and the subsequent decline of subculture as the preferred descriptor of socio-musical praxis, social organization and relevant spaces of sociality and production.

Although it persists in popular culture and has pertinence to online and fan cultures more closely aligned with forms of fashion rather than specific musical genres or subgenres (e.g. steam punk, dark academia), 'subculture' has largely fallen out of favour in scholarly work on live and popular music in the twenty-first century. While other terms have replaced it as more effective descriptors of socio-musical practice (van der Hoeven et al. 2020), until recently, the concept of scene has been the dominant scholarly framework for understanding the social organization of music making and the various domains of cultural consumption and production associated with musical practice. As van der Hoeven et al. state, 'the scene approach has been arguably the most influential one in popular music studies, and one that has been developed from music research to begin with' (2020, p. 23). While subcultures still have relevance within the broader study of popular culture, in terms of small live music venues and the modes of participation in live music events that they host, subcultural theory remains too fixed and rigid for application within the context of this book.

For the sake of further clarity, this chapter will provide a brief overview of 'subcultures', 'scenes' and other analytical and ontological frameworks through which live and popular music cultures are currently discussed. Such a discussion is pertinent to this book's broader theory of live music and small venues as it allows for an understanding of where small venues are placed within modern practices of cultural consumption and production, and their significance as sites of such practices. An understanding of the intersection between the social organization of live music (i.e. scenes) and the political, material and cultural infrastructure of live music (i.e. the 'live music ecology/ecosystem') is fundamental to an appropriate evaluation of small venues.

This chapter offers an original contribution to the study of live music, in that it marries the established concept of music scenes (Straw 1991) with the more recently conceptualized ecological approach to the study of live music (Behr et al. 2016b), positioning them as complementary methods for describing the production and consumption of live music specific to space, place and other material concerns. This contribution builds on similarly aligned but distinct work by my peers (Bennett & Rogers 2016b; van der Hoeven et al. 2020). Further, in this chapter I reject 'subculture' as an increasingly irrelevant descriptor of contemporary forms of cultural consumption, identity and music-making practices. This is an important conceptual distinction, as I specifically position small venues as unique points of convergence between informal, fluid and 'horizontal' forms of sociality (such as music scenes) and more concrete, rigid and 'vertical' structures (e.g. the live music ecosystem), demonstrating how small venues operate at the site of this intersection and are symbolic of the messy collisions and tensions between intangible forms of value and very real demonstrations of power. This theoretical repositioning will distinguish small venues as niche spaces of cultural production, illustrating the cultural work that they do alongside the sociality they facilitate, demonstrated via historical case studies and recent ethnographic research in Part Two of this book. However, first a critique of these terms and their precursors is necessary.

Music scenes and subcultures

Subcultures

Scenes differ significantly from subcultures, and Straw's definition of 'scene' is distinctly post-subcultural (Bennett & Rogers 2016b, p. 13). As an academic term, 'subculture' rose to prominence as a descriptor of various music, fashion and political movements in the late 1970s. Although originally coined and established by the Chicago School of Sociology in the 1920s (van der Hoeven et al. 2020, p. 22), a coherent theory of subcultures was not developed until the 1970s. Emerging from the Birmingham Centre for Contemporary Cultural Studies (BCCCS) and its associated figures (Hall & Jefferson 1976; Hebdige 1979; Willis 1978), class was central to the BCCCS's definition of subculture and its relationship to popular music. This definition drew on Marxist notions of power, Althusser's (1969, 1984) writings on ideology and Gramsci's (1971) concept of hegemony to analyse a variety of youth cultures such as punks, skinheads, mods and teddy boys (as cited in Bennett & Rogers 2016b, pp. 13–14).

The BCCCS defined subcultural activity as resistance articulated through music-related youth movements defined by specific visual characteristics, physical affectations and styles. These initially included punks (Hebdige 1979), mods (Hebdige 1976) and skinheads (Clarke 1976a), but later came to take in goth (Haenfler 2010; Hodkinson 2002), straight edge (Haenfler 2004, 2006; Nilan 2006; Wood 2003) and a multitude of others (Gelder & Thornton 1997; Haenfler 2014). These 'subcultures' used music, fashion and lifestyle choices to articulate themselves as group identities with an identifiable homology,[3] creating 'new social identities and reclaim[ing] cultural space for youth within a dislocating parent culture' (Bennet & Rogers 2016a, p. 14). Herein lies the primary point of distinction between 'scene' and 'subculture', as

> the study of 'subcultures' reads into the activities and textual production of social actors as an articulation of group identity and resistance, while 'scene' defines such articulations as multiplicitous at the level of the individual and asks what this means for subjectively lived out cultural identities.
>
> (Driver & Bennett 2015, p. 104)

---

[3] Willis defines homology as 'the continuous play between the group and a particular item which produces specific styles, meanings, contents, and forms of consciousness' (1978, p. 191). Homology is often read as the overlapping characteristics and identifiers of fashion, musical taste, social sensibility, disposition and socio-economic background that intersect to form a coherent subcultural identity.

This distinction also relates to class identities, as definitions of subculture are strongly informed by homological signifiers associated with socio-economic status, whereas scene allows for more casual membership (i.e. participation) that includes and cuts across multiple socio-economic indicators (Taylor 2012, p. 154).

As an ontological framework, a 'subculture' is often defined as a form of collective identity. Those members demonstrating individualistic, non-subcultural characteristics are usually regarded as outlying variations on a theme rather than as distinct from the subcultural style. Subcultures themselves are often aligned with political movements apparent in the music, art, fashion and cultural artefacts aligned with each. Scene, on the other hand, allows for a subjective experience of culture, one that is complex, eclectic and does not necessitate politics or a defined ideology, although such ideologies are often still implicit.

Another feature of subcultures as they were defined by the BCCCS and other subcultural scholars are their implicit autonomy or remove from mainstream society and those signifiers of power and capital associated with hegemony. To be *sub*-ordinate to or a *sub*-set of culture, subcultures require a parent or 'hegemonic' culture to articulate themselves in opposition to or in distinction from. This is problematic in the current age of fluid and performative identity under late capitalism, as sites and practices of cultural production and consumption are often subsumed by mass culture and cannot be easily separated from it.

The concept of subcultures, as Kahn-Harris argues, also 'clashes with contemporary concerns about globalization, the ambiguities of resistance and the heterogeneity of identity' (2000, p. 14). Articulations of identity through practices of consumption and taste have become more multifaceted and complex in the postmodern age of cultural omnivorousness, online media and globalization. These new 'ways of being' challenge the assumption that subcultures and the parent culture that they are supposedly resisting or opposed to are somehow autonomous. Further, the concept of a 'subculture' implies that both it and the parent culture that it is set against or apart from are somehow consistent, homogenous sociocultural formations; that they are both monolithic. Yet 'contemporary youth cultures are characterized by far more complex stratifications than that suggested by the simple dichotomy of "monolithic mainstream" – "resistant subcultures"' (Weinzierl & Muggleton 2003, p. 7).

Within the literature, belonging to a subculture is often framed as a totalized way of being that does not allow for the kind of broad cultural consumption that has come to define life and youth cultures in late modernity

(Peterson & Bennett 2004, p. 3). These contemporary modes of consumption have significant implications for subcultures, as previous understandings of the term implied 'a tight-knit, rigidly bounded, implacably "resistant", male-dominated, geographically specific social space (if such formations ever did exist)' (Kahn-Harris 2000, p. 14). Subculture therefore cannot effectively account for the modern way in which music is produced and consumed nor the transience of music scenes, as neither are homogenous or monolithic. The ineffectiveness of the term to appropriately account for the pluralism and diversity of cultural participation and engagement with live music cultures means that it is not a useful way of discussing or analysing the types of sociality, cultural consumption and production that occur in contemporary small live music venues. Whereas subcultures certainly accounted for significant youth and music cultures in the past, groups that no doubt gathered and socialized in small live music venues, they do not accurately represent the types of sociality implicit within modern small live music venues and the nuanced, multifaceted ways in which identities are articulated within them.

I avoid 'subculture' as a descriptor of sociality and musical practice as 'it presumes that a society has one commonly shared culture from which the subculture is deviant ... [and] that all of a participant's actions are governed by subcultural standards' (Peterson & Bennett 2004, p. 3). Unlike subcultures, music scenes are articulated via social activities, shared musical interests and a sense of common ground between participants, yet are ultimately transient and adhere to an anti-essentialist definition of identity (Bennett 1997, 2004; Bennett & Rogers 2016a, 2016b; Bennett, Stratton & Peterson 2008; Peterson & Bennett 2004; Straw 1991, 2001). As Driver and Bennett state, '[a] key value of scene as a conceptual framework is the more affective, emotive, fluid, and trans-local qualities that it brings to our understanding of musicalized meaning and practice in everyday life' (2015, p. 101). Its transience is the result of the dispersal of culture through globalization and the repositioning of popular music in people's everyday lives, engagement with and access to which has increased exponentially due to the proliferation of the internet, mobile devices and streaming services. Thus, while the work of the BCCCS can still be regarded as pioneering, 'they no longer appear to reflect the political, cultural and economic realities of the twenty-first century' (Weinzierl & Muggleton 2003, p. 5). We must therefore move towards a post-subcultural understanding of music making, live music cultures and, thus, small venues.

Scenes

The term 'music scene' is typically used as a descriptor of everyday manifestations of collective musical life (Driver & Bennett 2015, p. 99). However, as it is a conceptual framework and not a theoretical or methodological approach, scene studies vary deeply in their application and 'scene' has been used to describe a variety of music-making activities. These vary from live performances and record production specific to a genre within a time and place (Grazian 2013; Shank 1994), to translocal connections between scenes linked by genre across a variety of locales (Hodkinson 2004; Kahn-Harris 2000, 2007; Laing 1997; Petersen & Bennett 2004; Straw 1991); and both the virtual (e.g. chatrooms, forums, listservs) and physical infrastructure (e.g. venues, record stores, rehearsal rooms) of musical movements co-located within a specific neighbourhood, town or city that are linked more by the social actors participating in them than a coherent genre or style (Cohen 1991; Finnegan 2007; Rogers 2008; Stahl 2004). The ability for scene participants to dip in and out of scenes as they like, engaging with them to varying levels of degree and commitment without necessarily embodying or completely immersing themselves in one or the other, is one of the defining features of scene. In particular, the concept allows for the practice of omnivorous cultural consumption and participation common in late modernity, a practice that is significant within the everyday context of small venues and the casual sociality that they encourage, while also emphasizing that shared spatiality is defining in its limitations (i.e. the local scene).

Will Straw provided an early scholarly definition of 'scene' as 'that cultural space in which a range of musical practices coexist, interacting with each other within a variety of processes of differentiation, and according to widely varying trajectories of change and cross-fertilization' (1991, p. 373). As is implied, the term was initially associated with the study of musical forms in time and place (Shuker 2013, pp. 210–1), and early scene studies often focused heavily on locality, spatiality and specificity of place, often a *local* music scene. Straw's formal definition has served as the concept's primary description since it first appeared in print, with various proponents adapting it to their topic of enquiry and purpose (Baulch 2007; Olson 1998; Stahl 2004). Influenced by Barry Shank's (1988) work on the music scene of Austin, Texas – who later defined 'scene' as the interactions between distinct musical practices and their practitioners in a specific location – what made Straw's definition persuasive as a distinct conceptual framework for understanding musical practice and cultural participation were the distinctions made between scenes and previous descriptors such as 'musical communities', along with his convincing case studies of early 1990s alternative rock and dance music.

Building on the work of Shank (1988), Finnegan (1989) and contemporaries such as Sara Cohen (1991) and Holly Kruse (1993), Straw (1991) makes the distinction between a contemporary understanding of scenes and previous notions of 'musical communities', which were conceptualized as relatively homogenous cultural groups whose heritage contributed to the production and dissemination of traditional musical idioms native to that group. Examples of these kinds of 'musical communities' include those social and ethnic groups associated with traditional and folk music, with strong ties to cultural identity and place (Bennett & Rogers 2016b, pp. 16, 50). Although such musical communities have persisted and continue to grow, hybridizing with popular music forms, any contemporary music to develop out of such cultural groups is often articulated in the context of each community's distinct heritage, with strong continuing ties to that heritage. In contrast, Straw (1991) stresses that modern music scenes are composed of a range of musical practices coexisting together and, more importantly, interacting with each other. 'Scene' therefore allows for the kinds of aesthetic cosmopolitanism and cross-fertilization of musical styles typical of cultural forms in late modernity (Regev 2013), as well as the fluidity of cultural identity, consumption and participation associated with contemporary engagement with popular culture (Bennett & Peterson 2004; Peterson & Bennett 2004). Scene also considers the widely felt impact of globalization on the modern cultural industries, providing a framework for discussing and analysing music making *in situ* and as it relates *to place* while simultaneously acknowledging the 'placelessness' of contemporary popular music.

Another defining feature of music scenes are their mundanity, their *everydayness*. Music scenes are not spectacular subcultures, embodied with accompanying flair in the cultural practices and styles of their participants. They are instead made up of ongoing everyday interactions between those involved with music making in a time and place, or across several spaces and places linked by such interactions. Whether these interactions are casual, professional, driven by lifestyle choices or are simply 'something to do on a Friday night' does not bar participants from inclusion within the scene or scenes. However, this penchant for loosely bounded spheres of participation has contributed to critics of the concept's primary point of complaint: the term's elasticity and vagueness.

Indeed, the concept of a music scene has often been expanded to the point at which it becomes slightly meaningless (Straw 2001, p. 248) or is used purely as a method for circumscribing social actors participating in a very specific musical community (van der Hoeven et al. 2020, p. 24). In the context of these applications, the term is rendered merely descriptive rather than analytical (van der Hoeven et al. 2020). Proponents of an ecological approach to the study of live music have also criticized the concept of scene for its inability to account for materiality, built environments, policy settings and the impact of social actors and policymakers otherwise removed from the scene (Behr et al. 2016b). Further, scene studies have also been criticized for their methodological application, or lack thereof.

The study of music scenes is often approached from the methodological perspective of ethnography. Such ethnographic approaches to music scenes often draw on qualitative interviews and participant observation, privileging the voices of 'insiders' and scene participants, as well as emphasizing the voices – or at least the 'gaze' – of the researchers themselves. Scene studies have therefore often been criticized as insider accounts of cultural production and consumption that are exclusive, niche and self-absorbed (Hesmondhalgh 2005; Straw 2015). While this is true to an extent, ethnographic studies of music scenes offer a helpful way of observing the role of social participation, meaning making and interpersonal relationships within the formal music industries, and the impact that these have on broader popular and live music cultures from the intimate perspective of those best positioned to report on these matters. Immersive accounts of music scenes also provide further insights into hidden modes of sociality and the organization of informal music-making practices that often go unseen by casual observers or those without the tacit knowledge through which to engage with such practices (Lobato 2006). Therefore, despite its insular and narrow lens, ethnography remains a valid means through which to map, analyse and assess music scenes, their participants and their contribution to the musical life of cities and towns.

Music scenes thus remain the most effective method for conceptualizing participation and interaction with music making in the postmodern age of cultural omnivorousness. They provide insight into the complexity and nuanced ways in which such participation takes place, particularly in the era of late modernity wherein cultural engagement is increasingly diverse and eclectic. As common, regular and often default gathering spaces for music scenes, small live music venues have an integral role to play in the development of music scenes.

Previous scholars have defined scene as 'forms of collective activity that engender strong feelings of membership but do not spring from an ongoing community' (Bennett, Stratton & Peterson 2008, p. 593), and 'a specific kind of urban cultural context and practice of spatial coding' (Stahl 2004, p. 76). They state that music scenes can be both geographically specific spaces for the articulation of multiple musical practices and musical communities that are articulated simultaneously, in many spaces and across a range of sites. Further, 'scenesters need not be committed to a single scene, but may participate in several' (Bennett, Stratton & Peterson 2008, p. 593). The nebulousness of the term is what gives it its potency, as 'no musical practice can take place entirely separately from social processes. The implication is that scenes include everything … since all contribute to and feed off a larger space(s) of musical practice' (Kahn-Harris 2000, p. 25). This inherent interconnectedness between musical practices and social processes is central to my definition of small live music venues and the sociality inherent within them.

The term 'music scene' denotes a group of participants who are tied to music making by way of participation and interaction. This positions live music as something of collective and contributory value, as music scenes are 'not tied to preexisting notions of community grounded in class and tradition but rather facilitat[e] new forms of collectivity and connectivity that centre upon shared participation in more recent forms of material culture' (Driver & Bennett 2015, p. 101). The sharing of mutual interests and casual exchanges of cultural capital between scene participants is fundamental to any music scene. The scene itself is therefore articulated in the interactions and exchanges between participants and the spaces in which these take place, shaping them in turn.

Much of the experience of engaging with live music and the forms of sociality that encircle live music events (i.e. music scenes) is dependent on venue spaces. The role of 'social space'[4] in facilitating music scenes is apparent in small venues, as these spaces exist on the level of the local, the everyday and the commonplace, and are part of a cultural field with a strong relationship to place. Participants engage with small venue spaces on an everyday level and are more likely to be 'locals' or 'regulars' – demonstrating loyalty – than the broader demographic of participants encompassed in larger concert audiences. Such small venues are part of a network

---

[4] 'The term "field" is most often used to describe forms of social action or interaction in which geographic space is less important than social action and given more or less attention depending on the analyst. "Social space", in contrast, is a concept for which the question of the relationship between social and physical or geographic space is central' (Reed-Danahay 2015, p. 70).

of spaces otherwise defined as the 'live music ecosystem', which encompasses much of the physical infrastructure, policy settings and influence of non-scenic actors on small venues. However, before discussing and defining this ecosystem and its formal ontology – the 'live music ecology' (Behr et al. 2016b) – in more detail, the multiple modes through which scene is articulated must first be defined.

Indeed, unlike subcultures, scenes are not clearly defined or replicable and are either tethered to a specific place or a group of participants. Subcultures, on the other hand, are articulated as a set of ideas, aesthetics and symbolic markers that make up something identifiable (Clarke 1976b, p. 179; Willis 1972). Instead, scenes exist only insofar as there are participants engaging with them.

Scene studies: The social study of live music

Will Straw's seminal 1991 article marked the beginning of a coherent body of work within popular music studies known as *scene studies*. Such work has often concentrated on the social organization of popular music making within a specific locale (Overell 2014; Quader & Redden 2015; Rogers 2012; Stahl 2004) – highlighting the concept's emphasis on spatiality (Straw 2015) – but has more recently expanded to include translocal (Hodkinson 2004; Kahn-Harris 2000; Schilt 2004) and virtual music scenes (Bennett 2004; Hodgkinson 2004). These works have been instrumental in building an understanding of informal music-making practices that elucidate the hidden meaning(s), labour and social practices embedded within popular music cultures beyond the perspective of music industry and business-focused research. Whereas music business studies (Graham 2019; Tschmuck 2006; Tschmuck, Pearce & Campbell 2013) take a more market-focused lens to the topic, scene studies consider much of the hidden sociology of popular music making not explained by supply and demand curves. The concept of music scenes has therefore been adapted by cultural studies and sociology scholars as a useful and coherent method for explaining those parts of popular and live music cultures that are not necessarily aligned with any sort of market-based ideology but are more closely associated with informal modes of sociality, hobbyist cultural production and ideas of friendship, *communitas* (Sardiello 1994) and belonging. Following its origins in popular music studies (Kruse 1993; Shank 1988; Straw 1991), scene has also been adapted as a label for those types of social groups that gather around cultural objects and activities outside of popular music (Straw 2015).

The purpose of 'scene' as a term is not to designate cultural spaces (e.g. small venues) as specific to one scene or another but to examine 'the ways in which particular musical practices "work" to produce a sense of community within the conditions of metropolitan music scenes' (Straw 1991, p. 373). The sense of community found in local music scenes springs from a collective experience of participation that, although influenced by international styles and a globalized musical aesthetic, is enacted on a local level, giving rise to social activities based around musical styles and the venues in which they are performed (Straw 1991). Furthermore, music scenes are grounded in 'the ongoing transformation of social and cultural relations – and of alliances between particular musical communities – occurring within the context of the contemporary Western city' (Straw 1991, p. 375). This implies social exchange, particularly those exchanges that occur at the point where scenes intersect. The building of musical affinities and interactions across scenic boundaries all contribute to a scene's sense of identity (Straw 1991, p. 373).

The boundaries of music scenes are what both defines and distorts them as social phenomena and it is easier to distinguish scenes in terms of how they are constructed rather than what they are constructed of. However, as Straw suggests (1991, p. 375), the study of scenes has often been urban and centred on Western case studies. Although there have been deliberate and substantial attempts to shift the focus of scene studies away from cities (Bennett et al. 2020) and a Western perspective (Janotti & Pereira de Sá 2013; Quader & Redden 2015), the density of relationships, social actors, infrastructure and formalized music industries in Western metropoles, along with the highly networked nature of postmodern cultural consumption and production, has meant that music scenes tend to proliferate in urban centres across developed countries. This is not to say that they do not exist outside of these contexts, but they are otherwise more hidden, hybridized and disparate (Quader & Redden 2015; Wallach & Clinton 2013). A key recommendation of this book is for further research into music scenes outside the familiar and increasingly over-analysed context of the contemporary Western city. This would counteract the growing saturation of research on Western music scenes, with live music studies and scene studies gaining considerable momentum since the early 2000s.

Indeed, due to the prominence of 'scene' as a means of studying the social organization of music making in spaces and places, much of the literature on music venues and live music is framed in terms of scenes. Research on venues in Australia (Gallan 2012; Gallan & Gibson 2013; Quader 2022a, 2022b; Smyly

2010), Canada (Mouillot 2018, 2021; Stahl 2003a, 2004), New Zealand (Rochow & Stahl 2016; Stahl 2018), the UK (Bennett 1997), France (Spanu & Seca 2016) and the United States (Grazian 2013) have all drawn on the concept of scene to discuss the modes of sociality and interactions live music participants engage with. The study of small live music venues – specifically the social actors that make up the network of participants that frequent and populate these spaces – is therefore the study of music scenes. However, as I will discuss throughout this chapter, this framework is somewhat incomplete.

Local and translocal scenes

Since the advent of the internet, definitions of music scenes have become fragmented and complex (Bennett & Peterson 2004; Stratton 2008). *Local* music scenes are bound by space and geographical boundaries; a network of participants engaging in music-making practices within a demarcated, tangible place. Local scenes extend beyond musicians and their fans to incorporate venue owners, staff, booking agents, other cultural gatekeepers, publicists, label representatives and local enthusiasts. Here 'the notion of music scene becomes a form of collective association and a means through which individuals with different relationships to a specific genre of music produced in a particular space articulate a sense of collective identity and belonging' (Driver & Bennett 2015, p. 100). The role of identity and place making is particularly strong in local music scenes, and it is in the everyday practices of participants that scene bears the most similarities to a 'musical community' (Straw 1991, p. 373). However, unlike a musical *community*, local scenes are sustained by global trends and practices, and are further influenced by co-located and often rival local scenes that compete for many of the same spaces, resources and participants (Bennett, Stratton & Peterson 2008, p. 594). For example, while the entire live music scene of Melbourne, Australia, can be defined as a 'local music scene', genre-specific scenes connected to specific venues and musical practices also fit the description of a local scene. Melbourne's inner north, which includes many of the case study small venues discussed in Chapter 3, can be viewed as its own distinct scene. However, as local scenes do not exist in a vacuum, many of them function as nodes of participation in broader translocal networks.

Translocal music scenes are built upon inter- and intra-scene communication between disparately located musicians, participants and enthusiasts dedicated to the same types of music across geographical space. Translocal scenes are reliant on the nexus between musical consumption and lifestyle, as participants build strong ties by sharing and participating in ways of living that are associated with the music they love (Peterson & Bennett 2004). This definition also fits Straw's (1991) observations of the North American 'alternative' music scene of the 1980s and early 1990s. The ubiquity of 'alternative music' in the 1980s and 1990s – the fact that it was both (a) a manifestation of quasi-standardized musical practices to be found in all major urban centres and (b) a national and, with the advent of 'grunge', soon-to-be-global movement – lent 'alternative rock' a distinct sense of translocality.

Rising from the DIY practices of punk and hardcore, 'alternative rock' relied on the same independent modes of production, distribution and dissemination as punk. The infrastructure (or 'ecosystem', as I will define it later) that developed out of the local punk scenes of the 1980s (the independent record labels, small venues, networks of promoters and bookings agents etc.) were later utilized by a variety of other musical activities, forming a network of scenes across the United States and Canada. However, 'alternative rock' had less to do with aesthetic concerns and more to do with time, place and modes of cultural production and distribution:

> As the centrality of punk within local musical cultures declined, the unity of alternative rock no longer resided in the stylistic qualities of the music embraced within it. Rather, that unity has come to be grounded more fundamentally in the way in which such spaces of musical activity have come to establish a distinctive relationship to historical time and geographical location.
>
> (Straw 1991, p. 375)

This decentralization lent the role of localism in alternative rock a paradoxical status. By relying on region-specific modes of production and distribution, alternative rock scenes were inherently local, yet the musical practices of alternative rock were easily dispersed, replicated and reproduced, encouraging a uniformity of style that facilitated the translocal nature of the scene. In other words, '[t]he development of alternative-rock culture may be said to follow a logic in which a particular pluralism of musical languages repeats itself from one community to another' (Straw 1991, p. 378). This reflects a translocal mode wherein 'a particularly stable set of musical languages and relationships … has been reproduced within a variety of local circumstances' (Straw 1991, p. 379). The 1990s alternative rock scene of North America was, therefore, a translocal scene.

Other examples of translocal scenes are evident throughout the literature and popular music press. Bennett and Peterson's 2004 edited collection *Music Scenes* documents many of these, such as the translocal goth scene of northern England (Hodkinson 2004), riot grrrl (Schilt 2004), and the North American anarcho-punk scene of the 1980s (Gosling 2004). Recent studies of translocal scenes have looked at non-Western scenes within the context of globalized music cultures, raising interesting questions regarding what makes these scenes specific to the places they inhabit and the impact of local specificities on their articulation, but also how they relate to broader music cultures that go beyond the context of these specificities (Brown et al. 2016; Kahn-Harris 2001). Translocal music scenes also continue to serve as a framework for the discussion of emerging popular music trends such as hyper pop (Battan 2021; Grogan 2021; Kornhaber 2021) and others that have sprouted from disparate pockets of popular culture but contain many similarities and overlapping influences.

Further developments

Expanding on his initial writings in 2001, Straw elaborated on scene's elasticity as a term, stating: '"Scene" is used to circumscribe highly local clusters of activity and to give unity to practices dispersed across the world. It functions to designate face-to-face sociability and as a lazy synonym for globalized virtual communities of taste' (p. 248). Ten years after its initial conception, Straw refers here to the increasingly broad application of 'scene' to all communities of taste, regardless of specificity or their relation to common spaces of practice. However, in an effort to reclaim its value, Straw's 2001 realignment of 'scene' places an emphasis on the concept's social implications and the way in which the everyday activities that make up the scene are submerged in a kind of common sense or 'doxa'[5] (Bourdieu 2000, p. 16). The role of *everyday* sociality in music scenes and the rituals through which such sociality is enacted are evident here. Such everyday sociality needs locally oriented spaces of common experience and engagement, and small venues are ideal for such activities. The patterns of behaviour and

---

[5] Here, 'doxa' is defined as 'pre-reflexive, shared but unquestioned opinions and perceptions ... which determine "natural" practice and attitudes via the internalized "sense of limits" and habitus of [social] agents' (Deer 2012, p. 115). Doxa are the everyday norms that guide cultural consumption and influence how social agents – in this case music scene participants – interact with both culture and each other. Furthermore, although doxa 'lose visibility within the mundane activities of buying drinks or discussing shared interests ... they are perpetuated within such activities, absorbed within the thicker tissues of urban sociability' (Straw 2001, p. 256).

'tacit knowledge' (Lobato 2006) necessary for scenes to proliferate are reliant on small venues as common nodes of participation and interaction. Such everyday experiences of live music articulated and experienced in a local venue space familiar to those involved in the scene are further evidenced by Andy Bennett's (1997) research on northern English 'pub rock'.

Discussing the modes by which audiences and musicians mutually engage with live music, Bennett focuses on the sense of enjoyment local musicians gain from participating in musical practices that facilitate a distinctly social environment, such as those that occur in small live music venues. According to Bennett's participants, the positive characteristics of such an environment include familiar faces and spaces, an ongoing rapport between musicians and their audience, and the opportunity to drink and socialize as 'both musicians and audience become highly attuned to the commonality of social experience that bonds them together … playing a decisive role in framing the politics of performance and reception' (Bennett 1997, p. 99). Small venues are instrumental in facilitating such commonalities, as the inherent spatial limitations of small venues encourage proximity and intimacy between performers and audience, fostering the bonds mentioned previously. Such bonds form the web of social organization and interaction that music scenes are reliant on for their articulation.

Scenes, vernacular culture and place making

The role of the social in any notion of scene influences the very nature of the scene. Music scenes are composed of social actors, who contribute to how scenes are articulated through their interactions. A description of people gathered in a bar, a live music venue or any other cultural space as a 'scene' 'presumes that moments of seemingly purposeless sociability are caught up in the production of conspiratorial intrigues, projects and group identities' (Straw 2001, p. 250). Participants in music scenes create, promote and sustain identities that are bigger than themselves through collective participation and an identifiable group dynamic. This is enacted in Straw's so-called purposeless sociability, an ongoing process that is perpetuated by 'the mundane activities of buying drinks or discussing shared interests' (Straw 2001, p. 256), yet sustains music scenes on a fundamental level.

The spaces in which this 'purposeless sociability' takes place are imbued with a sort of collective history – what Gallan and Gibson refer to as 'vernacular cultural history' (2013, p. 174). In the context of live music venues, vernacular culture[6] implicates cultural heritage (MacKinnon 1994, p. 66), musical memory (Cohen 2013b, p. 580), small-scale musical activities (Homan 2008, p. 253), street-level culture and traditions (Jayne, Holloway & Valentine 2006, p. 459) and the grassroots cultural industries that depend on small venues to give them meaning (Waitt & Gibson 2009, p. 1234). Bennett and Rogers' (2016a, 2016b) work on music scenes and cultural memory further refines the concept of vernacular culture as it relates to music scenes, demonstrating how it is informed by collective memories or a kind of mutual cultural capital. These become textured by participants' experiences of venues, forging associations between musicians, audiences, scenes and the venues that make them up (Bennett & Rogers 2016a, p. 490).

Previous ethnographies of small live music venues, such as Brendan P. Smyly's (2010) doctoral thesis on the Sandringham Hotel and Ben Gallan and Chris Gibson's (2013) article on Wollongong's Oxford Tavern, have focused on specific live music venues. These venues are framed as sites of vernacular cultural history (Gallan 2012; Gallan & Gibson 2013; Rahnema 1997; Shorthose 2004), which give such spaces character and identity. Vernacular cultural history is shared cultural capital reified in space, an articulation of cultural capital that participants benefit from collectively through their engagement with the venue space.[7] This informs vernacular culture, which is shared between participants in a perpetual state of change.

Previous research on vernacular culture and music scenes centres on ideas of place making, documenting the oral histories of venues and exploring how the stories and narratives of their patrons imbue them with meaning. In this context, '[s]cenes extend the spatialization of city cultures through the grafting of tastes or affinities to physical locations' (Straw 2001, p. 254). As spaces of performance (i.e. cultural production and consumption) and sociality, music venues act as repositories of vernacular culture. They are not only performance spaces but also places wherein performances are experienced, appreciated and discussed. Venues can therefore be reframed as a unique type of 'social space'. The commonality of experience shared between musicians and their audience plays a significant role in framing discourses of performance in such social spaces. The small venues in which these experiences take place are therefore aligned with specific sets of sociocultural norms (i.e. doxa), through which the scene itself is

---

[6] Vernacular culture is that which is collectively imagined, enacted and re-told by those who participate in said culture. It is informed by the vernacular knowledge and experience of its participants and the articulations of social identity from which such knowledge arises.
[7] See Chapter 4 for further discussion of the relationship between cultural capital and venue spaces.

re-perpetuated and reproduced. Here, the concept of scene overlaps with Pierre Bourdieu's 'fields of cultural production'[8] and, although they are distinct – as fields are more preoccupied with questions of taste, power and capital and less with questions of space and place than scene (van der Hoeven et al. 2020, p. 22) – several similarities can be observed.

We can draw parallels between live music scenes and Bourdieu's understanding of 'cognitive structures' – those internalized, embodied structures that social agents implement through their practical knowledge of the world (Bourdieu 1984, p. 468) – in that 'scenes' are often taken for granted by individuals and are engaged in without substantial reflection. The assumptions of music scene participants are maintained across the scene, perpetuated in the interactions that take place. These assumptions are often internalized and lack reflexivity. Such biases categorize and define venues, musicians and scenes through processes of distinction, resulting in an understanding of most music scenes that is aligned with Bourdieu's idea of a 'common-sense world' (1984, p. 468).

The cycle of social and cultural practices that inform the 'common-sense world' of music scenes repeats, becoming more potent and entrenched as the field of the local music scene grows, taking in new spaces and participants. This cycle tends to favour the mundane over the spectacular, as the 'everyday' takes precedence over the extraordinary. As Straw states, '[s]cenes regularize these activities within the rituals of drinking or dining, or subject them to the frequency of accidental encounters … In this process, the spectacular loses visibility, dispersed within multiple sites of encounter or consumption' (2001, p. 255). The everyday practices of scene participants strengthen the scene's presence in the globalized context of the city and form part of 'a creative process whereby members of particular local scenes construct shared narratives of everyday life' (Peterson & Bennett 2004, p. 7). Such narratives add to the discourse of musical activity and the role of small venues on a grassroots level.

Scenes, globalization and localism

It is no coincidence that the concept of scene became dominant in popular music studies throughout a decade defined by a warp-speed increase in globalization and its effects, as well as a strong reaction against it embodied in the reassertion

---

[8] For further discussion of Bourdieu's 'fields of cultural production' and its relevance to live music research, see van der Hoeven et al. (2020, pp. 21–2).

of radical localism. Indeed, the increased frequency of cultural exchange between local and global musical practices that took place in the 1990s aligns with the growing interest in translocal scenes exemplified in Straw's (1991) initial translocal case studies, but also the renewed study of global dance music cultures (Browning 2002), goth (Hodkinson 2007; Spracklen & Spracklen 2018) and punk (Goshert 2000; Pearson 2020). Despite the growth of translocalism, regional re-workings of global cultural resources into local sensibilities have been inevitably influenced by the practitioners that enact them (Bennett 1997, p. 98), putting the local inside the global and positioning local music scenes as always distinct, despite their shared characteristics and the ongoing impact of globalization. We can refer here to the influence of cultural geography on scene studies, prominent throughout much of the literature (Connell & Gibson 2003; Gibson 2003; Gibson & Connell 2005; Luckman et al. 2008; Lyons 2016). Such an influence implies:

> If 'geography matters', and if place is important, this is not only because the character of a particular place is a product of its position in relation to wider forces, but also because that character, in turn, stamps its own imprint on those wider forces.
>
> (Morley 1992, p. 282)

Therefore, scenes and the small venues that house them occupy a point of intersection between social and cultural practices specific to space and place and globalized musical aesthetics dominant throughout niche spaces of cultural production across the globe. Small venues are both a microcosm of hegemonic popular music cultures, such as that of the Western pop-rock canon, and places for the exploration and proliferation of local music practices, some of which are far removed from the Western canon.

Following an established understanding of the impact of globalization and localism on scenes, we can therefore distinguish two defining factors in modern music-making practices: one that grounds them in local music heritage, and another that encourages pluralization and eclecticism. The former is influenced by the types of music dominant in a particular place, which may have arisen out of long-term and ongoing music scenes, tied to specific venues and musical communities. The latter is a product of globalization, shaped by globalized musical styles and their widespread impact on popular culture, wherein hegemonic cultural forms (often those of North America) have created a homogenized pop-rock aesthetic (Regev 2013).

In this context, the 'local' small music venue cannot exist apart from the influence of a globalized cultural aesthetic (Peterson & Bennett 2004, p. 3). But as such venues are tied to place, the musical practices that they facilitate are always somewhat characteristic of their surroundings. The influence of 'city cultures' emphasizes the venue's role as a cultural transistor, as an outpost of global cosmopolitan culture. 'Scene' is particularly useful here, as it 'seems able to evoke both the cosy intimacy of community and the fluid cosmopolitanism of urban life' (Straw 2001, p. 248). A city's music scene fulfils both, straddling community and culture. Straw's assertion also reflects those made previously regarding Australian city cultures, in that 'urban scenes will almost always be perceived as lively, productive social spaces' (Straw 2001, p. 256). A city's music scene and its cultural resources sustain it beyond the context of globalization. City cultures feed on international trends but also sit apart from them. The internet has played the largest role in this exchange, contributing to the rise of the so-called virtual scene.

Virtual scenes

As defined by Peterson and Bennett, a virtual scene 'involves direct Net-mediated person-to-person communication between fans ... the creation of chatrooms or list-servs dedicated to the scene and may involve the trading of music and images online' (2004, p. 11). Virtual scenes centre on new types of interactions that occur between musicians and fans by means of participatory communication technology and the Web 2.0 phenomenon (Bennett 2002a, 2004). Increased internet access since the 1990s has also resulted in fan sites dedicated to cult and obscure artists, monitored by groups of disparate yet interconnected fans. These virtual scenes have increased the popularity of these artists (Kibby 2000), along with improving access to their work and repertoire for young artists and new fans. However, some scholars have argued that unless they exist purely online and do not have equivalent material meeting spaces or places of performance (e.g. vapourware), many so-called virtual scenes are merely digitally mediated *translocal* scenes, albeit ones that rely heavily on such mediation.

As the internet, social and other digital media have grown as the dominant means through which to organize, promote and coordinate live music events as well as the distribution of popular music and commentary around it, all scenes have taken on virtual/digital aspects. This does not necessarily mean that they are *virtual* music scenes, existing entirely in cyberspace, but are simply local, translocal or otherwise dispersed music scenes mediated through digital communication. Clearly materiality still matters within the context of music scenes. However, it has often been observed that the dominant conceptualization of music scenes does not go far enough in accounting for it (Behr et al. 2016b, p. 6). Specifically, discussion of the actual built environments of venue spaces themselves, as well as other physical infrastructures that regularly serve the scene, seems missing from many accounts.

Further, discussion of the impact of agents and social actors outside of the scene is also absent from most scene studies, as is a coherent explanation of systemic factors, policy settings and the way in which interdependencies between scenic and non-scenic actors have a fundamental impact on the shape and capacity of most local music cultures. In response to this, an ecological approach to the study of live music has been posited. Such an approach is essential to the study of small venues, as much of their value is articulated as spatial value and other material concerns (van der Hoeven & Hitters 2020). The intersection between 'music scenes' and the 'live music ecology', and their value as distinct yet overlapping concepts relevant to the study of small venues, must therefore be further explored.

The 'live music ecology/ecosystem'

The 'live music ecology' has recently emerged as an alternative or complementary descriptor for how live music cultures – their participants, material infrastructure(s), relevant social actors (both engaged and those removed from it), interdependencies and the live music event itself – work in practice. Specifically, this ecological approach is concerned with 'the different relationships that enable the social events of concerts' (Behr et al. 2016b, as cited in van der Hoeven et al. 2020, p. 28). As a conceptual framework for understanding live performance, this approach aims to explain how the live music event is staged and has come to be, as well as considering place-based factors and the limitations of materiality (e.g. venue spaces, density of production, infrastructures).

Stemming from a large-scale and long-term research project on the British live music sector – the 'UK Live Music Census' (Behr et al. 2020; Webster et al. 2018) – this ecological approach to the study of live music was first properly outlined in Behr et al.'s 2016 article 'Live Concert Performance: An Ecological Approach', and has since been built on and utilized by various scholars (Hitters & Mulder 2020; Mulder, Hitters & Rutten 2021; van der Hoeven et al. 2022; Whiting 2019). As van der Hoeven et al. describe it:

> It views the live music ecology as a (inter)local network of different social actors within live music (e.g., musicians, concert organizers, agents) and beyond (e.g., regulators, policy makers, sponsors). The ecological perspective pays due attention to the material aspects of live music, such as the size of music venue and the urban setting in which music events take place.
>
> (2020, p. 28)

More than accounting for the impact and influence of materiality, space and place, the 'live music ecology' was posited as a means of accounting for the types of infrastructures, relationships and interdependencies that were not included in definitions of 'scenes' or 'subcultures' (Behr et al. 2016b). These include those social actors outside of the scene – the police, regulatory authorities, licensing bodies, local, state and federal governments, cultural advocacy groups, funding bodies and other institutions – that have an undeniable impact on live music venues and their ability to operate in a financially sustainable manner but are not active participants in music scenes or otherwise included in scene studies. The ecological approach also includes an acknowledgement of the materiality of venue spaces themselves – their size and the urban settings in which they are situated – and the impact of this materiality on the capacity and limitations of the live music event, something scene studies had not previously explored in depth.

Finally, the ecological approach accounts for the interdependencies between all factors discussed above and argues that such an ecology cannot function effectively without these interdependencies. As van der Hoeven et al. state, '[a]n ecology approach allows for an integrated analysis of the local, national, and internationally interwoven structures of the (live) music industries' (2020, p. 28). It is therefore comparable to previous cultural industries ontologies such as 'agglomerations' (Grodach, O'Connor & Gibson 2017; O'Connor 2004; Pratt 2004; Scott 2000) and 'creative milieus' (Costa 2012; Hessler & Zimmerman 2008; Meusberger, Funke & Wunder 2009). These ontologies similarly account for forms of 'competitive collaboration' (Bonink & Hitters 2001; Hitters & Richards 2002; Taylor 2015) that defy the common logic of consumer capitalism, in that multiple co-located SMEs[9] (i.e. small venues in a shared neighbourhood) compete for consumers while also sharing in a pool of cultural labour (i.e. regularly gigging musicians and often bar staff). For example, small live music venues compete as small businesses but, as they benefit from the same policy adjustments, the same funding announcements[10] and the same media and digital infrastructures, they are similarly affected by the same changes and shifts within the live music ecology. Although small venues might fill distinct niches within the local market for hospitality and live music experiences, they are too interconnected with each other to exist as isolated businesses. Their interdependencies and density of co-location are what make them viable as long-term projects, as spaces of cultural production. Such spaces need city cultures, music cultures and scenes to thrive. As a means of properly documenting and discussing this, the live music ecology 'allows a holistic approach to the connections between diverse actors and the material conditions in a sector' (van der Hoeven et al. 2020, p. 27). However, although it is a very effective and useful descriptor of the material realities of live music and its demands, 'ecology' is somewhat of a misnomer, as the term refers to the study of ecosystems rather than the conditions of the ecosystems themselves.

While the ecological approach posited by Behr et al. is a helpful ontological framework, what we are really talking about when we talk about the 'live music ecology' as it relates to specific locales and places – those that are delineated or bounded in some way, either by geography or networks – are live music *ecosystems*. My definition of a localized and tangible live music ecology as an 'ecosystem' reflects a recent statement by MusicNSW, the peak body for music industries in New South Wales, in which it described these industries as a 'complex ecosystem with many moving parts' (New South Wales Parliament 2018, p. 12). The importance of such a network has been previously discussed (Homan 2014; Stahl 2003b)[11] but has only been recently defined (Behr et al. 2016b). Further, the term

---

[9] Small to medium enterprises.
[10] Throughout the COVID-19 pandemic, hospitality and music venues collectivized and petitioned governments on behalf of these sectors. Such advocacy work was successful in pushing state governments towards direct financial support packages (see South Australia's Live Music Support program (Music Development Office 2022) and Victoria's Live Performance Support program (Creative Victoria 2022) for specific examples).
[11] For example, Shane Homan (2014, pp. 149–50) described key aspects of a live music ecosystem – a network of bricks-and-mortar spaces and interdependent relationships that coalesce to form the infrastructure of a 'music city' – without giving this infrastructure a formal name.

'ecosystem' rather than 'ecology' is dominant within the policy literature on the live music industries (Homan 2016; Martin 2017; New South Wales Parliament 2018; Rozbicka, Behr & Hamilton 2022), and work on venue spaces in particular frames their connections and interdependencies in this manner (Carah et al. 2021; Gu, Domer & O'Connor 2021; Hunt, Gedgaudas & Seman 2020). This is a necessary distinction to make in the context of live music, space and place, specifically regarding small live music venues. In the following section I define the 'live music ecosystem' as a distinct term. To make this distinction clear, the term also needs to be juxtaposed with 'scene'.

'Scenes' and the 'live music ecosystem'

In terms of their relevance to the topic of this book, music scenes relate specifically to the sociocultural aspects of small live music venues; the networks and social interactions happening within, between and across venue spaces. Such scenes are loosely affiliated groups of people co-mingling and organizing musical labour and participation within a cultural and spatial context. Such organization of cultural labour is foundational to the live music ecology and forms the basis of much of the work that live music ecosystems do. However, it is my contention that 'scene' and 'ecology/ecosystem' are distinct yet overlapping terms that are both useful and necessary in any analysis of local music-making practices and the venues in which they occur. Yet before this discussion can take place, a clear distinction between the terms needs to be made.

For clarity's sake, music scenes include the following characteristics:

- **Participants in a cultural practice**, in this instance local music making. This not only includes the musicians but also those other 'insiders' that are engaged with the scene – either peripherally or directly – such as the door staff, the bar staff and shift managers, casual and dedicated patrons, venue owners, and other music industry workers and audience members. These scene participants are engaged in an ongoing process of identity construction and disruption, as scenes change and develop through their continued and/or discontinued participation.
- Scenes also include **the social processes that develop around these participants and their cultural practices**. Certain social and cultural relations might be specific to a scene, and therefore identified closely with it.

These might include musical genres, performance styles or a particular type of ensemble. Venues play a role here too, as scenes might coalesce around a selection of venues or perhaps even just one. Thus, the material conditions of a scene's infrastructure serve to shape the social and cultural relations of music scenes, although this materiality is not broadly acknowledged within scene studies (Behr et al. 2016b, p. 6). Such social and cultural relations contribute to the sense of identity that scenes hold, yet this identity is not rigid but porous and fluid.

- Finally, **time and place are integral to discussions of scene**, especially local music scenes. The popularity of certain musical genres and the influence of key players in certain scenes shifts and changes over time. Their prominence is often specific to a geographical place, although the boundaries of this place are also subject to change. Further, despite the rise of translocalism and digital media, place remains central to live music scenes because all scenes have local manifestations, as live music performance must always take place *somewhere* (van der Hoeven et al. 2020, p. 29).

Through an understanding of these key characteristics, it becomes clear that music scenes, as they are defined throughout the literature, are closely associated with people, their actions and interactions, as well as the time and place wherein these interactions occur. However, while spatiality (i.e. space and place) is inherent in any discussion of music scenes (Straw 2015), what is apparent is the lack of a discussion of material concerns, in particular the materiality of venue spaces, their limitations and facilities, as well as other infrastructures. Also missing is a discussion of 'outsiders': social agents that are not scene participants but whose actions greatly affect the scene itself. These might include the police, policymakers, building developers, the Environmental Protection Authority (EPA),[12] liquor licensing officers and other outsiders whose actions and agency have an impact on music scenes. Finally, scene is lateral in its articulation and does not account for the way in which live music events are scalable, requiring a variety of spaces to function and facilitate an ongoing and sustainable live music culture, from the pub to the stadium (Behr et al. 2014).

---

[12] In Australia, for example, the EPA is responsible for monitoring 'noise pollution' in urban environments and therefore has the capacity to limit and shut down live music activities.

To clarify, a live music ecosystem is often affected by outsiders. An arts policy advisor or representative of the EPA might not have much to do with Melbourne's live music scene, but their power over its live music ecosystem – and underlying scene by extension – is far-reaching. Similar can be said of academics, politicians and corporate sponsors (Walmsley 2016, p. 286). This power is articulated in the form of symbolic and economic capital, those types of capital that are the most concrete, tangible and readily convertible (Bourdieu 1997). More integral to music scenes are cultural and social capital. A system of associations, exchanges and human interactions (i.e. social capital) that supports and encourages the flow of ideas (cultural capital) between individuals (the scene) and institutions (the live music ecosystem) can be seen to exist (Landry 2008, p. 133). In this context, the scene is made up of individual participants. The venues these participants regularly visit, as well as local government bodies, advocacy groups, 'outsider' agents and other organizations whose influence affects these venues and the scenes articulated among them, form the live music ecosystem. Scenes are therefore distinct from the ecosystem itself, but intrinsic in its makeup.

More than music scenes, which are ephemeral and porous, live music ecosystems are dependent on the materiality of venue spaces and how readily (and frequently) such venues can be adapted for the performance of live music. An ecological approach to musical performance must therefore take materiality into account, as live music ecosystems rely on venue spaces for their reification, whereas music scenes are more obtuse, based primarily on social interaction and exchange. As an ontology, the ecological approach also considers the influence of social actors that operate outside of the scene. Finally, unlike scenes, which are more transient 'moments', live music ecosystems are reliant on an ongoing live music culture and those things that facilitate such a culture, such as infrastructure, policy, audiences and density of production and consumption.

Within their seminal article, Behr et al. (2016b) outline the three main areas of investigation that an ecological approach to live music draws attention to. The first is the materiality of venue spaces:

> Such buildings may or may not have been constructed as musical sites; even when they are, the musical ideology inscribed in their physical and acoustic design may or may not be compatible with the physical symbolization of contemporary musical communities. Either way, buildings do not just exist in people's minds.
>
> (Behr et al. 2016b, p. 19)

The second is the interdependence between otherwise disparate social actors:

> A musical event is not just cultural, the result of ideological agreement among actors who, in coming to such agreement, form a musical world. A live music event also involves constant negotiation with people who are not part of a shared ideological construct. The role of the promoter is often overlooked as they intersect and interact with multiple actors to ensure the live music event goes ahead.
>
> (Behr et al. 2016b, p. 19)

The final area is the sustainability of the resulting live music culture:

> When policymakers are considering how to sustain a local musical culture or bolster a national musical economy, it is important that they understand the relationship between all the factors ... Similarly, while the primary goal of commercial promoters is to pursue their own profits, they too need to be aware that a policy which, in competitive terms, makes it impossible for small promoters or venues to survive will, in the long term, have a decisive impact on their own sustainability.
>
> (Behr et al. 2016b, p. 20)

I utilize these three points as a means of framing discussion around the value of live music ecosystems, the role of small venues within them, the social agents that impact their functioning and sustainability and how they differ from previous definitions of music scenes.

To make a further distinction, if scenes are transient and exist across multiple spaces and places simultaneously both locally and translocally, then live music ecosystems are more fixed and refer to those spaces and institutions that serve as infrastructure for each scene. These may be run by scene participants, such as independent record labels or live music venues, or might be official government bodies that are removed from the scene, such as the Arts Council of Australia, a federal cultural funding body. As van der Hoeven et al. state in reference to the ecological approach:

> This perspective is useful to analyse the structure of social relations between different actors and how that contributes to the qualities of the live music sector and the sustainability of live music cultures, including the material aspects of live music (e.g., characteristics of the music venue) and intangible dimensions (e.g., the histories associated with a specific venue).
>
> (2020, p. 29)

Building on this perspective, a live music ecosystem can be framed vertically as a pyramid 'whereby different venues – of all sizes – display interdependence, alongside different promotional practices' (Behr et al. 2014, p. 3). Within this analogy, small venues – 'the so called "toilet circuit"' (Behr et al. 2014, p. 5) – comprise the ecosystem's foundation, upon which the rest of a city's live music ecosystem is built. Scene, by comparison, is more lateral in its articulation. Organizations and institutions included in an ecosystem wield more power than individual participants in scenes. That is not to say that scene participants do not hold power, but that this power is articulated through social and cultural capital within the scene, all of which is difficult to transact and exchange outside of the scene without engaging with ecological agents.

Why 'ecology'?

The term 'ecology'[13] has experienced increased usage across academic studies of popular music and culture in general. Ernst Haeckel defined it via an analogy to free market economics, describing it as 'the economy of nature' (cited in Stauffer 1957, p. 141). Indeed, nature has often provided inspiration for human values to be organized around and 'music ecology' has its own body of literature, one that is varied and often conflicting (Keogh & Collinson 2016, p. 8). In the arts more generally the ecology trope has often been deployed to legitimize and 'naturalize' capitalistic and neoliberal systems of power, and the term 'cultural ecology' has been utilized by governments to promote competition and market principles between arts organizations. In this context, 'ecology' is used to submerge systems of power that dictate flows of capital, sinking these in a web of metaphor, as '[t]he cultural ecology model – one based on a pastoral idea of nature – has the ideological effect of naturalizing power relationships, masking conflict, and legitimizing hierarchies by exscribing them' (Keogh & Collinson 2016, p. 11). Further, when referring to for-profit cultural enterprises, the term 'cultural ecology' takes the neoliberal edge off, reducing such organizations to a state of passivity, masking the corporate boards and executive decisions that drive the so-called creative industries.

---

[13] 'Ecology' has been applied in a broad variety of ways in contemporary humanities. This has caused confusion between the term's multiple applications, as '[e]cology has been used across the social sciences to contextualize aspects of social and cultural life since the mid-20th century' (Keogh & Collinson 2016, p. 1).

Although it has been criticized as too broad to account for the complexities of the music sector (Keogh 2013), the ecology trope is still useful when describing the economic and social networks responsible for live music and for answering questions of how and why a particular concert event happens (Behr et al. 2016b, p. 5). I follow here the definition of 'live music ecology' initially outlined by Simon Frith and his colleagues (Behr et al. 2016b). In this context, the term was first utilized to describe the network of live music production, social connections and events that link local DIY artists to massive multinational corporations, such as Live Nation (Frith 2010, p. 3), and it was further defined in publications by Frith's colleagues at the Live Music Exchange (Behr et al. 2016b, 2014; Frith 2012). This ecological approach prioritizes the material and logistic, emphasizing production.

Such an emphasis on the production of culture is juxtaposed against previous cultural studies approaches that have focused primarily on cultural consumption and reception (Straw 2010), and scene studies, which focus on issues of participation, social identity and cultural memory (Bennett & Rogers 2016b). Such approaches tend to focus on more passive elements of engagement with live music, whereas the ecological approach is fixated on material and logistical concerns of how live music is produced. Although scene is still a useful descriptor for similar types of activities, the live music ecosystem places an emphasis on the live music event and its catalysts. Small venues play a central role here, placing them at the nexus of live music ecosystems and local scenes.

Music scenes and live music ecosystems intersect at multiple levels and are dependent on each other for their mutual manifestation. Live music ecosystems are inherently more localized than scenes as they are dependent on the materiality of venue spaces and the interdependence of local social actors to give them form (Behr et al. 2016b). This contrasts with definitions of 'scene', which 'describes a social process of music meaning-making which is not limited by the materiality of place' (Behr et al. 2016b, p. 6).

The materiality of venue spaces is a core concern of this book. The built environments of venues are a very real factor in the roles they perform. Therefore, live music ecosystems serve as valuable frameworks in discussions of place, space and the music scenes threaded throughout. Although proponents of scene might argue that the concept already takes issues of the live music ecology into account (Bennett & Rogers 2016b), scenes are more concerned with the fluidity of identity and organization of social practice than the materiality of venue spaces. Further, '[a]n ecological study of live music means studying social agents which are not in any coherent ideological way members of the social networks that are described by Becker's art worlds, Bourdieu's cultural fields, or Finnegan's social pathways' (Behr et al. 2016b, p. 6). These social agents influence live music ecosystems despite not otherwise acting as participants in the scene. Therefore, the ecological approach is a more holistic ontology for understanding the factors necessary for a live music event to take place and small venues along with them, as key sites for the production of live music. Ecosystems are also useful in accounting for the impact of policy, funding and policymakers.

Following the above discussion of music scenes, subcultures and the ecological approach to the study of live music, it is my contention that 'scenes' and 'ecosystems' are complementary terms for overlapping social, cultural and economic phenomena occurring within similar spheres of influence. While scene encompasses the social and cultural elements of a musical culture, the ecological approach accounts for the materiality of such cultures, the non-scenic actors that facilitate, hamper or permit such cultures, and the infrastructure necessary for such cultures to continue. Both ontologies have a role to play in the study of live music and small venues, and therefore both will serve a valuable function throughout the course of this book.

Part Two

Vibrancy

2

Live music and the city

As a concept, an ideal type and a material environment, 'the city' plays a fundamental role in shaping both popular understandings of live music spaces and how venues are positioned within cityscapes. Cities influence and impact venues as both brick-and-mortar spaces that have often been repurposed or adapted from previous uses (Kronenburg 2011, 2013), and as spaces of imagined community that contribute to a collective narrative of cultural participation (i.e. a vernacular culture). The intersection between urban planning policy, the character of local neighbourhoods and the broader cultural diet of urbanites shapes the identity of small venue spaces, and vice versa. Many venues manifest the cultural vibrancy and interests of those living nearby through their programming. Others might disrupt such homogeneity and attract patrons from further abroad, serving as a novelty within their locales. Either way, city cultures are synonymous with the night-time economy, and live music venues – particularly those that are hidden, small or niche – play an established role in such cultures. Further, small live music venues have historically been associated with urban and post-industrial environments, and the density of small venues in inner cities, along with the way in which they are highly networked and interdependent, impacts their financial sustainability and growth as well as their limitations as cultural enterprises.

The relationship between cities, live music and small venues is dense and intersects at many levels. Yet despite the focus on live music in urban centres that has dominated previous venue research (Bennett, C 2020, p. 602), it is also important to include regional and rural settings in discussions of small live music venues. These provide an important contrast to urban spaces, demonstrating how historical, geographic, political and economic factors affect venues differently. This chapter will explore these contextual elements and how small live music venues are affected by these through a discussion of the 'music city' paradigm and an analysis of two case study 'music cities', with an emphasis on the Australian context. These will be juxtaposed against the regional and rural context for small live music venues, concluding with a reimagining of how small venues might be better positioned within urban public policy discourses.

Small venues and the city

Live music's influence on experiences of nightlife is self-evident, and the mix and density of live music spaces on high streets and throughout cultural clusters further impacts experiences of the city and its night-time economy. A network of small venues co-located in a shared environment will often serve niche interests and cater to diverse audiences, although the clientele of each specific venue might be quite homogenous. Despite ever-present issues of homophily common within the creative industries and other cultural sectors (Luckman et al. 2020, p. 5; Millward, Widdop & Halpin 2017; Taylor & Luckman 2020), and the complicity of live music venues in entrenching such issues (Whiting & Carter 2016), a variety of small venues densely agglomerated within urban space can serve up unique and distinct experiences within only a few metres of each other. Such density encourages interdependencies to the point that such venues and cultural clusters effectively function in a state of 'competitive collaboration' (Oakley 2006; O'Connor 2007). Such conditions challenge the usual standards of capitalistic competition for market share and are defined by more rhizomatic understandings of how cultural spaces exist in a web of interconnection and interdependence, that is, the live music ecosystem. However, the ideal conditions for a well-functioning live music ecosystem are rare and rely on a multitude of factors.

Policy settings are a major factor affecting live music ecosystems, as are the regulatory norms established within certain locales. These are further dependent on environmental and legislative factors. The intentions of a newly elected state or local government might meet significant resistance from residents, developers or advocacy groups, and vice versa. Building planning codes and liquor licensing authorities have entrenched laws and processes that are monolithic and often do not account for the nuanced differences between hospitality and cultural spaces (Ballico 2016; Burke & Schmidt 2013; Homan 2008). Such laws and processes are often slow and difficult to change without substantial public pressure. Efforts to facilitate a more dynamic live music ecosystem within cities therefore require consistent lobbying.

The regulation of built entertainment and cultural spaces in urban environments – compounded by noise restrictions, residential developments, pre-existing cultural, political and social issues, and the dominance of commercially oriented spaces in the night-time economy – often makes hosting live music in the city a difficult task. Each city has its own distinct contextual and historical issues that inform planning codes and other legislation, as well as precedents set by previous use of urban and semi-urban spaces. Small live music venues are often at the mercy of these, although many campaign and advocacy groups have emerged to try to foster amenable conditions for small venues in the city (Homan 2011a, 2011b).

In concert with these, 'music city' policy and planning consultancies have become a global and officiated standard for advocacy, with consultancy group Sound Diplomacy serving as a primary example. However, grassroots campaigns specific to local issues are also prevalent in many major cities. Prominent Australian examples include Save Live Australia's Music (SLAM), Fair Go 4 Live Music, the Renew campaigns in Newcastle and Adelaide and Sydney's Keep Sydney Open (which is also now a political party in the state of New South Wales). These groups have sought to assist and redefine the role of live music in the city. However, as the ideal type for a 'music city' continues to be propagated and justified by a growing global cultural policy assemblage of handbooks, consultancies and cultural intermediaries (Bennett, T 2020), the definition of 'live music in the city' has increasingly narrowed, or at least become more curated in its articulation.

Much like the 'creative city' (Florida 2002; Landry 2008), the 'music city' has now become instrumentalized and similarly weaponized as an influential and equally problematic method for generating urban 'vibrancy' through a 'just add culture and stir' approach. Although more nuanced and specific to cultural production than consumption (which the 'creative city' model relies on heavily), such instrumentalization of the music city is often based on the same normative assumptions that have been heavily criticized throughout research on cultural industries–led urban regeneration and development (Bennett, T 2020; Whiting, Barnett & O'Connor 2022), particularly that of creative city proponents Richard Florida (2002) and Charles Landry (2008). These issues continue to impact small live music venues as they persist in 'music city' policy discourse. To this end, this chapter will consider the policy and planning phenomenon known as the 'music city', various critiques of this concept, and how cultural and urban planning policies derived from the 'creative cities' model – such as the 'music city' – have influenced the small live music venues and local music scenes of two Australian cities: Brisbane and Adelaide.

The 'music city'

The term 'music city' has entered popular usage over the last twenty years, predominantly as a promotional and marketing paradigm specific to urban cultural policy.[1] Its popularity has increased alongside the rise of 'creative cities'-led urban regeneration policies and has persisted long after such policies have been discredited by even their own authors (Florida 2017). Such policies have reshaped the traditional cultural industries – rebranded as the post-Fordist 'creative industries' (McRobbie 2011; Moor & Littler 2008; Pacella, Luckman & O'Connor 2021a, 2021b) – as drivers of economic growth, determinants of infrastructural and residential development (which often, paradoxically, leads to the demise of the aforementioned culture), and magnets for investment and labour markets. As an extension of 'creative cities' policies, the 'music city' has emerged as a distinct method for drawing on an urban centre's reputation for, history of and relationship with (usually, but not always) popular music[2] to reframe it as a lively and culturally significant place worthy of attention, flighty capital and footloose professionals.

As a marketing device, the *music city* evokes a sense of vibrancy and access to organic, street-level culture that is immediate and calls to mind a range of signifiers. These vary from the carnivalesque atmosphere of New Orleans during Mardi Gras, the subterranean high-street gig pits of Glasgow's cellar venues and the multi-story nightclubs of Sydney's prominent LGBTQI+ district Oxford Street. Beyond popular music, the paradigm is also used to describe historically significant music cities, such as Vienna (Graf 2019; Zacharasiewicz 2018), as well as more recently named music cities with deep connections to establishment arts, such as Adelaide, Australia (Franklin, Lee & Rentschler 2022). Indeed,

---

[1] Handbooks have served as the primary method for disseminating the ideas and policy 'toolkits' necessary for enacting the music city within cityscapes, with *The Mastering of a Music City* (Terrill et al. 2015) serving as a primary example. Such handbooks seek to justify and legitimate the 'music city' as effective urban cultural policy, often using competing logics and antagonistic modes of valuation to do so (Bennett, T. 2020, p. 6).
[2] Vienna has consistently marketed itself as a city of music given its strong historical connection with the classical traditions and their composers (notably Haydn, Beethoven and Mozart). Its historic concert halls and opera theatres are still in frequent use today.

due to its deployment towards a multiplicity of meanings, the 'music city' has become a mnemonic prompt that means different things to different people, eliciting diverse imagined communities and experiences. However, what these associations often have in common is an ideal-type urban setting wherein live musical performances are engaging, accessible and frequent.

It is interesting to note the exclusions implied here. The 'music city' is not for those who seek the quiet life, nor those who ascribe to hegemonic or establishment ideas of culture. Even the reputations of those music cities built on older cultural forms often have a contemporary and dynamic underbelly of edgy performance culture and are heterogeneous in their articulation as 'music cities' (Fürnkranz 2021; Reitsamer 2011). Regional settings are also neglected from popular imaginings of the music city. Instead, the common themes that dominate shared understandings of the music city reflect the way urban cultural economies have been instrumentalized to attract various forms of capital and labour, and the commodification of live performance and cultural consumption more broadly. In this context, the music city is the latest in a long line of buzzwords that governments and civic leaders – convinced by consultancy groups and urban planners – have deployed to drive economic development and shore up cultural status via promotion of the cultural and creative industries, often by (over)emphasizing their ill-defined 'economic impact' over and above their cultural contribution (O'Connor 2016). This link between cultural policy and urban development has become a key feature of discourse around live music and the city and has its origins in 'creative cities' policy work that gained popularity in the late 1990s and early 2000s (Florida 2002; Landry et al. 1996).

The 'creative cities' school of socio-economics and urban planning, from which the music city is derived, has greatly affected the way in which cultural industries are managed, regulated and promoted by local governments (Lobato 2006; Luckman 2017). Coined by Charles Landry (2008), the 'creative city' concept centres on the notion that cities are built on 'hard' and 'soft'[3] infrastructure. These are both resources themselves as well as points of attraction for skilled labour, particularly that of knowledge workers and 'creative' professionals. Prominent urban studies theorist Richard Florida expanded on Landry's 'creative city' concept in his book *The Rise of the Creative Class* (2002), taking Landry's 'soft

---

[3] Landry defines soft infrastructure as 'that system of associations, exchanges and human interactions that supports and encourages the flow of ideas between individuals and institutions' (2008, p. 133).

infrastructure' and its constituent workforce of highly skilled labour – dubbed 'the creative class' – and running with it. Florida's work has since become synonymous with creative industries–led urban regeneration policies that have dominated urban planning discourse since the mid-2000s, much of which has influenced the notion of the 'music city'. This is despite Florida himself disowning, amending and correcting many of his ideas with the publication of his book *The New Urban Crisis* (2017), which is not quite a *mea culpa* but as close as one would expect. Regardless, his original 'creative class' thesis marches on in planning and policy documents and continues to be re-tread in university design and architecture faculties not engaged with their colleagues in cultural studies, sociology and the critical humanities. Florida's ideas are therefore still worthy of further critique, as they are very much alive.

Establishing a link between economic development and concentrations of technology and media workers, artists, musicians and other 'high bohemians', Florida asserts that music plays a central role in the creation of identity and the formation of communities in urban environments, stating that 'music is a key part of what makes a place authentic, in effect providing a sound or "audio identity"' (2002, p. 228). Florida (2002, p. 184) also emphasizes the appeal of 'street-level culture': thoroughfares lined with clusters of small-scale cultural producers, including coffee houses, art galleries, live music venues and boutique bars. He describes these kinds of accessible cultural hotspots as organic, native and 'of the moment'. Further, Florida's street-level culture implies the idea of a local scene – a network of social relationships built around a specific location that facilitates interaction by means of work, play or a combination of both[4] – albeit Florida's use of 'scene' is decidedly more neoliberal than Straw's (1991, 2001), and emphasizes consumption specifically, whereas Straw's definition of scene is more participatory. However, what is common across the creative and music cities literature is the consistent instrumentalization of cultural production – whether it be design work, the visual arts or music making – in favour of largely economic markers of success such as 'job creation, economic growth, tourism development, city brand building and artistic growth' (Terrill et al. 2015, p. 13). This frames urban cultural policy as essentially urban *development* policy, a tension that – as discussed below – is ultimately paradoxical.

---

[4] This intertwining between work, play and socialization aligns with Gill and Pratt's (2008) concept of 'immaterial labour' and Wittel's (2001) 'network sociality'. These specific modes of instrumentalized cultural and social capital, and the blurring of these with performative cultural labour, are often inherent in the cultural and creative industries.

Emerging from this tension, music city policy work builds upon the creative cities model while acknowledging the specificities of localized live music scenes, ecosystems and their reliance on grassroots spaces of cultural production. Small live music venues play a fundamental role in the 'music city' and are positioned within music city policy discourse as a vital tool in its development. However, these discourses remain aimed at persuading planning departments and other components of government of the benefits of music city policy (Bennett, T 2020) and are therefore modelled to be enacted via a top-down approach. Although the problems of this can be countered, such a model cannot account for the historical and political circumstances of every city, as some issues and problems are both entrenched and contingent. Addressing such issues and problems often requires significant shifts in the attitudes of several tiers of government regarding risk, alcohol licences, noise abatement, development, land-use value and so on. Not only this but local stakeholders and residents, many of whom hold significant amounts of political power and capital – albeit often non-economic forms such as social and symbolic capital (Bourdieu & Wacquant 2013) – also require convincing of the value of music cities and their perceived benefits. These community groups, stakeholders, landowners and other long-term residents are often deeply resistant to change and development of any kind and can cause various problems in the planning or advocacy for musical or performance activities, let alone an entire 'music city'. It is for these reasons that a uniform model for a music city is almost an impossible task to enact, as cities are too diverse and subject to too many historical and social variables. To adequately consider the role of small live music venues within the music city, we must therefore consider the problem with the 'music city' as an ideal type, a policy object and a cultural icon.

The problem with the 'music city'

Florida's work has been the starting point for discourse surrounding the 'music city' in much recent urban and cultural policy, specifically the broader instrumentalization of popular music policy in urban environments. In particular, the music city hinges on the premise that talented young people across a range of professional fields – the 'creative class' – are attracted to thriving music scenes and that live music culture is a major contributing factor in recruiting these well-educated, talented and highly mobile workers (Terrill et al. 2015, p. 27). Indeed, small live music venues are fertile grounds for the kinds of street-level culture Florida promises, as they provide a spatial focus for participants to group themselves around, and their grassroots performance culture is symbolic of the creative city generally. However, Florida and other proponents of the creative city/music city model are not without their detractors, and there has been serious criticism regarding this thesis, which even its proponents have largely accepted (Florida 2017). Government intervention to encourage 'creative cities' has largely failed (Watson & Taylor 2014), corrupting a process that might have been more successful despite government rather than because of it. Further, the model has been roundly criticized for speeding up the process of gentrification, threatening the very street-level culture that it relies upon.

Kate Shaw's work on the cultural sector criticizes creative city strategies as being no more than economic development plans that instrumentalize culture, expediting gentrification, pushing rental rates up and threatening the tenure of the cultural producers that these strategies rely upon for their success. Such a policy direction creates a paradox: '[t]he particular problem for cities that want economic development and cultural vitality is that one tends to occur at the expense of the other' (Shaw 2013, p. 340). The impact of gentrification on 'cultural infrastructure' (Gallan & Gibson 2013, p. 174) – such as small live music venues – is clear, demonstrating how the instrumentalization of culture used to attract investment and encourage development only serves to increase the problem, pricing out artists and cultural producers. Gentrification is therefore not only a by-product but perhaps the goal of creative city strategies and has resulted in the large-scale residential development of previous 'cultural clusters' and other post-industrial 'creative' neighbourhoods in cities and urban settings in the West. Such developments have been a particular concern for small live music venues and a catalyst for disputes over noise (Burke & Schmidt 2013), leading to the closure of many venues (Gibson & Homan 2004) and tensions between residents, local cultural workers and music scenes.

As a counterpoint to Florida's 'street-level culture', Shaw's research focuses on recently colonized 'cultural clusters', emphasizing the closely placed operation of 'indie creative activities' and their interdependencies. These activities are defined as low cost and low profit, but of high cultural value:

> Independent creative subcultures,[5] in their various hybrids of music, theatre, art, and new and old media, are the primordial soup of cultural evolution. It is

---

[5] Although Shaw uses the term 'subculture' as a descriptor for the types of localized creative production typical of cultural clusters, her use of the term stems from cultural geography and does not have the same meaning and legacy as that of cultural studies and the BCCCS that popularized it.

> within these indie subcultures that the new work begins, often with very low entry thresholds as, unlike other productive activities, participation does not demand much initial skill or experience.
>
> (Shaw 2013, p. 333)

The social and cultural benefits of such grassroots cultural production are significant, as such activities might encourage individuals to transition from consumers to producers of art and culture or motivate further engagement in the form of more exhibitions, performance opportunities and live music venues.

Other cultural theorists and academics have offered alternatives to Florida and Landry's creative industries–led strategies for urban regeneration and development (Banks & O'Connor 2017; Pratt 2004, 2015; Whiting, Barnett & O'Connor 2022). These thinkers have emphasized the highly networked nature of the cultural economy and systemic factors affecting it, as well as a political economy approach to the study of culture that acknowledges the role of policy and governance in directly supporting arts and culture rather than the market-first ideology of the 'creative city'. They point to the kind of nuanced approach to urban policy and small-scale cultural production first pursued by the Labour-led Greater London Council (GLC) in the 1980s. Such policies resulted in the rich variety of independent record labels, galleries, studios and other hyper-local cultural production that the 'creative city' approach sought to capitalize on. However, rather than emphasizing cultural *production* like the GLC, creative/music city polices have chosen a *consumption*-led approach, leading to the homogenization of such culture globally and ultimately its failure as a social concept.

In line with the theories and alternatives offered by critics of the 'creative cities' approach, I posit that small venues serve as a local live music scene's infrastructure for the production of 'indie creative activities', as Shaw describes them. They are essential to the vitality of live music scenes, the sustainability of live music ecosystems and the cities that rely on these ecosystems for their cultural vibrancy. On the other hand, live music's role in 'creative cities'–led cultural policy and the effect these policies have had on local night-time economies are worthy of consideration here (Homan 2011b).

The Floridian school of neoliberal urban planning and socioeconomics has had a large impact on Australian cities, with even small towns developing their own 'creative city' plans, while the larger capital cities have planned theirs in terms of regional and global competition (Homan 2011b, p. 97). Further, live music is a major asset in 'creative cities' strategies, as a city's 'liveability' – an increasingly opaque and meaningless term in global policy contexts (Paul &

Sen 2020) – is based on consumer access to leisure, entertainment and 'street-level culture', of which live music and music venues form a significant part. Live music culture, music venues and government policy are therefore tied closely to concepts of city branding and the marketing of culture (Homan 2011b), yet music cultures and small venues are part of the grassroots networks of cultural production that allow local music scenes to thrive, and therefore need protecting from the multiple evils of such branding and marketing (i.e. gentrification and overdevelopment).

A city's nightlife and music scenes are almost always assumed in discussions of cultural vibrancy. Festivals, concerts and other cultural initiatives all rely on the realm of social encounter and play associated with the night-time. However, 'as an object of cultural policy [nightlife] has been strangely marginalised' (Lovatt & O'Connor 1995, p. 130). Indeed, within the context of much urban cultural policy, particularly in Australia, 'it seemed that this nightlife was not a legitimate object of attention other than as something to be regulated and contained … In short, a problem' (p. 130).

Dominant perceptions of nightlife cast it as a site of transgression, 'a time of crime and desire' (p. 130) and a space for encounter with the 'other'. Therefore, the night-time economy continues to be viewed as something that must be policed, curtailed and sanitized. This is problematic, as it is evident that a city's nightlife is an integral part of its broader cultural verve: a vibrant space and time of socialization that needs to be addressed and valued as such. Research has called for government policy on nightlife to shift from the perspective that it is a problem to be policed to the view that it is a social practice to be protected (Lobato 2006), acknowledging the social and cultural value of live music specifically (van der Hoeven & Hitters 2019; van der Hoeven et al. 2022). This draws attention to the nature of pubs, clubs, bars and other small venues as sites of networking, exchange and the production of a distinct form of cultural capital previously referred to as 'tacit city knowledge' (i.e. the 'lived and learned' experience of a city acquired only by being a local; O'Connor, 2004). Further, '[n]ightlife is not only about hedonism; it is also a site for the exchange of ideas, gossip and speculation – the tacit knowledges which underwrite creative cities' (Lobato 2006, p. 72). Therefore, a city's live music ecosystem is a particularly valuable and vibrant cultural asset, and one which must be protected, safeguarded and encouraged accordingly. This requires careful consideration of the role of grassroots culture and smaller live music spaces, a balance that governments and policymakers often forget when making reforms to cultural and entertainment sector policy.

Music cities: The Australian context

Since the publication of Straw's (1991) seminal essay on music scenes, translocal scenes have remained a topic of focus within the study of popular music, particularly the way in which such scenes are organized and interdependent across considerable distances and geography (Hodkinson 2004; Kahn-Harris 2007; Laing 1997; Schilt 2004). As a musical culture and network of live music ecosystems that is heavily affected by processes of globalization as well as the localized practices and limitations of its major cities, the broader Australian music scene is decidedly a translocal scene, as are the genre-specific scenes that traverse the country's major urban centres. These scenes, perhaps more than most, are significantly affected by geography due to the way in which the country's densely concentrated population is grouped in each state's capital city (Bennett, Stratton & Peterson 2008, p. 595). Australian live music scenes are therefore more noticeably influenced by 'city cultures', rather than a homogenous national music culture (Bennett, Stratton & Peterson 2008, p. 595), although the influence of the syndicated national youth broadcaster Triple J[6] certainly has a reinforcing effect on the latter. Despite this, city cultures dominate the musical landscape of Australia (Brunt & Stahl 2018), with the music scenes of each city often referred to by practitioners, participants and enthusiasts as distinct (e.g. the 'Melbourne music scene' or the 'Brisbane music scene').

A diversity of inner-urban community radio stations,[7] dynamic city-centric live music ecosystems served by strong networks of small heritage venue spaces, and until the 2010s a largely decentralized music press have all served to reinforce the influence of city cultures on music making in Australia. However, although local scenes exist on an accessible and everyday level in the major cities, genre-specific translocal scenes exist between and across Australia's regional and urban centres. Bands and artists that identify with these genres often tour together and will collaborate on releases remotely. The advent of the internet has made it easier for translocal scenes to articulate themselves,

---

[6] Triple J is an Australian national radio station and public youth broadcaster. The station was syndicated across the country in the late 1980s and early 1990s and sits under the auspices of the taxpayer-funded Australian Broadcasting Corporation. It has a national monopoly on the broadcast of new, Australian, alternative music focused on a younger audience.

[7] First launched as part of a national 'University of the Air' programme, major universities in most of Australia's capital cities received funding from the federal government to establish dedicated radio stations in the 1970s. Most of these continue to operate today, and have been lightning rods for radical politics, new music and the organization of small-scale cultural and social activities in Australia's capital cities for many years.

and in a country as geographically isolated as Australia (particularly from the rest of the Anglophone world), such translocalism is ever important, as global live music scenes – such as heavy metal (Kahn-Harris 2007) and dance (Laing 1997) – are more difficult for Australian artists to access given their distance from international touring circuits. This distance has created a two-tiered system within the Australian live music industry, one based on domestic touring, regional fame and hobbyism, and another focused on international markets, with their more densely populated touring routes and larger audiences (Rogers & Whiting 2020). This distance further emphasizes the role of space and place as they relate to local music scenes.

In the Australian context, local scenes are clearly defined by space, place and each city's urban boundaries, whereas translocal scenes – influenced by genre and musical aesthetics – criss-cross state borders and draw on local scenes for context and cohesion. Australia is therefore an interesting case study in the relationship between localism and translocalism, as geographically isolated and disparate local scenes feed into the translocal network and influence the broader aesthetic discourse. A national, Australian live music ecosystem can be seen to exist, as local scenes, dominated by those in the major cities, grow and make connections with translocal scenes.

Although steps have been made to promote Australia's music industries as monolithic and singular, the nation's local music scenes remain concentrated in urban centres that are quite distinct, particularly the larger east coast cities of Brisbane, Sydney and Melbourne. The relationship that local music scenes share with the cities they inhabit is particularly visible in the Australian context, emphasizing a translocal, national live music ecosystem that frames the local music scenes of each urban centre as nodes of participation, production and consumption in a broader translocal network. Thus, the musical practices of Australia's music scenes are defined in similar terms to Straw's understanding of 1990s 'alternative rock', in which 'the relationship of different local spaces of activity to each other takes the form of circuits, overlaid upon each other, through which particular styles of alternative music circulate in the form of recordings or live performances' (1991, p. 379).

This definition reflects modern understandings of place and their intersection with sociality, such as a scene as a series of 'moments' in time and place that intersect with the social relations that make up a participant's day-to-day activities (Massey 1994). Like scenes, 'some of these relations will be ... contained within the place; others will stretch beyond it, tying any particular locality into wider relations and processes in which other places are implicated too' (Massey 1994, p. 120). Drawing on this understanding of place, each Australian city features its own discrete music scenes that exist on a translocal scale, intersected by touring networks and influenced by an increasingly homogenized national music culture. We can therefore observe Australian music scenes in both local and translocal terms, with small live music venues playing important roles in each.

Historically, Sydney and Melbourne have usually been positioned as Australia's premier 'music cities'. Indeed, most of Australia's media and performing arts companies, particularly those associated with mainstream broadcasters but also the establishment arts (theatre, dance etc.), are based in Sydney. Sydney also has a rich history of popular music and local live music culture, although much of that has been diminished over a thirty-year period, beginning with the introduction of poker machines in most licensed venues in the early 1990s (which replaced live music as the default entertainment option of choice across Sydney's night-time economy) and more recently by the punitive lock-out laws introduced by Mike Baird and conservative Liberal–National Party state governments throughout the 2010s (Homan 2019). This has effectively pushed much of Sydney's live music infrastructure and music scenes into the inner-western suburbs, where they must contend with increasingly ambitious and aggressive property developers and residential pressures not normally conducive to performance cultures and small venues. Despite this, live music in Sydney continues to struggle on, albeit fragmented but thriving in diverse corners of the Greater Western Sydney conurbation.[8] The increased cost of living and housing in Sydney has also made establishing a coherent and ongoing live music ecosystem increasingly difficult (Ballico & Carter 2018). Melbourne, on the other hand, serves as a case study in how the cultural economy and the political economy remain deeply entwined, despite similar macroeconomic pressures.

Unlike NSW, poker machines in Victoria fall under specific gambling licences and most licensed live music venues have resisted their introduction as potential subsidies or replacements for live entertainment. As a result, much of the rich inner-city pub and venue culture in Melbourne has survived, and its live music

---

[8] Blacktown, Penrith and other Greater Western Sydney suburbs, such as Mount Druitt, have become hotbeds for cutting-edge music in the genres of metal (Tesolin 2015), hardcore (Rose 2022), hip-hop (Cunningham 2022) and drill rap (Fazal 2020), representing a diversity of sociocultural groups and youth cultures that have been left to create their own music at a remove from traditional live music ecosystems and relevant infrastructures. Such artists and genres have proliferated often despite and not because of the live music ecosystem in Sydney and have been successful due to their translocal links to globally connected genre-specific music scenes.

ecosystem is significantly more resilient than Sydney's due to several other contextual and policy settings.[9] A more detailed discussion of Melbourne as a music city continues in Chapter 3, but to illustrate the relationship between small venues and 'the city' more clearly, I turn now to two smaller Australian case studies: Brisbane and Adelaide.

Brisbane, Australia

The capital of the 'deep north' state of Queensland, Brisbane is a peculiar yet dynamic model for what could be considered a 'music city'. Having overcome a troubled political history[10] that has significantly shaped the city's cultural life, Brisbane has consistently punched above its weight in terms of both musical exports and its grassroots local scenes. Much of this talent and activity has emerged from the city's often improvised, typically inchoate and largely temporary small live music venues.

A hub for local farming communities during the colonial era, Brisbane has previously been described as a 'big country town' or otherwise lamented as Australia's 'third city' in comparison with the southern and historically more cosmopolitan capitals of Sydney and Melbourne. However, given Brisbane's rapidly growing population (Hinchliffe 2022), its increasingly dominant role within the Australian live music market (it is a staple on international and domestic touring routes) and the announcement that the city will host the 2032 Olympic Games (Foth et al. 2022), the dominant view of the city in popular and academic music literature as somehow 'second-tier' or 'marginal' (Bennett & Rogers 2018) is at best quaint and at worst wildly inaccurate. Although it has not previously been regarded as a hub for global cultural tourism or diverse night-time economies, despite humble beginnings, Brisbane is now a burgeoning centre for many creative industries, including

---

[9] These include a confluence of policies, such as the 'small bar licences' introduced in the late 1980s which revolutionized nightlife and venue-based entertainment in Victoria (Age 2006), the recently introduced 'agent-of-change' principle (Music Victoria 2014), placing the onus on developers to pay for soundproofing if adjacent to existing live music venues, and the prominence of European-style 'high-street culture' (O'Hanlon 2010, p. 109), which emphasizes community and civic engagement.

[10] The state was run by the very conservative National Party government of Joh Bjelke-Petersen between 1968 and 1987, an administration hostile to cosmopolitanism and rife with corruption (Coaldrake & Wanna 1988). However, Brisbane itself is seen as a progressive capital within an otherwise conservative state, with the Australian Greens Party having won most of the urban and inner-suburban seats in the city in the 2022 federal election.

animation (Potter 2021), videogame design (Banks & Cunningham 2016) and the music industries (Bennett & Rogers 2014; Darchen, Willsteed & Browning 2022; Homan 2011b), with many of Australia's successful international musical exports and popular domestic acts hailing from the north-eastern capital.

Split in two by the wide and snaking Brisbane River, the city shares many similarities with another prominent 'music city': Austin, Texas. The resemblance extends to factors of climate, geography, demographics and constituency. Like Austin, Brisbane is the densely populated, culturally and politically progressive capital of an otherwise large and conservative state, with a similarly warm climate and population known for their laidback and friendly attitude. Also, like Austin's Sixth Street, the Fortitude Valley – 2 km north-east of Brisbane's CBD – is a concentrated nightlife district featuring many venues and clubs packed into just a few thoroughfares and alleyways. Previously the city's red-light district, the Valley (as it is colloquially known) continues to house several strip clubs and adult venues alongside various mega-clubs, prominent LGBTQI+ inclusive pubs and clubs, and half a dozen established alternative and small live music venues that have served the local music community on and off for decades under various business models, managements and ownership. The suburb usually teems with activity on a Friday and Saturday night – 50,000 people on a weekend evening, as estimated in 2011 (Devilly & Srbinovski 2019, p. 57), nine years prior to the COVID-19 pandemic – and has been the natural home of live music in Brisbane since the early 1990s, when the area first opened up to residential and commercial development beyond its previous seedier uses. Given the similarities already apparent between Austin and Brisbane and following the popularity of 'music city' urban development policies globally – many of which point to Austin as an ideal-type 'music city' – there have been dedicated efforts to model Brisbane's cultural and urban development on Austin, both in terms of city planning, infrastructure and local music industry events.

South by southeast: Brisbane and the Austin legacy

Founded in 2002, the annual Queensland music industry conference and showcase event BIGSOUND represents a conscious effort by Brisbane music advocacy groups, industry representatives and peak industry body/quango QMusic to replicate South by Southwest (SXSW) – the hugely successful and influential music, film and media event that takes place in Austin each spring – in a local context. Further, to protect its nightlife precinct from noise complaints and over-development, which began to negatively impact the area during the early 2000s following increasing gentrification (Burke & Schmidt 2013; Homan 2011b), the Queensland state government created a specific policy zone called the Fortitude Valley Special Entertainment Precinct (SEP), wherein venues could operate at louder volumes and for longer trading hours. In an interesting case of policy cloning, the East Austin Entertainment District is a dedicated nightlife area with specific development and planning regulations much like the Valley's SEP. Austin's and Brisbane's urban planners and policymakers have clearly drawn on similar 'music/creative city' policy precedents and planning decisions (Darchen et al. 2022; Grodach 2012).

These similarities in event and planning policies represent the replication of the 'music city' model discussed earlier in this chapter, with many of Brisbane's music advocacy bodies, industry and planning infrastructure seeking to import the success of Austin as a music city to the Sunshine State of Queensland, Australia. This push to make Brisbane the Austin of the South Pacific was particularly prevalent throughout the 2000s and was documented throughout popular media and street press at that time, with similar discourse continuing until recently (BDAC4B 2018; Svert & Caldwell 2016). Music industry groups in Brisbane also hosted a variety of guests and keynote speakers from SXSW to speak at BIGSOUND, and QMusic ran numerous workshops aimed at local artists and industry professionals focusing on how to successfully market local acts at SXSW, positioning SXSW as somewhat of a holy grail for the Brisbane music industry and the Australian music industries generally. This relationship has continued over the years, with SXSW now hosting a regular Bigsound Brunch at the festival in collaboration with music export peak body Sounds Australia (QMusic 2022).

Like Austin, Brisbane's street-level small live music venues have played an important role in shaping the city's cultural significance. However, these have been marked by transience and instability, as various zoning and planning regulations have impacted venue growth in different ways. However, recent music city policy cannot solely account for structural and systemic issues within a city's live music ecosystem, and the political history of Queensland has left scars on the state's capital that have impacted its ability to nurture grassroots spaces of cultural production such as small live music venues long term. This is particularly apparent in Brisbane's lack of traditional 'pub' style venues, a result of both historical political corruption and over-development.

Pig city

Queensland's political history casts a deep shadow over its musical life. The deeply conservative and corrupt state government of Joh Bjelke-Petersen's Country (later National) Party oversaw what has been described as 'a police state' (Bennett & Rogers 2018, p. 114). In power from 1968 to 1987, police corruption during Bjelke-Petersen's premiership shaped Brisbane's nightlife, which in the Valley was characterized by sleazy strip joints and private casinos, often frequented by the police themselves (Stafford 2006). Alternatively, grassroots popular music culture and live music spaces were regularly pushed out of the inner city and adjacent Fortitude Valley red-light district by crony capitalist developers, emboldened by the corruption in Queensland's regulation and policing bodies. This tension and its continued facilitation by the state were demonstrated quite vividly in the demolition of Cloudland Dance Hall, a prominent music and entertainment venue in Bowen Hills, a suburb 2 km to the north of the Valley.

A staple venue within Australian and international touring circuits throughout the 1950s, 1960s and 1970s, Cloudland was demolished overnight on 7 November 1982 to make way for apartments despite consistent calls for its preservation and a listing by the National Trust. The demolition was done by the Deen Brothers, a demolition company often used by the Bjelke-Petersen government, the Brisbane City Council and the 'white shoe brigade'[11] for controversial demolition projects. The demolition took place despite there being no permit and the venue's National Trust listing.[12] This act of state-sanctioned vandalism was typical of the era, during which time many of Brisbane's heritage buildings were torn down to make way for new developments, often under suspicious circumstances. The Bjelke-Petersen government oversaw the destruction, sale and dereliction of many venues and premises traditionally adapted for live music purposes, resulting in a lack of dedicated or pre-existing drinking and entertainment spaces across the city, traditional 'public houses' or 'pubs'.

As a result of this period of over-development and the destruction of historic buildings – buildings often adapted for cultural and entertainment purposes – unlike Sydney, Melbourne and Adelaide, Brisbane does not have the same proliferation of traditional public houses dotted throughout its central

---

[11] A colloquialism referring to wealthy Queensland property developers perceived as aggressively commercial, showy and politically conservative. The specific reference is to the white shoes worn by these developers during the 1980s.
[12] Cloudland's destruction was later immortalized in Australian rock band Midnight Oil's popular 1988 single 'Dreamworld'.

suburbs, with many of its current live music venues having been built in the years following the 1980s or heavily adapted from previous industrial use, such as the Triffid (Hough & Burgemeister 2015), or recreational spaces.[13] This lack of what is often the default small live music venue in urban areas – the local pub – and therefore the built infrastructure necessary for a dynamic live music ecosystem has resulted in a live music culture largely based around informal, appropriated venue spaces (Bennett & Rogers 2016a; Rogers 2008). Warehouse parties, 'house shows'[14] and other unofficial and often unlicensed performance venues were popular throughout the 1980s, 1990s and 2000s.

Although Brisbane now has a strong network of live music spaces, particularly in the Valley (Carah et al. 2021), this current live music ecosystem emerged out of years of shifting uncertainty, venue closures, refurbishments, changes to management and 'an almost ever-present sense of instability within the city's venue infrastructure' (Bennett & Rogers 2018, p. 115). As a result, informal venues such as warehouses and rehearsal spaces have remained popular performance sites for those involved in the city's independent music scene (Bennett & Rogers 2016a, 2016b) and have shaped much of the city's live music culture. Such sites have often seemed more reliable than licensed venue spaces, as the official night-time economy has undergone multiple periods of disruption and change (Carah et al. 2021).

The political conservatism of the Bjelke-Petersen era also resulted in much out-migration of musical talent (Bennett & Rogers 2018, p. 114).[15] It was not until the 1990s that musicians chose to remain based in Brisbane while pursuing careers abroad. This was followed by a period of growth in the Brisbane scene, albeit one characterized by informality, 'making do' (Bennett & Rogers 2018, p. 115), and a proliferation of makeshift and underground venues alongside steady growth in the official night-time economy.

In the years immediately following the Bjelke-Petersen era, Brisbane's small-town ennui bred a thriving live music culture during the 1990s and 2000s. Several significant and popular bands emerged from the scene throughout this time, assisted by the expansion of the national youth music broadcaster

---

[13] Prominent Brisbane venue The Zoo was previously a pool hall.
[14] House shows refers to live performances taking place in private residences.
[15] 'Although Brisbane provided notable additions to the punk and post-punk canon of the late 1970s (featuring bands such as the Saints and the Go-Betweens), the city was generally considered something of a police state where local musicians clashed with authorities and worked in an entertainment sector often administered by organized crime' (Bennett & Rogers 2018, p. 114).

Triple J. Mainstream Australian rock icons Powderfinger, radio-friendly alt-rockers Regurgitator, power-pop trio the Grates, mainstream pop duos Savage Garden and The Veronicas, and grunge revivalists Violent Soho all came to prominence during this time, while the majority of their members remained based in Brisbane (Bennett & Rogers 2018, p. 114; Flew 2008, p. 14). Many of these bands' emerging careers were nurtured in the small venues of the Valley, which became an incubator for original live music and home to a critical mass of creative industries spaces during the 1990s (Carah et al. 2021, p. 622):

> The founders of key venues in the Valley in the 1990s described their DIY ethos in moving into an area without a nightlife market and negotiating with landlords and liquor licensing in order to create spaces for live music performance … These early venues were 'seen as the first stage that emerging bands would play on' (Taylor et al. 2018).
>
> (Carah et al. 2021, p. 628)

One of the venues established in the early 1990s was The Zoo. Founded in 1992, The Zoo has served as a mainstay venue of the Valley's music scene and still operates today despite multiple ongoing changes to the suburb's built and policy environment.

The Zoo

A former pool hall, The Zoo occupies a warehouse space built above a retail strip on the Valley's Ann Street and has a capacity of 500 patrons. Consistent booking policies have emphasized a diversity of prominent and emerging local bands as well as established international acts. This has positioned The Zoo as the premier venue for milestone local gigs (album launches, showcase events, other special occasions etc.) and mid-tier touring acts.

Indeed, The Zoo's long-term success is in part due to its capacity and size. The venue is an exemplary small music venue, with an open floorplan featuring the stage at one end of a long, wide room, and a bar at the other. There is no separation between drinking and viewing areas, and the venue opens only for performances. Although this niche appeal as a dedicated independent music venue might limit the venue's business potential, savvy booking policies (including performance embargos for local bands) and a reputation as the go-to venue for medium-tier touring bands – as well as acting as a showcase venue during industry events (such as BIGSOUND) – has ensured The Zoo's continued success, servicing a niche within Brisbane's live music ecosystem. Yet, despite this success, dedicated original live music venues have struggled to maintain a presence in the Valley, as the area has become densely populated with clubs and bars aimed at maximizing profit – often at the expense of live performance or other cultural experiences specific to 'alternative' music venues (Gallan 2015, p. 556; Gallan & Gibson 2013, p. 180) – muscling small venues out of the area.

This density of hyper-commercialized nightlife (Carah et al. 2021, p. 622) was further exacerbated by the introduction of the Fortitude Valley Special Entertainment Precinct (SEP), legislation that was aimed at protecting the local night-time economy, but which has ended up somewhat consolidating it while sacrificing much of its iconic diversity. This is due to the way the SEP paved the way for those venues with surplus financial capital – usually mega-clubs and larger drinking establishments, like sports bars – to expand rapidly and at scale once the policy settings were amenable to them, buying up smaller alternative venue spaces and expanding their footprint within the local night-time economy. In this way, the Valley is exemplary of live music ecosystems and their interdependencies; there are multiple overlapping factors which, when a certain component shifts, can impact the rest of the ecosystem in unforeseen or unprecedented ways.

Previously an unfettered mismatch of strip clubs, sports bars, niche retail spaces and independent music venues initially attracted to the lack of an established regulatory framework, the Valley now features a dense nightlife precinct that is home to Brisbane's largest concentration of nightclubs, bars, and live music venues (Carah et al. 2021, p. 622). As a young musician, I started gigging in the Valley with my indie rock band Nikko before any of us were of legal drinking age. During this time (*c.* mid-2000s), Nikko usually played at Visible Ink – a community-run warehouse space aimed at hosting youth-focused events for teenagers – and Ric's Bar, 'a key venue in the music scene during the 1990s and 2000s' (Carah et al. 2021, p. 625).

These two venues – Visible Ink and Ric's – are symbolic of the two types of small live music venues commonly found in Brisbane: (a) an unofficial live music venue run in an appropriated private or rental space, usually as a not-for-profit, and (b) a licensed for-profit music venue featuring original live music whose primary revenue stream is liquor sales, which also offers a niche cultural experience. These two types of venues – unofficial/informal and official – represent much of the diversity of small live music venues throughout the global North (Bennett & Rogers 2016a), although ownership and management structures, revenue streams and staffing differ significantly (Holt 2020; Kronenburg 2019).

Ric's

Ric's Café-Bar is a licensed venue[16] that had particular significance within Brisbane's nightlife as a gateway performance space for bands emerging from the house party and 'unofficial venue' scene. It served primarily as a space for such bands to perform their first public shows in a semi-professional environment. This was largely due to the venue's small size and stage, an area that could only host around 80–100 audience members, making it ideal for new and emerging acts without an established audience to perform their debut.

The initial venue space was a small narrow bar, with the stage planted at the front of the venue directly adjacent to Brunswick Street, the Valley's busiest thoroughfare. Although this allowed a certain degree of access to live music from the street, it was also a constant point of tension for the venue, as sound easily passed through its front doors and noise complaints tended to take precedence over local desires for live music activity. Ric's struggle with noise restrictions was characteristic of many venues in the Valley throughout the 2000s prior to the introduction of the SEP, as pre-existing clubs and venues competed with new residential developments built during the Queensland state government and Brisbane City Council's decades-long love affair with Floridian 'creative cities' policy (Flew et al. 2001).

During the mid- to late 2000s many established venues in Fortitude Valley were threatened with closure due to continued noise complaints from new residents (Burke & Schmidt 2013). An antidote to this tension was proposed by the Brisbane City Council after consistent lobbying from live music advocacy groups. The Fortitude Valley Special Entertainment Precinct (SEP) was created in 2006 to be a suburb-wide special zoning[17] that would allow for increased volume above what was permitted in residential or mixed-used areas, as well as various licence-by-licence permissions for later trading hours (Carah et al. 2021, p. 623). Although initially created to protect live music venues, this regulation has had the unintended effect of consolidating the power of many of the bigger, more 'nightlife-oriented' players in the Valley's night-time economy:

> the creation of a dedicated nightlife precinct dramatically accelerated the commercialisation of the area over the past two decades. The Valley was transformed from a post-industrial inner-city area with a diverse mix of pubs,

---

[16] My bandmates and I had to be chaperoned by our parents to each gig while we were still under the Australian legal drinking age of eighteen.

[17] The Valley has two overlapping precincts. The special entertainment precinct was created in 2006 to provide regulatory certainty for live music venues. The safe night precinct was created in 2016 subject to the Tackling Alcohol-Fuelled Violence legislation and was designed to place further regulations on liquor licensing and trading hours in the form of lockouts and ID scanners.

clubs and performance spaces into a dense late-trading nightlife economy dominated by large venues oriented toward high volume or premium alcohol consumption.

(Carah et al. 2021, p. 622)

Able to operate at full capacity and full volume until late into the evening, the Valley's larger pubs and mega-clubs began to grow in terms of both capital resources and physical size, buying out the smaller remaining independent venues that had been characteristic of the Valley since the early 1990s:

> While the SEP gave certainty to venues that staged live original music, it also laid the foundation for the commercialisation of the area as a nightlife district. The policy and licenses gave all nightlife venues within the precinct confidence that their trading conditions would not be curtailed ... This brought competing interests into the area, with commercially motivated operators creating strong competition for tightly held premises. Large nightclubs, bars, and pubs – that at one time traded one suburb over in the city centre – now dominate the nightlife trade in the area ... Most of these venues are concentrated in a 150-metre radius around the Brunswick Street Mall.

(Carah et al. 2021, p. 623)

For example, the business licence for Ric's was subsequently purchased by neighbouring sports bar RG's, and their shared carpark was converted into a large open-air beer garden. This change in management resulted in a reduced emphasis on live, original music at Ric's, with bands performing at the venue often having to compete with an amplified cover act just next door at RG's. The resulting cultural clash and burgeoning profitability of 'indie club nights'[18] meant that it was also often cheaper to put on a DJ rather than a live band, and as a result 'live original music has become a more marginal part of the business model of venues like Ric's' (Carah et al. 2021, p. 625). Meanwhile, while licensed small live music venues were having the squeeze put on them by the Valley's club scene in the late 2000s and 2010s, the informal live music venues that had been the unofficial home of the Brisbane independent music scene during the 1990s and early 2000s experienced a significant resurgence.

---

[18] Themed and licensed dance parties marketed towards Millennials featuring playlists of popular 'alternative' music, usually from the 2000s. These became popular in the late 2000s and continue to this day as Millennials have aged and their consumption and entertainment practices have consolidated, alongside their incomes. It is an excellent example of the commodification of nostalgia for relatively recent pop culture.

Brisbane's 'unofficial' small venues

During the late 2000s and early 2010s, Lofly Hanger, a rehearsal space and venue housed in a disused warehouse (underneath an adult entertainment store) in the inner-western Brisbane suburb of Red Hill, epitomized the DIY spirit synonymous with Brisbane's unofficial venue scene (McMillen 2011). The venue operated infrequently and informally, with cover charged at the gate (most of which went directly to the bands) and a BYO policy on booze. Bands would play in a long and narrow warehouse space (previously a mechanic's garage) in front of a wall of old TVs, décor that significantly heightened the sense that this was an appropriated venue space.

Lofly (as it was commonly known) hosted a variety of acts and genres including punk, hardcore, experimental, folk, instrumental post-rock, post-punk, noise, metal and almost anything that fell under the broad umbrella of local and independent, although the venue also hosted its fair share of touring interstate and, occasionally, international acts. Founded by several local musicians and friends, the venue brought together various scenes and communities of musical practice (jazz, punk, experimental etc.) that might not have otherwise crossed paths. The BYO policy on alcohol gave the venue a distinctly informal air, and the melting pot of genres meant that the venue became a hub for the diverse independent music scenes that made up Brisbane's underground at the time (2007–10). This was typical of unofficial small live music venues in Brisbane, which were strongly and distinctly 'scene-oriented' in their articulation.

Two other prominent examples of such spaces were Browning Street Studios, in the bohemian inner-city suburb of West End, and Sun Distortion Studios, in post-industrial Albion, both rehearsal and recording studios that were appropriated as performance spaces. These two venues were active during the early 2010s following Lofly Hangar's cessation as a venue space, and such unofficial or appropriated venue spaces have consistently cropped up throughout the history of popular music in Brisbane, often as a means of filling gaps in the official live music ecosystem. This lack of investment in the city's formal live music infrastructure seems to be historical. As Bennett and Rogers state:

> The development of Brisbane music has been aided by a large number of state and academic initiatives but the immaturity of the venue business sector, and its comparison to Melbourne in particular, seems to suggest that only so much

stimulation can counteract the city's problematic past and the longer arc of cultural disinvestment.

(2018, p. 115)

Due to such cultural disinvestment and the destruction of heritage venue spaces throughout the Bjelke-Petersen era – resulting in a lack of built infrastructure amenable to regular and everyday live music performances in Brisbane – an ongoing tension remains between official 'scene-oriented' small live music venues (Carah et al. 2021) – always somehow under threat due to the financial precarity of running a dedicated music space for profit – and unofficial venue spaces.

Such informal, unofficial venues are by their nature transient, ephemeral and often subject to specific zoning requirements. They are usually repurposed private, residential or industrial buildings not built to host live music events and vulnerable to a range of complaints from hostile neighbours, local councils and the police. Following this discussion and these examples, a typology of small venues can be observed that includes (a) not-for-profit unofficial venue spaces, often adapted from residential or private use, (b) 'scene-oriented' (Carah et al. 2021, pp. 627–30) or 'cultural capital-oriented' (Scott 2017, p. 67) official live music spaces dedicated to providing a platform for original music and local acts (i.e. niche spaces of cultural production) and (c) 'nightlife-oriented' (Carah et al. 2021, pp. 630–1) or 'economic capital-oriented' spaces (Scott 2017, p. 68) that host cultural and entertainment events but are motivated primarily by profit.

As the Valley has continued to be developed, both as a hip residential district and as an entertainment precinct known for its density of nightlife and clubs, original live music or 'scene-oriented' venue spaces are disappearing. In their research on the impacts of the SEP on dedicated live music venues, Carah et al. emphasize that they

> are concerned about the fate of scene-oriented venues not out of an essentialist nostalgia for yesteryear, but because they were one kind of venue that is now less likely to appear in the hyper-commercialised nightlife precinct. With their disappearance goes some of the diverse texture of our music culture.

(2021, p. 633)

This recent research emphasizes the way in which live music ecosystems and the small venues that act as their bedrock can be easily disrupted by policy interventions and legislative actors seeking to assist such an ecosystem.

Small venues, 'music cities' and the legacy of the Fortitude Valley Special Entertainment Precinct

When the SEP was first developed, it would have been difficult to foresee that its extension of trading hours and repeal of restrictions on volume would lead to the eventual homogenization of the Valley's night-time economy. As it was the Valley's small independent venues (such as Ric's and The Zoo) that had suffered the most under noise attenuation laws and complaints from neighbours during the period of intense development and gentrification that defined the 2000s, it seemed as though these spaces had the most to gain from legislative reform. However, the specificities of live music ecosystems – their interconnections, interdependencies, and place-based nature – often mean that policies that impact one part of the ecosystem have flow-on effects throughout. Even disruptions not directly relevant to the night-time economy (i.e. changes to public transport timetabling and frequency) can have knock-on effects throughout the ecosystem. The SEP was a policy mechanism designed to increase the diversity and strength of live music and small venues within the Fortitude Valley's night-time economy, but instead has led to its flattening out. As Carah et al. state:

> All venues must adapt themselves to the cultural, commercial, and regulatory settings of a late-trading precinct organised around excessive consumption. The colonisation of this city space by high-volume or premium high-margin nightlife trade generates harm and reduces the diversity of cultural uses of urban space. While the history and mythology of the Valley's live music culture is invoked as a useful alibi for legitimising the late-trading nightlife economy, whether there is actually a music scene is increasingly immaterial. Cultural performances like live music in the Valley increasingly take place within the commercial and cultural setting of the high-volume, late-trading nightlife venue.
>
> (Carah et al. 2021, p. 622)

What Carah et al. allude to here is that live music and cultural vibrancy are generally considered either as afterthoughts or novel inclusions in many of the Valley's venues, rather than as an integral feature of their programming or curation, or a core contribution to Brisbane's cultural life. Such a shift in sentiment regarding the role of live music in the Valley is inevitable in policy and material settings where most brakes on development have been removed but where limited spatial boundaries[19] and the availability of real estate force those with tenure to compete for physical assets in a rapidly appreciating property market. This situation has now forced many small venues and other niche spaces of cultural production (which do not own the freeholds to their establishments) to either pivot or perish, applying financial pressures and other stresses on the same venues the legislation was designed to protect. The story of the Fortitude Valley SEP is another in the global experiment of so-called music cities, their complexities and legislative failings.

Adelaide, Australia

Adelaide is a smaller city on Australia's southern coast and the capital of South Australia, a state with a distinct past that has strongly informed its live music culture. A 'UNESCO City of Music' and a hub for various performing arts festivals, Adelaide has been late to embrace the same kind of 'creative cities' rhetoric that saw the SEP established in Fortitude Valley. However, after decades of cultural policy aimed at emphasizing and promoting establishment arts institutions – policy that was at the time quite revolutionary[20] – the introduction of small bar liquor licences in the early 2010s has opened the city up to a new night-time economy. This relatively recent policy innovation has disrupted the city's live music ecosystem in multiple ways, diversifying the city's night-time economy in terms of the availability of spaces, but allowing for a similarly qualitative homogenization of live music spaces to that of the Fortitude Valley's SEP. However, the contextual and historical circumstances of Adelaide are specific to the city, and, much like Brisbane, the historical context of Adelaide has greatly informed the practices of its small live music venues.

Adelaide's cultural awakening came during the 'Dunstan Decade' of the 1970s, a period marked by considerable social reform and cultural investment presided over by the progressive government of South Australian Premier

---

[19] The SEP is a geographically bound area.
[20] The 'Dunstan reforms' were some of the first large-scale implementations of cultural policy at a state-wide level in Australia and led to the establishment of many cultural institutions in South Australia (such as the Festival Centre, the South Australian Theatre Company and the South Australian Film Corporation). Labor Premier Don Dunstan's arts and cultural policies informed and influenced much of the progressive cultural policies of the incoming federal government of Prime Minister Gough Whitlam.

Don Dunstan. As well as funding the construction of many large arts venues (including the Festival Centre), Dunstan was instrumental in protecting much of Adelaide's built heritage spaces (Mosler 2007, p. 4) with the enactment of the South Australian Heritage Act 1978, a policy position that has aided Adelaide in retaining much of its original live music infrastructure, such as its inner-city pubs, bistros and corner bars. In contrast with Brisbane, Adelaide's CBD and inner suburbs have retained many of the traditional public houses typical of colonial architecture and city planning, often positioned at the intersection of popular thoroughfares and streets. These inner-city pubs continue to serve as the city's most consistent and long-term official small live music venues, with a network of these spaces dotted throughout the CBD and inner suburbs. The Exeter and the Crown and Anchor in the city's East End, the Metropolitan Hotel in its south-west and the Grace Emily Hotel (see Figure 1) in its north-west are three prominent examples operating in 2023 at the time of this book's publication. However, despite Dunstan's considerable reforms, his government was driven by a top-down policy agenda influenced by Keynesian cultural policy (i.e. the 'state as arts patron'), and his contributions to South Australian cultural life primarily emphasized establishment artistic practices popular with the middle and upper classes, a constituency that still holds much of the political, economic and symbolic power in the state. Such a political environment has not been particularly amenable to the kinds of grassroots 'independent subcultural activities' (Shaw 2013, p. 350) and alternative, cultural production that small live music venues are associated with. In fact, such activities have often struggled to find purchase within the socially conservative policy settings of South Australia, which have often sought to criminalize or punish those pursuing artistic activities outside of the jurisdiction and graces of the state (Ware 2013). Such a political setting was exacerbated by economic factors that took hold in the 1990s, namely the collapse of the State Bank (McCarthy 1996), hastening and accelerating the out-migration of young people from Adelaide that continued from the early 1990s until recently (ABC 2021; Evans 2021), colloquially known as the 'brain drain' (i.e. the phenomenon of young and talented people leaving the city for the Australian east coast or further afield) (Property Council of Australia 2013; Spence 2022). Such disruption and suppression of grassroots cultural activities has taken place alongside the championing of establishment arts in South Australia, which has seen it brand itself the Festival State (Higgins-Desbiolles 2018, p. 78).

Figure 1 The Grace Emily Hotel, Adelaide (Source: Author provided).

Elizabeth, South Australia

Adelaide's role as a hub for some of Australia's largest establishment arts institutions during the 1970s and 1980s (e.g. the Adelaide Festival, Adelaide Symphony Orchestra, South Australian Film Corporation) was preceded by an influential period in the history of working-class Elizabeth – an industrial city to the north of metropolitan Adelaide and included in its greater conurbation – impacting

Australian popular music culture at large. Home to a Holden car factory that was at the centre of vehicle manufacturing in Australia, Elizabeth attracted working-class families and youth from England, Ireland and Scotland, many of which arrived during the Australian government's '10-Pound Pom' immigration scheme (and the racist White Australia policy,[21] which underwrote it):

> Between 1954 and 1966 almost a quarter of a million British-born immigrants arrived in Australia ... Of particular significance is the uneven spread of these new immigrants. Over a quarter of them settled in South Australia ... of special importance was their intense concentration in Adelaide's new satellite city, Elizabeth, where, by 1966, almost 45 per cent of the population had been born in Britain.
> (Zion 1987, p. 294)

Many of these new migrants were teenagers and brought with them British youth culture, namely pop music. Bands and dance halls began to spring up throughout the township, and Elizabeth was at one point described as 'the cultural centre of rock music in Australia' (Zion 1987, p. 298).

British working-class migrants continued to arrive in South Australia throughout the 1970s and 1980s. During this period, Elizabeth produced some of Australia's most iconic rock acts, including Cold Chisel, the Angels and Glenn Shorrock (of the Twilights and Little River Band). Dance halls and youth centres served as prominent live music venues in the suburb, creating an alternative touring circuit outside of the central Adelaide performance spaces (Zion 1987, p. 298). In response, metropolitan South Australians were said to express 'distaste at the styles that were emerging in the nascent Elizabeth scene' (Zion 1987, p. 299). This highlights the cultural divide between the working-class migrant enclaves of the Elizabeth/Salisbury area and the naturalized middle-class tastes of Adelaideans. Regardless of this tension between the Adelaide and Elizabeth scenes, it remains a point of historical importance that 'a significant proportion of pop music performers in Australia were British immigrants who had settled in the Adelaide/Elizabeth area' (Zion 1987, p. 307).

Due in large part to the cultural significance of the Elizabeth scene and to the contemporary music scenes that sprang up throughout Adelaide in the 1980s,

---

[21] The White Australia policy made it incredibly difficult for migrants from non-English-speaking, non-Anglo-Saxon backgrounds to emigrate to the country. In a flailing attempt to prolong the doomed policy, from 1945 extremely cheap migration and visas were offered to British citizens to help populate the burgeoning former colony in the post-war boom years, formerly named the Assisted Passage Migration Scheme.

1990s and 2000s – scenes centred largely on the city's three universities – Adelaide was made a UNESCO City of Music in 2015. This designation was made partly in recognition of Elizabeth's contribution to Australian rock and pop, as well as the strength of establishment arts bodies such as the Adelaide Symphony Orchestra, its various festivals (WOMADelaide, the Fringe Festival etc.) and music education institutions (the Elder Conservatorium, etc.). However, despite its popular music history and the city's strong relationship with heritage arts, there remain doubts as to why Adelaide was awarded a City of Music designation over more established 'music cities' such as Melbourne, which features the most live music venues per capita in the world (Newton & Coyle-Hayward 2018, p. 6), or Sydney, which has its own vibrant history of popular music. Although Adelaide's musical life is certainly strong for a city of its size, its live music infrastructure is still small in comparison to Australia's eastern capitals. Indeed, the story of Adelaide's small live music venues is often a story of success despite the city's attitude to live popular music, not because of it.

The great south Australian bummer

Previously an industrial hub filled with factories, markets and warehouses, Adelaide city itself has also always been and remains a largely residential CBD, as well as a manufacturing and retail centre. In the early twentieth century, blue-collar workers lived in Victorian-era cottages in the western and south-western quarters of the city, close to the city's factories and markets, which were themselves linked by road and rail to Port Adelaide in the north-west. The land-owning and middle classes occupied North Adelaide, whereas much of the CBD featured working-class and service-class workers living in public housing (Shaw 2004, p. 184). Such class distinctions can still be observed in parts of Adelaide, albeit gentrification has taken hold of much of the city centre (Badcock 2001).

During the post-war period and the ensuing intense and sustained era of rapid globalization that resulted in the decline of manufacturing in the West, heavy industry began to leave Adelaide's CBD, as working-class communities moved north and west towards the manufacturing hubs in Salisbury/Elizabeth and the shipyards in 'the Port'. Further contributing to this exodus from the city centre was the rise of suburban malls in the 1970s and 1980s, anticipating the suburban sprawl that surrounds much of Adelaide's city centre, a CBD that is still characterized by a lack of density relative to European and American cities of a similar size. Although it was largely a feature of policy design, the problem of suburban sprawl has impacted much of Adelaide's city planning following the 1950s, and by the time of the State Bank collapse (and certainly following it), central Adelaide was largely empty of both industry and residents.

Following the collapse of South Australia's State Bank in 1991 (although its financial troubles began in 1989), the state entered a period of economic decline that it is arguably still recovering from.[22] This was exacerbated at the time by a national recession; the 'recession that Australia had to have' as Treasurer Paul Keating termed it (Tate 2014, p. 440). As a result of this large-scale and long-standing economic downturn, industry – and with it residents – began to leave South Australia, heavily affecting Adelaide's CBD, which was left in a state of neglect characterized by vacant lots and disused urban spaces until the late 2000s (Scott & Szili 2018) and beyond (Hanifie 2017).

Indeed, urban and office vacancy rates in central Adelaide remain high[23] despite concerted efforts to curtail these, driven at both a grassroots level (Scott & Szili 2018) and by local councils and state governments (Shaw & Sivam 2015). The aftermath of the 1990s recessions resulted in a particularly hostile environment for official small live music venues, fuelled by a lack of density, onerous liquor licensing and zoning laws, and an overly influential and well-heeled class of property developers buoyed by a political establishment and policy environment wherein land ownership equated very directly with political power (Lonie 1978). This was all set against the increasing 'pokiefication'[24] of entertainment venues and nightlife in Adelaide – much like Queensland and New South Wales – following the introduction of poker gambling machines in licensed venues in the 1990s (Homan 2002, 2008). This pokiefication led to widespread scaling back of live music in licensed establishments, as Shane Homan (2002) states:

> The introduction of poker machines to hotels and clubs in South Australia in 1994 was accompanied by a provision that venues provide entertainment if trading past midnight, yet many venue owners hired solo performers or duos and dispensed with larger groups.
>
> (ARE Entertainment 1996, cited in Homan 2002, p. 96)

---

[22] South Australia maintains the highest unemployment rate in the country (Eccles 2022).
[23] This is despite a massive squeeze on the residential property market triggered by a peaking property boom exacerbated by closed borders during the COVID-19 pandemic.
[24] Electronic gambling or 'poker' machines (otherwise known as 'slot machines' in North America) were introduced into many licensed venues in Australia during the late 1980s and 1990s, replacing much of the traditional entertainment in these venues, such as live music (Homan 2008; Taylor 2018).

Although the high rate of urban vacancies resulted in a brief wave of cultural investment in the city, with new venues and spaces opening throughout the 1990s, by the late 1990s and early 2000s this hollowing out of the CBD set the scene for developers to put the squeeze on those remaining venue spaces, contributing to a homogenization of the city's night-time economy concentrated in the red-light district of Hindley Street.

It is easy to point to this multitude of factors when discussing Adelaide's lack of cultural vibrancy during the otherwise boom years of the late 1990s and 2000s. However, several other social and cultural factors have led to the so-called South Australian 'brain drain'. Such factors are both historical and political, and all have implications for the ability of small live music venues to find a home in the city. The prominence of disused urban space in central Adelaide was precipitated by a long period of out-migration, both from the state and the city centre, and by the mid-2000s much of central Adelaide was devoid of cultural spaces save for the red-light district of Hindley Street and the high streets of Rundle and Hutt in the city's more affluent east. Indeed, the state government itself has also played a role in concentrating the night-time economy and pushing cultural spaces to the fringes of the city.

The dream of the 1990s was alive in Adelaide

After the State Bank collapse, the rise of urban vacancies and cheap rent following the flight of investment capital and development from central Adelaide led to a proliferation of live music spaces in the CBD during the early to mid-1990s, making use of cheap urban leases and semi-industrial zoning. After years of out-migration from the city due to the expansion of suburban sprawl, live music and other cultural spaces were able to operate relatively cheaply in the city centre for the first time since the early 1980s heyday of Adelaide pub rock. Prominent music venues at this time included the Exeter Hotel, the Crown and Anchor, the Austral Hotel, the Grace Emily and the Governor Hindmarsh, the majority of which are still operating today.

All-ages shows were also a viable option for several venue spaces at this time, which encouraged dynamism through youth access to live music and facilitating engagement with live music generally. Many of these gigs were centred on Adelaide's three universities and hosted and organized by their student unions. The Crown and Anchor (in the city's north-east) also hosted all-ages shows on Sunday afternoons. Such regular youth engagement with performance meant that young people formed bands earlier, facilitating a much younger entry point into the professional Australian music industries than what is common today. In fact, all-ages shows were commonplace in Australian cities in the 1990s, and the success and popularity of teenage bands at this time (Silverchair, Something for Kate, Jebediah etc.) can be seen as a direct correlation. Beyond youth music and all-ages shows, the University of Adelaide's UniBar (located within the university's CBD campus) regularly hosted live music on Thursdays. A multitude of small venues, such as Mad Love Bar on Synagogue Place (opposite the university campus), were also popular throughout the mid- to late 1990s.

Further afield, a network of venue spaces extended throughout the northern and southern suburbs, towards Glenelg in the south-west and up to Port Adelaide in the north. The majority of these were pubs, relics of settler colonialism and previous working-class populations. During the 1990s and early 2000s, the Holdfast Hotel in Glenelg East (away from the more gentrified shoreline)[25] was a mainstay live music venue of the southern suburbs. Given the diversity of venues and their spread across the city, interstate touring bands could string together a quick tour, playing in Glenelg in the south-west, then the CBD, then further out in the Port or elsewhere in the northern suburbs over the course of a weekend.

Due to Adelaide's relative isolation from the rest of the Australian touring network, its density of universities and youth arts infrastructure, and the network of venues yet to be overwhelmed by poker machines and gaming licences, a vibrant local scene sprung up throughout the city in the 1990s. However, this was relatively short-lived. In an attempt to further police and concentrate Adelaide's night-time economy, either to maximize profits, surveillance or development opportunities (or all of the above), a concerted push to centralize nightlife and entertainment venues on and around the west-end 'red-light' district of Hindley Street began in the early 2000s.

A developer's dream and a music fan's nightmare

The catalyst for this centralization was a variety of changes to liquor licensing and planning laws aimed at doubling the residential population of the Adelaide CBD. This was to be achieved via an active policy of rezoning previously commercial and industrial land for residential development and restricting

---

[25] The city of Adelaide is a square-mile grid built just south of the Torrens River (or Karrawirra Parri). The Torrens flows west towards the coast, and most of the city's beaches are located directly west and south-west of the CBD.

the availability and coverage of liquor licences, specifically by limiting licensed venues to a densely packed area around Hindley Street in the Adelaide CBD's West End. While the initial idea of increasing population density in the city centre would have assisted in promoting urban vibrancy, the policy approach was a stick rather than a carrot for most cultural venue operators.

Entertainment and hospitality zoning was limited to Hindley Street, and an anti-competitive clause was included within liquor licences so that existing venues (or even the police) could object to new licences in certain areas or could otherwise administer conditions that made new venues financially unviable.[26] Such restrictions made it more difficult for entertainment and cultural venues to operate outside of the dense areas of consumption centred in and around Hindley Street, in the city's 'West End' district. They also created the conditions for a new and aggressive wave of development to sweep Adelaide's city centre.

The sudden re-emergence of developers in the Adelaide CBD in the early 2000s led to disruption for many long-standing live music venues. The Exeter Hotel – a bastion of youth and alternative cultures given its proximity to the University of Adelaide, a variety of other cultural institutions such as Radio Adelaide's studios and the Palace Nova's East End cinemas – had to cease its popular beer garden performances when the carpark behind the hotel was demolished in favour of residential apartments. The Austral Hotel, also located in the East End, was forced to cease all live performances, despite years of support for the local music scene. This period of closures was concentrated within the early years of the 2000s, following the deliberate development of the CBD and centralization of nightlife on Hindley Street. While the policy intention was to increase the population of an otherwise severely underpopulated CBD (down from 50,000 people in the post-war years to just 8000 in the mid-1990s), local and state government pursued this by removing anything that could be seen as a disrupter to property value and incoming residents, with live music being one of the first things to go.

This led to the closure of several venues across the Adelaide CBD, not able to cope under the new liquor licensing models. Many of these venues were housed in built heritage spaces, such as the city's former public houses, resulting in a gap in the protection of these spaces when left vacant. Opportunistic developers took advantage of the shifting property market in the Adelaide CBD, buying

---

[26] These conditions were arbitrary and included such stipulations as not being able to sell certain types of beer if a similarly located venue already sold them, or not being able to sell wine without also serving food (interview, Dr Ianto Ware, 2021).

up vacant blocks and renovating disused space. This placed further pressure on surviving live music venues in central Adelaide, as new residential developments introduced a variety of noise and disorder–related complaints.

Increased development (mainly new apartments) and noise complaints from new residents began to negatively affect the Grace Emily (located in the city's north-west) and the Governor Hindmarsh (located in the north-western suburb of Hindmarsh). The Austral Hotel ceased hosting live music due to its adjacency to a neighbouring apartment block. The Producers Hotel on Grenfell Street and Hotel Tivoli on Pirie Street were also forced to cease live music due to residential development. The cessation of live music in various pockets of the CBD and the concentration of nightlife on Hindley Street that resulted also led to an increase in violence and aggression in the red-light district (interview, Dr Ianto Ware, 2021). The policy was extremely disruptive to the city's live music ecosystem and is a primary example of such an ecosystem's interdependencies.

An important point to note here, however, is how spatially centralized social and cultural life in Adelaide is. As its suburbs lack the vibrant high streets and village-style planning of inner Melbourne and Sydney, which facilitate autonomy from their respective city centres, policy aimed at reshaping density and the night-time economy in the Adelaide CBD had a significant effect on the city's broader live music ecosystem. Further, the impact of changes to the city's liquor licensing laws, which included multiple venue closures, was compounded by the phasing out of all-ages shows, the consolidation of alternative youth radio with the emergence of Triple J, and the dominance of the Big Day Out within the national touring and festival circuit, all of which led to a significant reduction in local audiences for small gigs and the venues that housed them throughout the early 2000s.

As a result of venue closures, limitations placed on live performance and the subsequent reshaping of Adelaide's night-time economy during this time, live music in Adelaide began to move into informal spaces across the city and its suburbs. These included rehearsal spaces, private residences and disused retail and hospitality spaces, often operating on an ad-hoc, semi-legal or often illegal basis. Due to the lack of official venue spaces throughout the early to mid-2000s, local Adelaide bands were primarily playing house shows. Carparks and other public spaces were also used for performances. While medium-tier venue spaces (such as the Governor Hindmarsh) continued to serve the national and international touring circuit, smaller and local bands were limited to playing informal, unofficial spaces during this period of Adelaide's live music history. These small venues and hangouts were precarious and often seen as illegitimate by local governments. Many were subsequently forced to adapt to a rather broad set of regulations for entertainment spaces or cease operation.

Meanwhile, disused urban space (mainly former industrial, retail and hospitality spaces) continued to remain vacant throughout the city's CBD. It was not until the Adelaide Fringe Festival[27] began making use of derelict spaces in the city for ad-hoc performances that those spaces already operating as informal and unofficial live music venues in disused urban spaces started to be seen as legitimate. Once the Fringe began initiatives to start making use of these spaces, hosting novelty performances and stage shows that utilized their unique settings, other venue operators became aware of their potential as long-term creative ventures. One of these spaces was Format (see Figure 2), occupying a neglected retail space in a laneway off Peel Street, itself a small retail strip off Hindley Street.

[27] An annual comedy, music and performing arts festival (running mid-February to mid-March).

Live Music and the City

Figure 2 Format (Source: Ianto Ware).

Format

Format was an arts space and small live music venue hosting punk, alternative and eclectic musical performances on an ad-hoc and semi-legal basis for the first few years of its existence. Housed in a disused retail space in an arcade adjacent to Peel Street, just off Hindley St, Format was close enough to the grit of Adelaide's red-light district while remaining at a slight spatial remove. The venue was spatially liminal, but liminal also in terms of its programming and cultural function.

As a collective, Format was established in the mid- to late 2000s by a group of friends booking events in venues sourced by the local Fringe festival:

> We'd get a temporary liquor licence and run it during the festival period. And then we couldn't get an ongoing licence. So, we would get one every, like, month for a weekend and just have these massive shows. And we had this basement space ... We would have, like, 300 people in this basement with only one fire exit.
>
> (interview, Ianto Ware, 2021)

This later expanded into its own small festival called Format Festival in 2009. Founder Dr Ianto Ware, a local young academic and activist, articulated Format's raison d'être in an interview, stating: 'We were interested in this whole idea of active access to the production of culture and a sense of agency, and trying not to get stuck in what we referred to as the "youth arts ghetto"'. Gradually Format became a stable venue space from 2009/10 onwards, albeit initially occupying a disused shop front and operating in a semi-legal capacity.

The venue was housed in a space between Peel and Leigh Streets,[28] two alleyways running off Hindley St, which are now full of small cocktail and wine bars but at the time were largely disused or otherwise derelict retail spaces. Format also included a gallery space above its cellar venue:

> So, the upstairs space we had as a gallery. Yeah ... We sort of recognized this crossover between people who were trying to put on visual arts kind of shows when there used to be more, small artist-run spaces, but they disappeared as well. And yeah, this sort of music scene, and it was ... I hadn't really thought about it, but it ended up being quite a successful crossover.
>
> (interview, Ianto Ware, 2021)

---

[28] The original logo for Format – a comma shape – is still etched into the walkway between Peel and Leigh Streets that was created when the space was renovated.

Although at the time Format was a bunch of young people trying to make something happen in an otherwise not-so-happening town, Ianto reflects now that the level of risk that Format's founders exposed themselves too was probably quite dangerous:

> I had no idea what building and planning, or liquor licensing compliance was. We took just terrifying risks. Signing a lease, we didn't know what a bank guarantee was, we could have put ourselves all in permanent bankruptcy and been stuck trying to pay off the space if the landlord had been pushy, or if something had gone wrong.
>
> There's no way I would do it now. Just the legal and the financial risk we exposed ourselves to … Nobody who knew what they were doing would do it. Absolutely terrifying … I'm extremely pleased that I did it. But no, I mean, the amount of risk we were exposed to was absolutely colossal.
>
> (interview, Ianto Ware, 2021)

Although it was short-lived, the emergence of Format started a broader conversation in the public policy space around the importance of small venues and their role in not only Adelaide's cultural economy but the urban economy more broadly.

Renew Adelaide

The Adelaide CBD is a unique mixed-use space in that it still features many historical residential premises, such as worker's cottages, alongside newer townhouses and apartment complexes. These are often occupied by older locals who have either lived in the city for many years or have downsized for lifestyle or economic reasons. Such residences are placed in tension with the city's burgeoning nightlife, which is concentrated in the north-western and East End of the city's four-quadrant grid. The creep of development, either by residential developers or by venue operators, has territorialized the city somewhat and raised questions as to what Adelaide's CBD is for. In the late 2000s and early 2010s, noise complaints and other zoning disputes were having a negative impact on Adelaide's live music infrastructure while vacancy rates of industrial and commercial spaces were still relatively high.

Led by Dr Ianto Ware and stemming from the various issues Format encountered when dealing with liquor licensing authorities and the building and planning code of South Australia, Renew Adelaide drew from a similar spirit to that of Renew Newcastle.[29] The idea was to partner owners of under-utilized or disused urban spaces with creative entrepreneurs and other cultural producers to make better use of these vacant spaces. Short-term leases were initially granted rent-free, and pop-up stores (e.g. garment makers, retail and hospitality spaces, live music venues) were able to open with low overhead costs. Once such enterprises were established as viable businesses, rent and other overheads were scaled up to a commercially appropriate level. The initiative has since developed further to become a feature of Adelaide's urban use discourse. As Scott and Szili comment, 'Renew Adelaide and other "vacancy fix" programs present a fiscally conservative program that temporarily aligns the interests of cultural entrepreneurs, landlords, and municipal governments' (2018, p. 26).

After seeing the initial success of the programme in the post-industrial port city of Newcastle, two hours north of Sydney, Ianto and several colleagues worked to establish the programme in Adelaide, founding the urban renewal not-for-profit Renew Adelaide in 2009:

> I went and did Renew because I could see how people really needed that kind of space. But how hard [Format] was to set up. It was really, really difficult. And it really kind of bugged me that we were taking on these massive risks, but there was no policy support around us … surely there must be some sort of guidance or policy support, or somebody helping us figure out the building and the planning issues. But there was just nothing. It was really obvious that there was no link between cultural policy and built environment at all … I remember talking to one of the planners after he'd left the council. He said, like, whenever your application got to the top of the pile, we would just put it at the bottom of the pile again. They must have done that for years, which is a massive risk to them. But I think they knew that what we were doing was good. But they also knew there was no way we could afford to go through the regulatory processes. I thought, 'Somebody has to set up a structure around this so that people aren't at this much risk'.
>
> (interview, Ianto Ware, 2021)

The initial idea was successful, and Renew Adelaide continues to shape the use of retail and hospitality spaces in Adelaide's CBD today. However, the major idea that the Renew model and its advocates introduced into the public policy space was the need for an amendment to the South Australian Liquor Licensing Act to allow small bars and venues to open and operate more easily.

---

[29] Founded by local activist, arts advocate and music venue operator Marcus Westbury, Renew Newcastle was the first of several urban and empty space revitalization schemes that have been rolled out in post-industrial, regional and otherwise underdeveloped cities in Australia since 2008.

Such reform of the liquor licensing legislation was met with initial resistance, as drinking and nightlife continued to be seen as a problem to be policed:

> So, a lot of my time with Renew was getting the organization up, legitimizing it, and getting it funded so that we could keep going ... People were still really into Richard Florida. So, they sort of had this idea of cutesy pop-ups and small bars as exciting. But people having the skills and the resources to set up their own spaces was seen as kind of risky and dodgy. And I think there was an idea that if you give people direct access to space, that they'll just turn them into these kinds of crazy, illegal bars.
>
> (interview, Ianto Ware, 2021)

In their pursuit of reform, the founders of Format and Renew Adelaide noticed that the same roadblock continued to arise time and again, namely the inaccessibility of liquor licences for small and often short-term hospitality spaces. This was identified as a structural problem by Dr Ware and other activists, who began to petition Adelaide City Council and the South Australian state government to amend legislation.

A range of contemporaneous factors assisted this advocacy work and implicit support was found at a high political level, as the then South Australian Premier pursued several initiatives to assist the programme:

> I mean, we dealt with a lot of people ... had really good government support from a high level. So, we had support from [Premier] Mike Rann, he was great ... I think they could see we were trying to do something that was quite interesting. And they were personally very supportive. Like, you'd meet them. And they were, you know, they actively looked for chances to give us money to get Renew up and going. So, there was kind of a commitment to doing things differently. And I think we benefited because Rann was kind of on the way out. So, he sort of did all these, like, pretty amazing hero projects. Australian Centre for Social Innovation, Integrated Design Commission, the Thinkers in Residence program, all of those things helped us. So, Tim Horton, who's [in Sydney] now, he used to run the Integrated Design Commission, and was probably one of the first people to teach me how policy works ... We got our first batch of funding for Renew through the Australia Centre for Social Innovation ... But we also got people who, you know, were introducing us to sort of higher levels of government so that we could try and learn the policies that were impacting on us and better advocate for how they were reformed. Which is sort of how I ended up doing the liquor licensing reform stuff.
>
> (interview, Ianto Ware, 2021)

This advocacy for reform eventually resulted in the Small Bars Licence, which has dramatically reshaped the Adelaide CBD. However, whether this has led to more small live music venues is arguable, as many of the 'small bars' are cocktail and other boutique drinking spaces, with minimal live entertainment:

> South Australia built, like, a kind of a planning pathway for small venues. My critique of it is always that [the result of] those reforms end up being you become a bar, and you're allowed to have music, rather than they are for people who are making dodgy art spaces. But I'd still say it was a more cohesive policy response than I've seen elsewhere, certainly. I mean New South Wales hasn't done that stuff very well.
>
> (interview, Ianto Ware, 2021)

Adelaide continues to develop as a city that is broadly supportive of culture, but slightly suspicious of grassroots spaces of cultural production. While their reforms were the product of a dedicated group of advocates and activists, the examples of Format and Renew Adelaide managed to shift the conversation around small venues and other niche urban cultural spaces several steps forward in a short amount of time. This leap in policy and planning discourse has resulted in several tangible outcomes in Adelaide's development as a 'music city' and has inarguably aided the functioning of small live music venues in the city, in their ability to both function and advocate for their social and cultural value in the face of multiple hostilities (e.g. escalating development, noise complaints, COVID-19 restrictions, economic downturn).

Significantly, discourse around the use of built space for live music resulted in the commissioning of the so-called Reverb report on the future of live music in South Australia, authored by Thinker in Residence Martin Elbourne and published by the Don Dunstan Foundation in 2013. The report made several notable recommendations that have since been actioned, specifically the establishment of the Music Development Office by the state government in 2014, a sub-department within Arts SA (and more recently the Department of Innovation and Skills) dedicated to the development of live music and career opportunities for the burgeoning number of local musicians. This also foreshadowed the addition of Adelaide to UNESCO's Creative Cities Network the following year.

UNESCO City of Music

In December 2015, UNESCO designated Adelaide its 'City of Music' in Australia. Although the local city council and state government were delighted, outsiders and sector advocates interstate were puzzled. This was because, in terms of the raw data, Brisbane, Sydney and particularly Melbourne all host larger, more diverse and more dynamic live music scenes than Adelaide. Indeed, prior to the COVID-19 pandemic Melbourne had recently overtaken Austin as the so-called Live Music Capital of the World, a branding exercise based on data pertaining to the number of performances per capita in an average week (Newton & Coyle-Hayward 2018, p. 8), but more importantly its significant number of venues (pp. 6, 11). Further, as outlined earlier in this chapter, Brisbane and Sydney both have legitimate claims to 'music city' status. Why then was Adelaide named UNESCO City of Music above Australia's east coast state capitals?

Certainly, Adelaide's festival season is sizeable, with many musical events programmed across both the Adelaide Festival and the Fringe. This includes WOMADelaide, the Australian edition of Peter Gabriel's WOMAD festival. However, most of the festival season's programming focuses on marquee events featuring 'out-of-town' talent, as well as 'out-of-towners' in general, as much of the season's success is measured by how many hotel beds it fills (Adelaide Fringe 2020, p. 5; Marsh 2020) rather than its engagement with local audiences, let alone local artists. The musical programming of these festivals is focused primarily on consumption, rather than production, and does not encourage long-term investment in arts and musical infrastructure beyond the temporary staging required to host such events. It is supply-side music policy, aimed mainly at importing artists for the consumption of interstate and international tourists (Franklin, Lee & Rentschler 2022). Although the sheer scale of these events may be enough to guarantee Adelaide the title of 'City of Music', it seems like a low barrier to entry.

Certainly, in terms of Adelaide's broader arts infrastructure, the city has the hallmarks of a city of 'institutionalized' music, featuring a prominent music school in the Elder Conservatorium (at the University of Adelaide), an established and pre-eminent orchestra in the Adelaide Symphony Orchestra, and the Festival Centre and Entertainment Centre providing world-class venues for large-scale performing arts events and popular music concerts. However, Brisbane, Sydney and Melbourne each arguably have all this and more, which is not to consider other South Pacific cities with prominent arts infrastructure and live music ecosystems such as Auckland, Wellington, Kuala Lumpur and Singapore. Perhaps UNESCO's previous designation of Sydney as a City of Film and Melbourne as a City of Literature meant that the top two contenders for an Australian City of Music had already been given status in UNESCO's Creative Cities Network, and therefore were disqualified from further recognition? Also, the fact that potential member cities can simply apply to be included in the network sheds further light on the question of Adelaide's induction. Either way, the prominence of festivals within Adelaide's live music and arts ecosystem would certainly strengthen any relevant application. Indeed, festivals have been such a prominent feature of the city's arts sector that South Australia has the moniker the 'Festival State'. However, it is evident that such spectacles of consumption for interstate and overseas tourists do not facilitate the long-term production of culture in the state, nor do they necessarily encourage the kinds of conditions for grassroots spaces of cultural production (such as small venues) to flourish.

While small venues (such as those discussed above) continue to serve a valuable role within the live music ecosystem of Australia's 'City of Music', a policy framework that supports the sustained production of local South Australian culture and that maintains the state's ability to stop local talent from leaving for greener pastures is yet to be developed. Although the COVID-19 pandemic may have temporarily relieved the effects of the 'brain drain', encouraging more local musicians and music sector workers to put down roots and invest in Adelaide's cultural economy, a considered campaign dedicated to fostering the social conditions amenable to artists and musicians (e.g. affordable housing, a diversity of venue spaces and built infrastructure such as rehearsal spaces, ease of access and density of live music activity) is needed in order to facilitate a more dynamic and productive live music ecosystem. This will take time and effort. Indeed, the arts community in South Australia, and arts policy by extension, has become overly reliant on cost–benefit analyses and economic impact studies carried out by large global consultancy firms for their legitimation (O'Connor 2022). This has reduced the capacity of the arts and live music sectors to make long-term decisions and requests of government based on their own experiences. A deliberate effort – such as that undertaken by Ianto Ware and his colleagues in the late 2000s and early 2010s – to reform arts and cultural policy to support local artists, musicians and venue owners will be needed to take full advantage of the opportunities Adelaide, and South Australia more broadly, are currently presented with.

Regional, rural and remote small venues

The role of small venues in urban spaces is distinct from those in regional centres, which are quite different again to rural or remote venues. As discussed in Chapter 1, small venues serve an important function as niche spaces of cultural production and consumption within both the live music ecosystem of a city or town and the local music scenes that feed this live music ecosystem with participants, performers and a sense of vibrancy. However, as spaces removed from the kinds of pre-existing or identifiable media and built infrastructures necessary for a functioning live music ecosystem (e.g. venues of various capacities and pertaining to a diversity of genres, local press/blogs, gig guides, community or local radio stations, resident promoters and other cultural intermediaries), small venues in regional, rural and remote contexts are specific to their circumstances and are heavily affected by these circumstances in ways that are dissimilar to small venues in urban areas.

Notably, small venues in regional and remote areas are both *less* and *more* affected by their relationships with other regional and remote venues, in that, as they do not necessarily interconnect to form a distinct live music ecosystem in the manner previously defined, relationships between these spaces often take on a traditional, capitalistic mode of operation, similar to small businesses competing for resources and audiences (Roberts & Whiting 2021). Further, as many regional, rural and remote venues are run as not-for-profit community spaces, much of this competition is for cultural resources rather than economic capital. Moreover, due to their not-for-profit or 'not-for-loss' business models, many regional and rural venues rely on the support of the state, which complicates their relationship with similar local venues further, increasing local competition for grants and other funding.

A helpful way of framing small venues in regional or rural areas is either as (a) nodes of participation and engagement between and across broader translocal scenes; (b) grassroots spaces of cultural production within a broader live ecosystem that may encompass the entirety of live music spaces across a state, principality or territory; or (c) both. This framing casts regional venues as both important stops on touring itineraries between 'anchor cities' (Johansson & Bell 2014, p. 317; Rogers & Whiting 2020, p. 451) and as spaces that encourage a more immediate and novel degree of engagement from audience members and performers than larger urban venues might. However, this framing is also problematic, as it positions regional venues as 'in-between' spaces and does not properly acknowledge the vital cultural and social purpose of these spaces. Of course, this is an oversight, and it is important to consider how regional venues function not only as significant stops on national and international touring routes but also as places of considerable social and cultural value to local communities, wherein regional identities are often articulated.

Beyond the divide between urban and regional small live music venues, further distinctions can be made between small venues in regional centres that might have a distinct night-time economy, and other venues that are more remote or isolated, and which do not have adjacent competitors in terms of nightlife. The former are often cast as 'alternative' spaces in juxtaposition with otherwise homogenous, 'mainstream' forms of entertainment (Gallan 2015, p. 556), whereas the latter are destination venues that require a commitment in terms of both time and travel to access and enjoy. In regional centres, 'alternative' venues might serve a function that little to no other spaces do, acting as a refuge for those disinterested in mainstream drinking and entertainment spaces (Gallan 2015, p. 556). Such regional small venues provide an opportunity to foster a unique musical culture unaffected by the types of competition and plurality of nightlife experienced by live music spaces in urban centres, including the niche aspects that serve as points of distinction between these. Remote and rural destination venues, however, must rely on novelty and the ability to provide a unique experience over and above more readily accessible regional venue spaces. However, small live music venues in both regional centres and more remote, 'out-of-the-way' venues offer opportunities for community engagement and place making distinct from live music spaces in the city, as, due to their relative scarcity, they are often the only spaces around which local music scenes and other musical activities can gather.[30] Therefore, less emphasis should be placed on regional venues in terms of how they function as live music infrastructure for larger music scenes and live music ecosystems, and more should be made of their role as hubs for certain musical or cultural communities that might not have access to spaces elsewhere in regional or rural areas.

A peculiarity of the articulation of small regional venues is that they often bring scenes and genres into tension with each other. With a scarcity of performance venues comes the necessity to host and facilitate styles and genres that would usually occupy distinct live music venues within urban environments. Despite the restrictions of regional venues in terms of distance, space and their disconnection from established live music ecosystems in the

---

[30] For example, the council-operated Byron Bay Youth Centre served as an important venue for the beachside town's burgeoning metal scene in the 2000s, despite local concerns as to its viability as an ongoing venue space (Gibson 2008; Whiting, Klimentou & Rogers 2019, p. 60).

cities, such a confluence of musical aesthetics is in keeping with a cosmopolitan definition of popular music (Regev 2013). The mishmash of genres and styles that occupy regional music venues is often what gives regional music scenes coherency, in that, although the characteristics are disparate, the solidarities that emerge are based on a practitioner-to-practitioner relationship developed within cohabitated spaces. Regional musicians find bonds through their commonalities as musicians in places that do not often accommodate such niche cultural production.

Although venues that host a variety of musical styles and genres often exist by necessity in regional centres, remote and rural venues must articulate their aesthetic characteristics more narrowly, as their ability to draw audiences is often premised on points of novelty. The Barn, a 'destination venue' in the Mid-North region of South Australia, offers folk, country and other acoustic-based acts as musical entertainment in a sit-down theatre format, hosted in a disused stable with exposed dirt floors (Roberts & Whiting 2021). The venue is a 'listening venue', in that use of the space is entirely given over to the performance. The audience is usually seated, and interactions between audience members during the performance are discouraged by signs and other visual prompts. Such a distinct and unique venue experience is used to leverage regular audiences, many of whom travel from up to two hours' drive away to participate. Such an element of novelty is often necessary to draw audiences to remote and rural venues from far afield.

Finally, regional festivals play a large role in the articulation and communication of regional identity and often rely on small venues as performance spaces, activating these in a way that is not comparable to their day-to-day function. However, festivals also attract participants and performers who might not otherwise engage with such spaces (Rogers & Whiting 2020, p. 457), offering vital albeit transient activation of these spaces (Gibson & Connell 2016). Such festivals have often been used to stimulate regional economic development (Gibson 2007), drawing on similar regeneration narratives to that of the 'creative' or 'music city'. However, unlike the 'music city', regional musical festivals *as* culture-led development strategies need to engage with local stakeholders to produce the event, and employ a vast number of full-time, part-time and casual staff in those regions directly, employment that might not otherwise be offered. As Chris Gibson stated in a now-legacy 2007 article, 'Just about every rural town in Australia now has a music festival, and they have become for the most part an accepted and popular part of the annual calendar' (p. 71). Further, regional festivals can facilitate the construction of venues and other built infrastructure for live music ecosystems that might otherwise be neglected by local governments and concert promoters:

> music festivals have been the basis for development strategies that have involved the construction of permanent facilities and venues funded by state government and other benefactors ... such facilities have either been designed as multi-purpose, or have been filled by councils staging festivals at other times of the year, such as Tamworth's Hats Off to Country Festival, held with moderate success in winter as a corollary to its enormous January event.
>
> (Gibson 2007, p. 73)

Clearly music festivals have an important role to play in the development of music scenes and live music ecosystems in regional areas (Gibson & Connell 2016). The function of small venues within such ecosystems – as host spaces for regional music festivals and as a potential outcome of such festival-led development – adds to their already established roles as social hubs for regional, rural and remote music communities, as well as important host sites for touring itineraries. Small venues therefore play a significant role within live music scenes and ecosystems both in the cities and outside of them.

Reimagining 'music cities'

To summarize, the concept of the 'music city' has become increasingly popular in urban and cultural planning policy. An extension of creative cities discourse, music city policy handbooks and city-branding events continue to have an impact on local, regional and state government cultural policy. Throughout this chapter I have discussed distinct case studies of so-called Australian music cities, as well as the regional context for live music cultures, to form an understanding of how live music is positioned in built urban and regional environments, as well as broader night-time economies. What is apparent from these case studies is that, although the 'music city' model may work as a decent template upon which to build a discussion of how best to foster live music ecosystems, cities are deeply influenced by their historical, geographical and political contexts, and a top-down planning model will always come up against localized issues specific to these contexts. Such issues are often more deeply entrenched than would first appear and require deep regulatory and legislated change to be ameliorated.

Despite this oversight and as demonstrated both within my own research and the strategic and academic literature, one thing that a thriving live music ecosystem and thus a music city requires is an agglomerated network of small live music venues that are both co-located and also offer diversity in terms of their amenity and plurality of host styles and genres.

Small venues are the wellspring of the cultural production and community necessary for a larger value chain of live music spaces and music industries to emerge. They promote diversity of style and genre and fill existing gaps in night-time economies. Such diversity and subsequent service to niche, specific audiences are often only compounded by density, as 'competition collaboration' becomes the primary dynamic of flourishing live music ecosystems. However, regulatory frameworks often work against small venues. As niche spaces of cultural production that walk a fine line between precarity and vibrancy, small live music venues require hospitable policy settings in which to thrive. The risk-averse nature of local councils and governments coupled with the profit motive of commercially oriented nightlife spaces can often suffocate small live music venues in a mire of legal red tape not fit for purpose, and unregulated competitors that have not only policy but capital on their side. Strategies that were designed to protect small live music venues, such as the Valley's Special Entertainment Precinct and Adelaide's small bars licence, often end up benefiting more commercially oriented nightlife spaces, pushing out the financially precarious small venues that foster and develop local cultural production.

A truly effective support framework for small live music venues needs to sidestep neoliberal desires for maximum use value of built space and property. This need not be anti-competitive in its makeup but should recognize that most small venues, just like other SMEs in the cultural and creative industries, exist in a state of competitive collaboration with similar spaces. The density of such spaces within cities promotes agglomerations of cultural and creative industries SMEs, creating cultural hubs or clusters (Shaw 2013). These clusters need appropriate policy settings to flourish, as 'creative activities tend to be clustered in areas characterized by low rents and non-residential uses such as retail and industrial areas, often without the proper permits' (Shaw 2013, p. 334). The small venues and cultural spaces that make up these clusters may not be financially viable on their own, but within a network of spaces localized to a sector of the city, they become entwined in an interdependent web of cultural production and consumption that not only sustains itself through localized participation but can also draw significant interest from elsewhere.

However, such density of small venues and a nurturing of the live music ecosystem from the ground up require a holistic approach to policy work. The role of place and space is far more pertinent here than policy consultants often realize, and such issues come with a myriad of historical and contextual specificities unique to each city.

The way in which small live music venues 'sit within' or 'slot into' pre-existing or established night-time economies has a major impact on their financial sustainability and success. A small venue positioned on a vibrant high street and surrounded by similar small-scale cultural spaces has a much greater chance of success than one in an outer suburb. This is due to not only factors of density but also access, as centralized nightlife districts are not only more readily accessible to audiences (via public transport, etc.) but also because participants within these emerging scenes often choose to live nearby, creating a community of practice specific to place. Not only does place matter in terms of geography, local demographics and the use of the surrounding built environment, but also the materiality of each venue space – whether it is positioned on a corner or shares walls with its neighbours in a terrace, or whether it is purpose built or adapted/appropriated – places a myriad of limitations on its ability to host live music and attract audiences. Such issues of space and place will be explored further in the following chapter. However, they are central to any 'reimagining' of the music city, as this 'reimagining' must happen with the complexity and interdependencies of the live music ecosystem in mind.

Small venues require specific policy settings in which to thrive. As small-scale cultural producers that are enmeshed within webs of competitive collaboration, small venues require a more lateral approach to the way in which policymakers, governments and the market perceive, conceive of and value cultural and creative industries and the role of live music within them. None of this is new and all of it has been posited previously. What is being proposed here, however, is a repositioning of small live music venues at the centre of all live music and music city policy. A centring of such spaces within policy and strategic planning would allow for a reprioritizing of regulations and built environment. This reprioritizing needs to allow the grassroots foundational spaces of live music ecosystems to thrive. It requires a 'freeing up of space' within policy frameworks but also a reframing that does not just allow commercially oriented nightlife spaces to 'take up space' in regulatory voids. Ideally such commercial activity will follow as a result of effective planning, but this activity should not displace small-scale cultural venues. Instead, nightlife-oriented spaces need to coexist alongside small venue spaces, adding to the diversity of entertainment options offered within a locality and attracting a diversity of audiences in kind.

For such a reimagining of the music city to occur, the impact of both built and imagined spaces and places needs to be included within any evaluation of small live music venues, local music scenes and live music ecosystems. This requires an engagement with both the regulatory frameworks that dictate the legal use of space and the acts of place making that transpire each night in live music spaces, shaping the way in which participants, locals and the public reflect on and value these spaces. The following chapter explores the material and policy concerns of place and space, alongside the role of heritage, participatory culture and imagined community that shape the way that small live music venues are regarded and valued.

3

Place, space and small venues

The live, small venue 'gig' is that most accessible and intimate of performances; those which take place in the local pubs, clubs and other small live music venues of a city. Gigs are specific to time and place; they contribute to the ongoing musical activities of a city, providing local participants – the scene – with a place to congregate and socialize. Although the internet has changed the way music scenes are organized, local scenes still articulate themselves in relation to small venue gigs and other events such as festivals. These give scenes context, a social event to organize themselves around, a space to meet and the means to construct collective identity. Regular gigging opportunities provide emerging musicians with exposure, income and the chance to hone their craft in front of a live audience, while audiences attending local gigs can engage with place-based music scenes on an accessible, everyday level, due to the ubiquity of small gigs and their low cost of entry. These local scenes rely on a sustainable live music culture of small gigs, providing musicians with performance opportunities and scene participants with a means to network and socialize. Without regular small gigs, music scenes would not flourish.

The link between small gigs and placed-based music scenes has led to the emergence of internationally recognized musical movements, such as the punk scenes of New York and London during the mid- to late 1970s and the grunge boom of Seattle in the early 1990s. Such scenes rely on a sustainable live music culture of small gigs, providing musicians with performance opportunities and scene participants with the means to network and socialize. Without regular live gigs performed on a local, everyday and small scale, music scenes would not flourish. The small live gig is what simultaneously grounds music scenes in local processes of meaning making and encourages their development into something bigger than the sum of their parts.

The effect of 'place' on music scenes and cultural narratives is significant, as a sense of place influences the identity of a scene. Scenes are impacted by geography and centre themselves around specific places and spaces. These places (suburbs, neighbourhoods, cities etc.) inform the nature of the music being made, informing new styles and genres. Indeed, '[l]ocations where popular musicians have been particularly active, or audiences and subcultures unusually vibrant, have become synonymous (and sometimes eponymous) with specific styles of music' (Connell & Gibson 2003, p. 90). The influence of place on popular music has been widely discussed, centring on themes of identity, style, genre and diversity (Connell & Gibson 2003; Regan 2019; Stratton 2003, 2005). Such work emphasizes how place influences the music created and performed, as live music scenes are complex systems of interpersonal connection and sociality that maintain a strong sense of localness about them (Strong & Whiting 2018, p. 153).

The ubiquity of local gigs and small venues makes 'the live gig' identifiable as a distinct phenomenon in live music studies. However, previous studies of popular music and place-based music scenes have focused largely on the relationship between the city, live music venues and musicians (Bennett 1997; Cohen 1991, 2013a; Finnegan 1989; Shank 1988, 1994). More recent research focuses on popular music and space, rather than place (Gallan 2012; Gallan & Gibson 2013; Holt 2014; Kronenburg 2011, 2013, 2019) and this shift in discourse is worthy of further consideration.

In this chapter I focus on the roles of space and place as they pertain to two small live music venues – the Old Bar and the Tote – and the local music scene

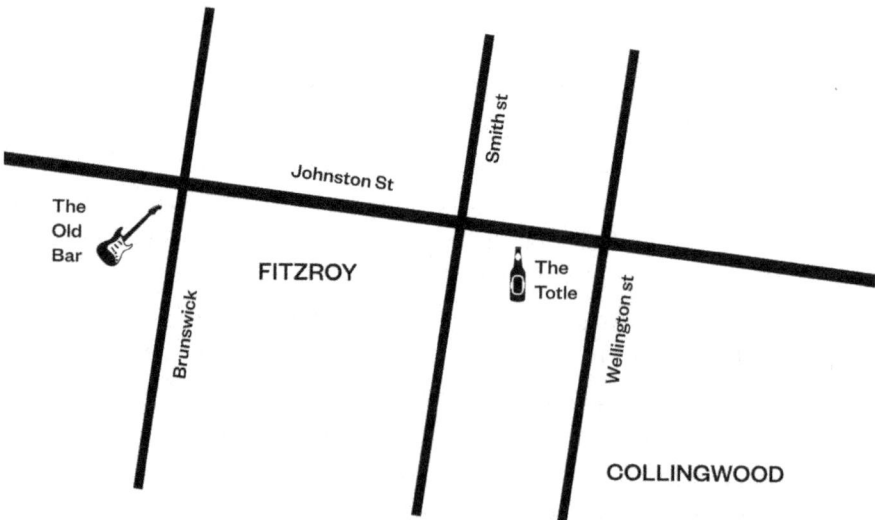

Figure 3 Map of inner Fitzroy and Collingwood featuring the Old Bar and the Tote (Source: Jacob L'Huillier Lunt).

of Melbourne, Australia. I discuss the historical settings of Melbourne and its inner-northern suburbs of Fitzroy and Collingwood, which feature these two case study venues (see Figure 3), examining how these areas have influenced local small venues and providing context through a brief history of these suburbs, the inner north and Melbourne in general. Finally, I position small venues in terms of the role of 'the local' – a meeting place for musicians and live music enthusiasts – and discuss how different intra-venue spaces – the front bar and the band room – impact and influence participants' experiences.

Space and place

Live music is inherently tied to notions of space and place. Although there have been persistent debates regarding definitions of 'liveness' in popular music studies (Auslander 2008, 2012; Holt 2010), these are often abstract, conceptual and do not necessarily account for participants' direct experience of live music. The definition of live music adopted here is the traditional 'live music experience', something Holt outlines as 'associated with co-presence in the here and now, and the strict meaning involves a face-to-face relation in the same physical space' (2010, p. 245).

Throughout the ethnographic literature on live music (Bennett 1999a, 2002b, 2003; Cohen 1993; Stahl 2003a), musician and audience experiences are often marked by descriptions of impromptu sociality – both with friends and with strangers – a distinct ambience, a connection between body and self (i.e. corporeality), a sense of intimacy, of physicality, of sweat, tears and sometimes – in the case of mosh pits – blood. Ultimately, the experience is shared in an embodied and collective manner. These descriptors are centred on proximity and synchronicity – being in the same place at the same time as those performing – and although much of what has been described above can be recreated on a living room dancefloor, the compounding factors of volume, fandom and a real-time connection between audience and performance elevates live music to something much closer to communion (Walker 2012, p. 3), that is, a unity of purpose. Much of the way that participants experience live music is influenced by notions of space and place: the immediate performance environment as well as its setting within the broader milieu of the city or landscape. Space and place are thus key to understanding live music and must be accounted for in any discussion of small live music venues.

Space

Small live music venues provide the means for music scenes to articulate themselves at the level of the local and commonplace. Further, the small gigs that these venues play host to are inherently shaped by the venue spaces in which they take place. Robert Kronenburg has written at length on the nuances of live music venues and their design, focusing on the architecture of performance spaces (2013), while creating a 'typology of venues'[1] (2011) and analysing the cultural and social effect of these spaces on the experience of live performance (2019). He argues that, throughout the literature on live music, 'place' has taken precedence as a descriptor, whereas small live music events are more clearly defined by 'space':

> Place can mean the country, region, city, neighbourhood and the actual venue. In recent years there has been considerable recognition of the importance of place as a defining factor in popular music development ... However, the vast majority of this illuminating research has dealt with geographical place rather than physical space – comparatively little has examined the location of popular music performance in terms of the building in which the experience actually happens.
>
> (2013, p. 5)

'Space', as I define it here, relates to music venues, performance spaces and other sites of music-making activity (e.g. recording and rehearsal studios) that are inherently related to musical practices. This definition frames space as 'a simultaneity of stories-so-far' (Massey 2005, p. 130), the collective value of which is cumulative and corresponds with the social and cultural significance of the activities that have occurred therein. 'Place' is broader and emphasizes geographic locations such as cities – Melbourne being the case study explored throughout this chapter – or distinct urban areas such as Melbourne's inner north, where most of the city's live music venues are located and where I centre my analysis.

The small live gig is dependent on both place and space to give it meaning and to shape the experiences of those engaging with the musical event. The idiosyncrasies of the small live music event are difficult to measure, record and reproduce (Kronenburg 2013, p. 4). No two small gigs are the same and

---

[1] This typology identifies adopted, adapted and dedicated live music venues. Adopted spaces are not purpose built for performance and are temporarily set up for music-making activities. Adapted spaces are altered from their original purpose for the continued and regular performance of music. Dedicated spaces are purpose built for musical performance (Kronenburg 2011, pp. 140–1).

their differences are articulated largely in the spaces in which they take place. The size of the venue, its decor, its clientele, the way patrons move through the space and how audiences interact with the musicians all contribute to an understanding of the small gig as either accessible and commonplace, or exclusive and hidden. Further, the materiality of venue spaces is key to their role within live music ecosystems (Behr et al. 2016b, p. 19). Their capacity, layout, use, type and the connections between intra-venue spaces influence their position within such ecosystems, as this position is always relative to other venues within the ecosystem. In line with this understanding, this chapter presents a snapshot – a 'moment' – in the musical life of two specific spaces – the Old Bar and the Tote – within a defined geographical place: Melbourne's inner north. These venues serve as examples for an exploration of 'space' and 'place' as distinct concepts, framed around their role as 'local' venues and the intra-venue spaces of the front bar and the band room.

Place

'Place' is defined here 'not as points or areas on maps, but as integrations of space and time; as spatio-temporal events' (Massey 2005, p. 130). Time is an important constraint to acknowledge in discussions of place, as places are always positioned in time. When we discuss place, we also discuss eras; the periods in which those places were defined. Melbourne today is quite different to Melbourne in the 1990s and is different again to the city in the 1970s. The popularity of certain venues and neighbourhoods for nightlife and live music has developed in peaks and troughs. These are dependent on various issues of population density, gentrification, demographic movement and changing regulatory environs. Both time and place are natural limitations on small venue spaces, and access to these spaces can be framed in terms of these (e.g. time of day, distance from cultural clusters and nightlife precincts, public transport), as,

> unlike many publicly funded arts activities, live music typically happens at night. This affects the ease, cost, and availability of public transport to and from venues, which are typically located in areas that make access and parking for private vehicles unrealistic.
>
> (Whiting & Carter 2016)

As surrounding areas change over time and with them the communities that patronize live music, small venues – fixed in place both physically and financially, as bricks-and-mortar small businesses – must adapt or face the consequences. Some stick it out, slowly changing their approach while holding steadfast to their core aesthetic and with it their original audience. This audience also inevitably ages, often moving away or changing their priorities. Other venues change management or are rebranded, sometimes becoming radically different and abandoning live music altogether. These shifts in venue identity, priority and the demographics of those who patronize them affect factors of inclusion and exclusion. However, other elements in which venues have further agency, such as programming, style, genre and the interface between habitus and field (discussed further in Chapter 4), also have a strong influence over who is excluded from and who is welcomed into small venues. In this sense, although places are collections of stories, they are also made up of disconnections and the relations not established (Massey 2005, p. 130): exclusions, a factor that is ever apparent in place-based live music scenes due to their specific and niche appeal.

Indeed, placed-based live music scenes are inherently exclusive yet also function as sanctuaries for artists, musicians and other cultural producers.[2] This guarded nature is a problematic yet unavoidable feature of niche spaces of cultural production such as small venues. The niche qualities of small venues – in that they cater to specific audiences and provide desired entertainment for a certain group – often mean that small venues have implicit limitations on who can access them. Indeed, their niche characteristics are what make them attractive, and employing a universal policy of access to them would alienate audiences that seek niche entertainment and nightlife experiences. This discussion is relevant to place as neighbourhoods and cultural hubs often feature a mix of venues that cater to specific audiences within a broader frame of reference that is both heterogeneous in the micro (i.e. each venue provides a distinct live music experience) and homogenous in the macro; cultural clusters cater to those demographics that live or work nearby, populations that are often specific to the area. In this sense, music scenes 'divide up' place into defined fields of cultural production and consumption and, although this might often result in exclusions, it also provides a sense of belonging and collective identity to those who may otherwise feel excluded from mainstream nightlife (Gallan & Gibson 2013; Lobato 2006). The paradox of place-based music

---

[2] This dilemma is reflected in broader discussions of place, as '[h]orror at local exclusivities sits uneasily against support for the vulnerable struggling to defend their patch' (Massey 2005, p. 6).

scenes is demonstrated in their ability to include some at the cost of excluding others. Of course, such spaces of refuge are valuable and needed for vulnerable and otherwise marginalized communities, proving that such exclusions are somewhat justified in their efforts to carve out space within place, albeit such justifications contain heavy caveats.

In this sense, place is often used to describe a delineated area of practice. This definition of place is one of meaning making, identity forming and everyday practice, as 'the idea that a deterministic relationship between place and culture exists – as musical styles and sounds emerge from different locations, and as musicians relate to their environment – remains powerful' (Connell & Gibson 2003, pp. 90–1). This intersection of the social, geographical and political resonates with the notion of social space (Reed-Danahay 2015), which can also be framed in terms of popular music's relationship with place and broader discussions of 'place making'. We can therefore think of local music scenes as limited not only by geographical borders, but also social ones too, implicating the notion of 'social space'.

Music scenes, social space, habitus and field

Just as music scenes can be defined as multiplicitous but at the same time discrete, occupying multiple spaces across a distinct network of activity, space too can be conceptualized as open yet demarcated, singular yet multiple. As Doreen Massey states: 'Space is a discrete multiplicity, but one in which the elements of that multiplicity are themselves imbued with temporality ... The argument here is instead to understand space as an open ongoing production ... that space itself is an event' (2005, p. 55).

Conceptualizing space as an event reflects a similar understanding of music scenes, defining them as a series of ongoing events within space. This allows for the transient nature of music scenes, yet fixes them to space and place, the materiality of which is fundamental to a live music ecosystem. A renewed focus on 'space as scene' presents a shift in the conversation around local music scenes, which in the past have been identified and aligned with a geographical place, that is, a region, city or town. This shift reorientates the discussion to centre on an understanding of venues as social spaces.

The notion of 'social space' can be transmuted into physical space and the two concepts are closely related. 'Social space' presents a way of discussing 'field' and 'habitus' that also accounts for spatiality and the movement of social actors through space. In this context,

> habitus is a position within social space ... It is part of everyday, common-sense understandings of one's social world and how to behave within it ... The orientations and dispositions of the habitus take on differing amounts of value within social space.
>
> (Reed-Danahay 2015, p. 81)

This value is shaped and illustrated in terms of capital, which takes on various forms – cultural, social and symbolic (discussed further in Chapter 4) – and can be accumulated, mobilized or converted depending on the context, that is, the field, or 'social space'. Here social space is used as a way of framing the field in terms of spatiality, as 'the term field is most often used to describe forms of social action or interaction in which geographical space is less important than social action' (Reed-Danahay 2015, p. 70).

Small live music venues are good examples of 'reified social space' (Bourdieu 2000, p. 134), as they are often aligned with a specific music scene or several scenes while also serving as the grassroots foundations for a broader live music ecosystem. Throughout his work, Bourdieu discussed the alignment between social and physical space, co-implicating the two and asserting that 'the places or localizations that people inhabit are related to their position in social space' (Reed-Danahay 2015, p. 81). Scene participants who frequent small venues occupy a similar social space to one another. This is what a scene is: social actors coming together to participate in the same social, cultural and physical space. Melbourne serves as an ideal case study here, as a city with not only a distinct and vibrant live music ecosystem, but multiple local music scenes spread across various pockets of the city and housed within a variety of venues, each their own distinct social space.

Melbourne, Australia

The social and cultural value of Melbourne's live music scene has played a major role in the city's growing reputation as the live music capital of Australia, and the city is now referred to as the 'Live Music Capital of the World' (Newton & Coyle-Hayward 2018, p. 11). This label, albeit self-appointed, reflects a self-conscious preoccupation with framing culture as representative of the city. Prior to the COVID-19 pandemic, Melbourne hosted over 73,000 live music performances annually and was home to 553 live music venues, accommodating an average of over 110,000 live music fans in its venues every Saturday night (Newton & Coyle-Hayward 2018, p. 6). Melbourne's live music sector previously generated approximately A$1.42 billion annually, which included an average Saturday night turnover of A$6 million (Newton & Coyle-Hayward 2018, pp. 6–7). With its cosmopolitan inner suburbs and abundant network of venues, Melbourne has fostered a highly competitive and successful live music ecosystem, creating demand for high-profile bands and larger audiences. This has resulted in a variety of performance spaces for live music across the city and throughout its surrounding suburbs.

As discussed in Chapter 2, live music has become key in city branding strategies around the world (Bennett, T 2020), and Melbourne has subscribed whole-heartedly to its assumed title of Australia's 'cultural capital' (Homan 2014, p. 152), with various tourism and media campaigns making statements to this effect (Nguyen 2017; Visit Victoria 2017). This title is not without its significance, as the relative success of the Save Live Australia's Music (SLAM) campaign and the continued advocacy for live music in the city has demonstrated (Homan 2014). However, the paradox of culture-led urban renewal strategies and the 'creative cities' model (Bianchini 1995; Florida 2002; Landry 2008; Montgomery 2004) – their reliance on culture to assist property development that eventually leads to gentrification, in turn threatening and diminishing that same culture – has raised a variety of problems for practitioners, local governments and the small venues that populate Melbourne.

For example, in 2010, the closure of the much-loved Tote Hotel provoked the SLAM campaign. The Tote closed due to new and severe liquor licensing laws that deemed music venues 'high risk' (Homan 2011a) and subsequently required all live music venues to hire security guards at a ratio of two for the first 100 patrons, with one extra guard for every further 100 patrons, in addition to the installation of CCTV cameras (Homan 2010). Many venues with thin profit margins could not handle the financial stress imposed by these new security costs, and the Tote announced its imminent closure following the policy's announcement. Instigated as a lobbyist movement, SLAM coordinated a 20,000-strong protest rally in Melbourne's CBD against the liquor licensing laws that had caused the Tote's closure (Homan 2014, p. 152).

Since 2010 and this initial wave of advocacy, the status of live music and the reform of live music policy has remained a topic of popular public debate and concern in metropolitan Australia. SLAM was successful in reversing the damaging effects of the licensing laws that had forced the Tote's closure and has remained active in local music scenes, particularly in Melbourne (Homan 2014). Another outcome of SLAM was the establishment of Music Victoria (Watson & Forrest 2012), an independent, not-for-profit organization that represents the contemporary music industry in the state of Victoria, run by former journalist and live music activist Patrick Donovan (Homan 2014, p. 152). Such victories have strengthened the formal processes that protect live music venues and have kept the debate around the cultural and social value of music alive in Australia.

The events that led to the closure of the Tote, along with the advocacy that arose as a reaction to this, are indicative of the way that live music ecosystems are affected and influenced by agents and factors operating outside of music scenes. Whereas scenes encompass artists, audiences and other participants engaging and interacting in certain delineated fields of practice, an ecological approach to the study of live music considers influences that come from outside of the scene. The temporary closure of the Tote and the disruption of other live music businesses due to external factors (Homan 2011a, 2011b, 2016; Walker 2012) demonstrate a need for live music research to consider both scene(s) and the live music ecosystem as mutually complementary conceptual frameworks.

The inner north

In the context of this book, 'place' refers to the lived environment of a delineated geographic locale and the experiences and encounters accessible therein. Various social and cultural forces may affect this lived environment. Gentrification,[3] for example, has had a considerable impact on place-based live music scenes across Australia and the world, and is no longer limited to the global North[4] (Atkinson

---

[3] 'Gentrification' was coined by Ruth Glass in 1964 to describe the ongoing colonization of London's working-class quarters by the city's middle class (Atkinson & Bridge 2005, p. 4). It refers to changes to local housing stock and the renovation of modest, smaller residences located in previously dilapidated neighbourhoods. These houses were upgraded to appeal to the gentry and subdivided for profit, with an inflated price tag to match. Further, according to Glass' definition, '[o]nce this process of "gentrification" starts in a district, it goes on rapidly until all or most of the original working-class occupiers are displaced, and the whole social character of the district is changed' (2010, pp. 22–3).

[4] Following the Second World War, gentrification has swept the globe, beginning in the Western metropolises of London and New York, and expanding to include the colonies of the former European empires and much of the global South (Atkinson & Bridge 2005). The shift to a post-industrial economy in the global North has further hastened gentrification's third wave. This has greatly affected the cost of living for musicians and creatives in Melbourne's inner north, and other parts of urban Australia.

& Bridge 2005, p. 1). Ironically, however, the success of such music scenes is usually a precursor to gentrification (Lobato 2006; Shaw 2005), particularly since the advent of creative-industries-led urban regeneration strategies supercharged this process from the early 2000s onwards.

The suburbs of Fitzroy and Collingwood are located north-east of Melbourne's city centre and are two of the oldest suburbs in the greater Melbourne area. Both are trendy urban districts catering for nightlife, dining and live music. Many small live music venues populate the area surrounding Brunswick Street and Smith Street – the high streets of Fitzroy and Collingwood, respectively – along with the main streets and highways that connect the two suburbs. These high streets are symbolic of each area's demographic and their associated 'street-level' culture.

Since the 1970s, Melbourne's inner north has been a refuge for artists and musicians looking for a sense of place. Many of their artistic practices have centred around cultural institutions, niche spaces of cultural production that rely on cheap rental space and low overheads to operate sustainably (O'Hanlon & Sharpe 2009, pp. 293–5). The diversity of venues and entertainment spaces established throughout Fitzroy and Collingwood in the late 1970s was part of a cultural boom taking place across Melbourne's inner north that continued into the late twentieth century.

The changing face of Melbourne's inner north bears resemblances to other post-industrial cities around the world. London and New York have both been through similar phases of transition, transformation and renewal, followed by periods of increasing gentrification (Dingle & O'Hanlon 2009, p. 67). Likewise, '[s]ince the 1970s, Fitzroy's social profile had changed, and its housing stock, once reviled as "slums", had become highly sought after and increasingly expensive' (Dingle & O'Hanlon 2009, p. 63).

Dingle and O'Hanlon cite the availability of cheap rentals as a primary incentive for emerging cultural and artistic institutions in Melbourne's inner north. These replaced former manufacturing sites, marking the early stages of gentrification in the area: 'In Victoria Street, Fitzroy ... the collapse of grocers Moran and Cato and footwear manufacturers Easywear Shoes provided space to a community radio station, a theatre workshop, an independent television production house, and alternative medicine training institutes' (Dingle & O'Hanlon 2009, p. 66).

The 'alternative' cultural institutions listed above were founded at the beginning of a long period of hospitality, arts and 'wellbeing' centres (e.g. yoga studios, gyms, massage parlours, osteopaths) colonizing the inner north in an ongoing process of gentrification. This process began with the replacement of the area's working class by artists and students and is now in its late stages with the increasing occupation of the area by Melbourne's professional class.

Throughout the 1980s and 1990s Fitzroy and Collingwood were closely identified with Melbourne's live music scene. Iconic venues the Punters Club, the Evelyn and the Rob Roy Hotel on Brunswick Street along with the Birmingham and the Tote hotels in Collingwood hosted many mainstays of Australian alternative rock during this time. This occurred as part of a three-decade wave of gentrification transforming the inner north, beginning in Carlton during the glam-rock era of the 1970s. Discussing the impact of local culture on identity, O'Hanlon states that 'Melbourne's high streets and their surrounding neighbourhoods are celebrated in film, literature, and song. In the 1974 song "Carlton", the band Skyhooks capture the night-time vibe of what was then Melbourne's most happening address' (2010, p. 108). This 'vibe' eventually moved east, sweeping from Lygon Street in Carlton, through Fitzroy and Collingwood:

> By the mid-80s Brunswick Street had overtaken Lygon Street as the heart of alternative Melbourne … Then it was Brunswick Street's turn to become too expensive and overrun by cafes and restaurants. So in the early 90s the inner north's scene moved on to Smith Street, which until then had been an eclectic mix of derelict old department stores, a Coles New World supermarket (that was stuck in the 60s), and a number of Greek cafes, Vietnamese restaurants and bakeries – as well as two-dollar and opportunity shops … But, like Lygon and Brunswick Streets before it, Smith Street's popularity is making it increasingly expensive.
>
> (O'Hanlon 2010, pp. 111–13)

As the 'alternative Melbourne' of the inner north articulated itself across these suburbs, venues came and went, as did the bands that frequented them. The small venues of Fitzroy and Collingwood were formative spaces for Melbourne's local music scene in the years following the iconic pub-rock era of the 1970s and 1980s. In addition to this, the boom of 1990s alternative rock also coincided with a property boom that has continued to shape the inner north to this day.

Following this bohemian phase of Melbourne's inner north, which saw live music venues take the place of the restaurants and corner pubs previously frequented by the area's working class, gyms and cafes have sprung up in the disused warehouses and commercial spaces that once housed shoe factories and other textile manufacturing plants. Such changes are symptomatic of late-stage gentrification as young professionals begin to move into the area. This new demographic has either prioritized lifestyle above the ability to purchase real estate or are wealthy enough to buy into the inflated Melbourne property market (Australian Bureau of Statistics (ABS) 2018), changing the social character of the area yet again.

The cultural narrative of Melbourne's inner north is well established in local popular discourse. The media, policymakers and scene participants themselves have constructed a narrative around the suburbs of Fitzroy and Collingwood, one typified by street art, boutique cafes, green spaces such as Edinburgh Gardens in Fitzroy North and Victoria Park in Collingwood, pub culture and live music. Both Collingwood and Fitzroy are former industrial areas that were transformed into cultural hubs by artists and musicians in the late 1970s. These 'creatives' took over the former factories and workers' cottages, attracted by their cheap rental rates and open-plan living spaces, which were desirable as potential studios and rehearsal rooms. This identity and the history of the area is known to local music scene participants, as former manager of the Tote and Old Bar staff member Therese Martschinke observed:

> Collingwood and Fitzroy were rough areas back in the day. So, rents would have been really cheap so artists and musicians would live here … And so then starts a little hub and people hear about that hub and want to be a part of it and then come over and then it just grows and grows.
>
> (interview, Therese Martschinke, 2015)

This narrative reflects historical accounts of the area as well as artist occupations of post-industrial suburbs in Melbourne and abroad (Shaw 2005). However, such occupations have often been harbingers of gentrification, and a clear line can be drawn between the arrival of the 'creative class' (Florida 2002) and the early stages of gentrification.

Despite this increasing gentrification and unlike other Australian cities, Melbourne has retained many of its high street shopping strips (O'Hanlon 2010, p. 109). Entertainment and nightlife have been central to the survival of these high streets and have heavily influenced their character and the aesthetic of the surrounding suburbs. These

> suburbs are known by name, but also by their major streets' style and ethnicity: Carlton evokes Lygon Street's Italian cafes; Fitzroy, Brunswick Street's alternative grunge scene; St Kilda, bars and entertainment in Fitzroy Street and European cake shops in Acland Street.
>
> (O'Hanlon 2010, p. 108)

The 'alternative grunge scene' of Fitzroy and Collingwood has clear links to live music, as the concentration of venues contributes to these suburbs' sense of place, identity and cultural value.

Fitzroy

The rise of cultural institutions in Fitzroy during the late 1970s and 1980s brought artists and musicians to the area. These 'creatives' patronized the suburb's corner pubs, bars and cafes, with many of them moving into the cheap workers' cottages nearby. The 1990s brought a boom in residential development following the recession, which saw the area transition from small businesses, artist studios, retailers and manufacturers, into a hub for nightlife, hospitality and leisure activities (see Dingle & O'Hanlon 2009; O'Hanlon 2010; O'Hanlon & Sharpe 2009). The 1990s was also a big decade for musical life in Fitzroy, as the Evelyn and the Punter's Club cemented their reputations as prominent venues. However, gentrification has had a disruptive effect on Fitzroy's potential as a hub for Melbourne's music scene, as few young musicians can now afford to live there (Dingle & O'Hanlon 2009, p. 66).

Recently, Fitzroy has become an expensive suburb in which to rent and buy property. As the Australian housing market has few substantive restrictions or regulations, prices have skyrocketed in the years following the residential boom of the 1990s (Wood & Dovey 2015). This has become particularly apparent in recent years, with the median sale price of a house in Fitzroy rising from A$945,000 in 2014 to A$1,465,729 in 2016 (ABS 2018), an increase of 50 per cent in just two years.

Since the early 2000s Fitzroy has experienced a great deal of gentrification, with disputes over noise pollution between new residents and established venues coming to a head. Indeed, 'Fitzroy, and Melbourne live music pubs in general, have been subjected to the same "urban renewal" pressures that have seen the closure of many venues in Sydney' (Gibson & Homan 2004, as cited in Smyly 2010, p. 84). The Fitzroy music scene, in particular, has suffered a slew of blows to its live music ecosystem, seen in the closing of many long-standing local venues along with continued pressure on existing venues to 'turn it down' (Shaw 2009, p. 195).

Live music venues in Fitzroy have been pushed out or forced to change their production practices in the wake of gentrification and its effects on the local urban environment. Adapting to these pressures is costly and many venues have struggled to meet the new standards imposed on them, as their budgets are tight and live music is not a lucrative business (Shaw 2013). A pertinent case study is Fitzroy's Rainbow Hotel, which suffered financial woes due to an ongoing dispute with neighbours over noise complaints:

> The publican of the heritage-protected Rainbow Hotel, a roots music pub in Fitzroy, says he was forced to spend AUD $80,000 in soundproofing (and fines and legal fees) to satisfy his new neighbours whose own levels of insulation were inadequate.
>
> (Shaw 2009, pp. 195–6)

Although it has continued to host live music – albeit largely acoustic performances – the case of the Rainbow is exemplary, demonstrating the damaging effect gentrification has had on Fitzroy's live music ecosystem and local music scene.

Despite this adversity, the Old Bar has remained steadfast in its resolve to host live music seven nights a week in the heart of Fitzroy. However, its owners are aware of their precarious situation. Venue booking agent Joel Morrison stated that 'noise complaints were a big threat to live music venues' and that '[j]ust from one person complaining it can cause a hell of a lot of trouble for you, the council can really clamp down on you' (Dowling 2012). Co-owner Liam Matthews stated:

> If you start waiting for noise complaints to roll in you are already too late. We try to stop as much noise as possible before people are put out. Within reason of course, people must also understand the area they are moving into and accept us to some degree.
>
> (Yarra City Arts 2015)

Here Matthews cites an active approach to dealing with noise complaints and other potential disputes. This approach has served the Old Bar well and the venue continues to host music at all volumes throughout the week.

Collingwood

Collingwood's history tells a slightly different story to that of Fitzroy. Although the two suburbs are situated alongside one another, Collingwood has taken slightly longer to gentrify, as local venue owners have made strong steps to combat development. It is only since the 2010s that the suburb has started to see the effects of gentrification changing its landscape and increasing rental prices in the area (O'Hanlon 2010, pp. 94–5).

Built on a swamp, Collingwood was a slum for most of the nineteenth and twentieth centuries. Demographic data from the early 1970s shows that manufacturing workers were heavily concentrated in the City of Collingwood at the time, making up 47.5 per cent of the municipal population (Dingle & O'Hanlon 2009, p. 54). However, this changed rapidly over the following thirty years:

> In Yarra, which is based on the old cities of Fitzroy, Collingwood, and Richmond, manufacturing workers [now] accounted for 9.6 per cent or only 3,451 people. Managers, professionals, and similar groups had become the dominant group in the inner city by 2001, comprising almost 45 per cent of the workforce.
>
> (Dingle & O'Hanlon 2009, p. 54)

By 2001, the inner north had become dominated by white-collar workers, a big change from the area's working-class roots three decades previous.

Collingwood's changing demographics have had a lot to do with the area's post-industrial transition to a lifestyle economy. However, the suburb's aesthetic appeal is built on an image of dilapidated housing estates, converted former factories and the grunge-chic of venues such as the Tote, the Bendigo, the Grace Darling, and Yah Yah's. Venues such as these and the local live music scene associated with them have attracted several musicians to Collingwood from regional areas across Australia.

Thomy Sloane (music industry worker and musician) moved from Goulburn in rural New South Wales, finding a scene in Collingwood centred around the Tote Hotel:

> I feel comfortable in this scene. I don't really look at it as if it's a scene, it's just where I'm happy to live/work. I want to play music, I want to see music. I want to be around people that are into the same shit. I'm happy in Collingwood, I've never really lived anywhere where I felt like this is where I want to be … I'm from a country town and I've lived in other towns as well that I've hated, I wasn't happy at all, and even in Melbourne, like when I lived in Thornbury,[5] it was depressing, I hated it, fucken hated it; and then when I moved to Collingwood I was just like, 'Fuck, this is awesome. This is Melbourne.' Every fucken night of the week there's something on.
>
> (interview, Thomy Sloane, 2015)

The urban environment of Collingwood is juxtaposed here against country towns and suburban Thornbury, which Sloane framed as 'depressing'. Like Sloane, many of my interviewees emphasized a feeling of belonging in the suburb. His

---

[5] Thornbury is an outer Melbourne suburb, north of Collingwood.

understanding of Collingwood is that of an authentic urban experience, stating 'This is Melbourne' in reference to the suburb's aesthetic. It is interesting that the built environment of the area – its sense of 'place' – is aligned closely with the 'scene', as though each influences the other. The Old Bar and the Tote have been dedicated venue spaces for this scene and many others over more than two decades and are regarded as institution by locals.

The Tote and the Old Bar

My case study venues – the Old Bar and the Tote – are located away from Fitzroy and Collingwood's high streets of Brunswick Street and Smith Street (see Figure 3). However, they both benefit from being close to these retail and hospitality strips. Johnston Street, which they both share, runs perpendicular to Brunswick and Smith, joining the two suburbs. Several retail outlets, liquor stores, cafes, restaurants and pubs are located on Johnston Street, between Fitzroy and Collingwood. However, this section of Fitzroy is primarily seen as a thoroughfare between Fitzroy and Collingwood, rather than its own cultural precinct. The Old Bar is located on the Fitzroy side of Johnston Street, between Brunswick Street and Nicholson Street, the western border between Fitzroy and neighbouring Carlton.

As small independent venues that host an eclectic array of artists and musicians, the Tote and the Old Bar represent a form of night-time leisure, entertainment and drinking space commonly typified as 'alternative'. These 'alternative' nightlife spaces are defined in comparison to 'mainstream' and 'residual' spaces:

> Mainstream nightlife spaces are corporate owned and managed pubs, nightclubs, cafes and styled bars, which come to dominate urban nightscapes. They are increasingly branded and themed, targeting financially lucrative consumer markets and identities. Opposite the mainstream are alternative nightlife spaces. These are usually smaller and independently run examples that cater to specialised youth cultures and identities, often associated with fringe fashion and music, but also diverse ethnicities, sexualities, and politics. Residual spaces are the traditional pubs, ale houses and taverns with strong community ties that are rapidly disappearing or deteriorating.
>
> (Gallan 2015, p. 556)

The Old Bar neatly fits the category of an 'alternative' nightlife space. However, due to its long-standing history and iconic status, the Tote straddles the border between alternative and residual drinking space, with an identifiable 'old guard' often mixed in with the venue's younger patrons. This old guard is represented both onstage and off, with prominent older Australian rock acts such as Warped, the Cosmic Psychos and the Hard-Ons performing at the Tote on a regular basis. The Tote therefore represents a dichotomy between a more established brand of alternative music – one that has its roots in the

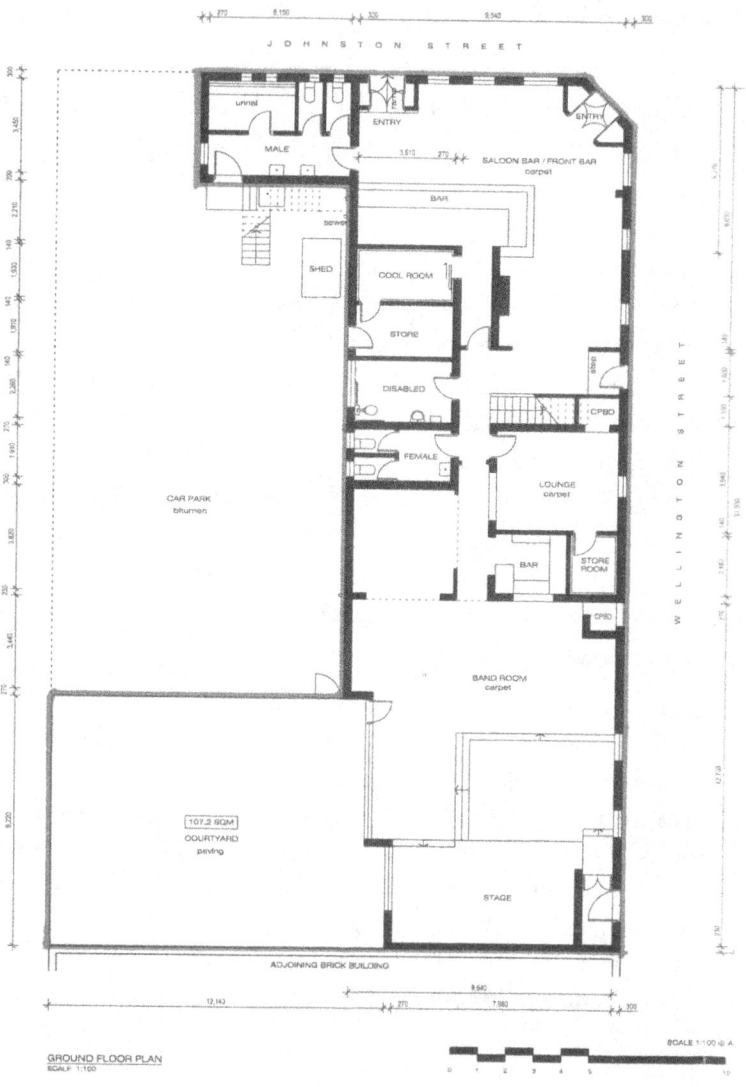

Figure 4 The Tote: downstairs floor plan featuring main band room and front bar (Source: The Tote).

grunge and 'alternative rock' of the 1990s – and a new, independent music scene represented in its eclectic booking policies. Interestingly, the Tote's management are wary of the venue's transition into a residual drinking space and are eager to combat it by employing young musicians and ensuring that a variety of diverse acts are represented across the venue's live music events (fieldwork interviews).

The Tote is a performance space for both emerging acts and established bands. The venue hosts live music five nights a week (Wednesday to Sunday), with multiple performance spaces throughout the venue. The Tote's main band room (see Figure 4) hosts headliners over the weekend, while smaller bands perform in the upstairs band room.

Sunday afternoon residencies take place in the front bar (see Figure 4). All these spaces rely on the materiality of the venue to give them form and function. The Tote's main band room (towards the rear of the ground floor) features a purpose-built stage ideal for big production headline acts, with enough room to host around 300 patrons. The saloon-style front bar, however, is poorly designed for hosting bands due to its L-shape and is therefore better suited for smaller groups.

Like the Tote, the Old Bar also has afternoon performances on Saturdays and Sundays. These are usually reserved for quieter, acoustic performances. However, the Old Bar is smaller than the Tote, approximately half its size in terms of floor space (see Figure 5). For up-and-coming bands, it is a natural choice for a debut show, most likely on a weeknight. Therefore, the Old Bar can be seen as an entry-level venue in the live music ecosystem of Melbourne's inner north, providing bands with some of their first performance opportunities.

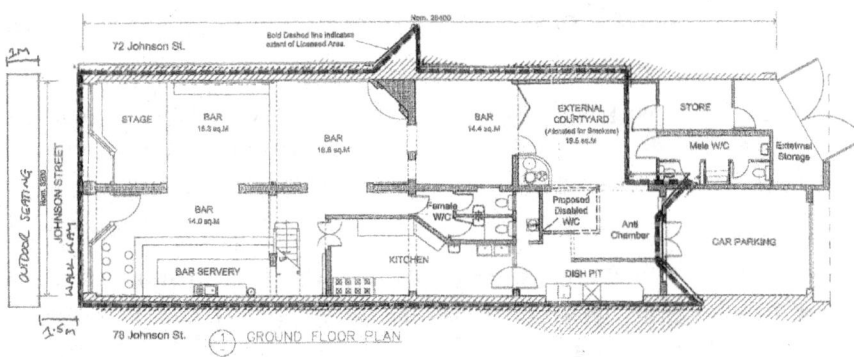

Figure 5 The Old Bar: downstairs floor plan featuring front bar (bar servery), band room and stage (Source: The Old Bar).

Weeknight and afternoon slots at the Old Bar act as testing grounds for young bands, with front-bar and upstairs shows at the Tote serving a similar purpose. Friday and Saturday nights at the Old Bar are reserved for headline acts and their supports. Therefore, a 'pecking order' can be seen between these spaces and the bands that perform there, giving the live music ecosystem a sense of structure as bands move through these performance spaces.

Melbourne has built a strong reputation for culture and music as part of its collective identity. Its small venues serve as ideal case studies through which to explore the role of the live music ecosystem and associated music scenes. These venue spaces play an important role in bringing new bands in contact with existing audiences as well as acting as social hubs for music scene participants.

The Old Bar

Nestled in the heart of Fitzroy on Johnston Street (see Figure 3), the Old Bar (see Figure 6) is a dedicated small live music venue and occupies a unique position in Melbourne's inner north, its local scene and the city's live music ecosystem. In hosting original live music every night of the week, the venue and its owners demonstrate a commitment to providing local and emerging acts with valuable performance opportunities. The small size of the venue (200 capacity) makes the Old Bar an ideal performance space for entry-level bands. The bar is also a dedicated late-night venue, with a liquor licence that allows it to remain open until 3 am. Following a night's performance, audience members and musicians stay late and socialize while the venue serves as an after-party destination for other scene participants.

Co-owner and venue booking agent Joel Morrison discussed the Old Bar's prioritization of live music and the importance of ensuring a positive experience for musicians:

> It's a good breeding ground. It's very welcoming to bands … We don't do food, we don't do anything else apart from the bands, that's the main focus and it's reflected well with the attitude of the staff and the patrons and the bands as well.
>
> (interview, Joel Morrison, 2015)

Many of the staff are musicians themselves. This adds to an understanding of the venue as a specific cultural field in the broader live music ecosystem of Melbourne, fostering feelings of commonality between the musicians, the

Figure 6 The Old Bar (Source: Sianne van Abkoude).

audience and those that serve them, and heightening a sense of place. Morrison discussed the benefits of hiring musicians as bar staff:

> If we hire a muso that we know and bands that we know, it's good because they have an understanding of the bar culture and the music scene – the live music venue culture – already, so they know what to expect and how to deal with things and have an understanding of it.
>
> (interview, Joel Morrison, 2015)

This 'understanding' is cultural capital, operationalized via each participant's habitus and the tacit knowledge that comes only with immersion. Cultural capital and habitus influence the practices of musicians, affecting the styles they engage with and influencing their social networks and the social capital gained from this. As Morrison stated, '[i]t's a breeding ground. A lot of bands start at bars. Musicians like to see other musicians play. All that sort of stuff, so if you're in the scene, then why not work in the scene as well?' (interview, Joel Morrison, 2015). These factors contribute to the Old Bar's reputation as a destination venue for those involved in the local music scene of Melbourne's inner north, aligning the Old Bar with a broader narrative of live music culture. However, this culture is often disrupted by social actors who are not active participants yet still have an impact on the space.

Speaking from my experience as a staff member as well as fieldwork data collected over the course of a longitudinal research project, a marked change in the clientele of the Old Bar occurs between the hours of 1 and 3 am on Friday and Saturday nights. As neighbouring bars, clubs and pubs close at 1 am, their patrons seek drinking spaces that remain open later. The Old Bar – with its 3 am licence – is an attractive option. Therefore, the venue is positioned not only as a small venue in Melbourne's broader live music ecosystem – offering a platform for emerging acts – but also as a space where participants meet after hours to socialize and 'compare notes' regarding their respective nights out. However, 1 am is also the time at which live performances at the Old Bar cease and therefore a certain portion of the crowd departs, allowing for a new clientele of late-night revellers to fill the space.

This mixing of clientele often causes tension, as patrons who are unfamiliar with the bar and lack the habitus appropriate for such a field pour into the venue space, mixing with participants and putting extra pressure on the bar and security staff. As the Old Bar identifies strongly with the live music scene of Melbourne's inner north, many patrons and staff see these new patrons as intruders in 'their space'. This can lead to a disconnect between the venue's regular clientele and those less familiar with the space, evoking an idea of the field as guarded, as well as social issues related to belonging, exclusion and access to live music scenes (Whiting & Carter 2016). This curation of clientele and the exclusion of non-scene participants is even more apparent during the Hispanic Fiesta, a street-long festival that occurs once a year and occupies Johnston Street between Nicholson and Brunswick Streets (two adjacent high streets).

The Hispanic Fiesta is an annual street festival bringing in tourists from all over Melbourne and abroad for one weekend in November. During this time the

Old Bar becomes a temporary drinking space for those revellers who may have never visited the venue before, disrupting the space in a manner that the regular clientele, staff and owners find to be a necessary evil. This is because the Hispanic Fiesta is one of the bar's biggest financial weekends and is integral to the bar's long-term profitability. The participants are the same types of disparate social actors described earlier, those that are not part of an identifiable local scene but still influence the ongoing sustainability of Melbourne's live music culture. Regardless, the Hispanic Fiesta is considered a bane for staff, as the disparity between these 'scene tourists' and the cultural field of the Old Bar manifests in a palpable sense of tension.

The begrudging tolerance of the Hispanic Fiesta by the Old Bar's staff and owners is indicative of the venue's status as a small business that caters to a niche local music scene. This was reflected in my interview with Joel Morrison, who specifically emphasized that music is their focus despite alcohol being their main source of profit:

> I'd say the main focus would be the music. We get all the money from the alcohol, but the music was the main sort of factor for it … So things like putting the door up front. When we first started, they used to have the door up halfway through the venue, so you could sit in the front bar and not pay for the bands or anything like that. So we wanted to get the bands as much money as possible while not making us bankrupt.
>
> (interview, Joel Morrison, 2015)

By prioritizing the musicians' needs above the venue's financial gain, Morrison aligns the Old Bar with the Bourdieusian notion of 'disinterest'[6] prominent in artistic fields; the so-called economic world reversed (see Bourdieu 1993). 'Disinterest' is common among businesses working in independent music scenes, 'where the rewards of the field are credibility and authenticity rather than financial gain' (Threadgold 2015, p. 58). By deprioritizing economic capital, Morrison and the Old Bar are awarded with credibility and authenticity in the field of the Melbourne music scene (Threadgold 2015, p. 57). However, this credibility and authenticity is also what the owners rely upon to bring revenue into the venue space.

---

[6] Disinterest can be observed in the 'symbolic practices [that] deflect attention from the interested character of practices and thereby contribute to their enactment as disinterested pursuits … Individuals and groups who are able to benefit from the transformation of self-interest into disinterest obtain what Bourdieu calls a "symbolic capital"' (Swartz 1996, p. 77).

The Old Bar is ideal as a case study for small venues with a capacity of under 200 people. The venue officially caps the number of patrons allowed into the venue at any one time at 180, which is counted by both the door staff and security guards. The average number of paying live music attendees – those that pay entry at the door – usually varies from twenty to thirty per night between Sundays and Thursdays. These nights often feature emerging bands that are yet to establish a strong local following. On the peak nights of Fridays and Saturdays, patronage averages around 100 people. These nights are usually reserved for more momentous live music events, such as album launches, touring bands, headline acts and special themed nights.

Although many participants are unaware of the financial risks of running a venue,[7] some see it as a point of respect, as it aligns with their understandings and beliefs regarding independent music scenes, specifically that of disinterest (Bourdieu 1993). As local music industry professional and publicist, Bek Duke stated:

> They are dedicated live music venues so they're not just a pub that puts on a band as a bit of a novelty. They exist and their managers and owners exist to support live music and that's something that's incredibly important to me, so anyone that is willing to put their business out there to support live independent music is going to get my dollar … because there's not a lot of money in running a live music venue … They could quite as easily just have a DJ or background music, put in more drinking spaces, and probably make a bit more money. But the fact that they're willing to have live entertainment and obviously genuinely care about it – they're the kind of people that I want to go and hang out with.
>
> (interview, Bek Duke, 2015)

Duke demonstrates an emotional investment in the cultural capital that comes with the risk of running a small venue and the associated symbolic value of disinterest in economic capital.

---

[7] Prior to the COVID-19 pandemic, the Old Bar spent around A$85,000 per annum on rent and around A$3000 on artist fees, with staff costs (including the three owners, twelve casual bar staff, four casual security guards, one door person and six casual sound engineers) reaching around A$15,000 per week. This amounted to a total cost of approximately A$868,000 per annum. Earnings on Fridays and Saturdays were roughly A$8,000 per night and A$3,200 per night from Sunday to Thursday, which came to a net total of A$1,664,000 earnings per annum. However, mark-up on products was approximately 80 per cent, leaving overall gross earnings at approximately A$1,331,200. This placed overall profit after basic costs at A$463,200 in a good year. However, there are many other variables and costs that are hidden in the administration and running of a venue, such as licence fees, utilities, insurance, maintenance, slow periods and other hiccups that are difficult to plan for. According to the owners of the Old Bar, their actual profit for the 2017/2018 financial year was A$18,000 (fieldwork interviews). This sort of low profit makes the day-to-day running of a small live music venue a precarious operation.

A former manager at the Old Bar's sister venue the Public Bar, Jarrod Brown, maintains an outsider's perspective. A native of the nearby city of Geelong and the distinct music scene of that city – having worked at iconic venue the National for many years – his position is less entrenched than other participants in the Melbourne music scene. However, Brown affirms the notion that the Old Bar's owners – including booking agent Joel Morrison – have intentionally curated it as a social space:

> You'll see the same heads there and I think they're people that Joel's really worked hard to get a relationship going [with]. Then you've got people that are maybe a bit more aligned with Liam [Matthews, owner] and Singajaya [Unlayati, owner], people that are there because they like those guys or used to work for them or whatever, a bit older.
> (interview, Jarrod Brown, 2015)

The music scene of the Old Bar is framed as being somewhat fragmented yet largely aligned with the vision of the owners as a space that fosters a sense of familiarity and comfort among its patrons, aligned with a distinct sense of habitus. This is founded upon the owners' physical presence in the bar, developing and maintaining a feeling of consistency throughout the venue space, and generating and mobilizing social and cultural capital for their conversion into economic capital. In this sense, the collective social capital of a venue space relates to the total amount of relevant connections and social networks maintained by the venue's staff, owners and, most importantly, their booking agents. However, this social capital is ephemeral and changes depending on context and circumstance. Therefore, it is not necessarily helpful to think of social or cultural capital as total, quantifiable values, but rather as individual powers that can be mobilized and leveraged from situation to situation. Further, social and cultural capital go some way towards imbuing each venue space with a certain amount of symbolic capital, which relates to ideas of merit, prestige, reputation and status. Regarding my case studies, consistency and a sense of 'unchanging familiarity' are fundamental to the idea of 'the local pub'. Joel Morrison and the other owners of the Old Bar have encouraged this sense of consistency by remaining present and visible in the physical setting of the venue, putting themselves on both sides of the bar and reinforcing the implicit culture of participation through this.

As a small live music venue hosting original music seven nights a week, the Old Bar's role in the live music ecosystem of Melbourne's inner north is established and has been so for the last two decades. Consistency is key and the

Old Bar's owners have maintained a steady aesthetic throughout their tenancy. This has resulted in a great deal of loyalty in their patrons, including Andre Fazio – a former bartender at the Tote, regular sound engineer at the Old Bar and practising musician:

> I think the social element definitely has something to do with what gigs I choose to go and see. If the same band was playing at the Workers Club[8] I probably wouldn't go [and] see the band. If I had a choice between going to see them a week later at Old Bar or a week before at the Workers Club I'd probably go to the Old Bar and I think that's got a lot to do with the social aspect of it and just the intimacy of it. I don't really like the layout of the Workers Club. There's something architecturally about the Old Bar which is also nice.
>
> (interview, Andre Fazio, 2015)

Space, social dynamics and a sense of intimacy are emphasized here as key reasons for Fazio's loyalty to the Old Bar. The materiality of the venue space is also mentioned as a large part of its appeal, which ties into how it functions in the broader live music ecosystem.

The Old Bar acts as an entry-level venue for local bands, feeding Melbourne's live music ecosystem by providing a launch pad for musicians yet to establish a strong local following. As a slightly larger venue, the Tote is seen as the 'next level up' or 'big sister' Old Bar, providing a performance space where bands are the main point of attraction. Many interviewees saw a relationship between the two venues, both geographically, culturally and socially.

Located near each other (less than a kilometre apart) on the same street (see Figure 3), the Old Bar and the Tote coexist in a similar geographical place and social space. This is not a competitive relationship, as was outlined by local sound engineer and musician Katie Harrigan:

> I mean they [the Old Bar and the Tote] seem pretty related. I think Liam [Matthews, Old Bar owner] was saying that, because they've got a matinee on Saturdays, they put it on a bit earlier knowing that the Tote has one in the later afternoon. So they're not really in direct competition, even though they would be rivals and they're on the same road [Johnston Street]. But I mean they're fairly similar in terms of getting the kinds of bands that they have in, I guess. Bookings are kind of the same. They're definitely related.
>
> (interview, Katie Harrigan, 2015)

---

[8] The Worker's Club is another live music venue in Fitzroy, featuring a separated front bar and band room.

This sense of coexistence is reflected in the thoughts of Old Bar owner and booking agent Joel Morrison:

> Well, the Tote's sort of like the granddaddy of the music scene in Melbourne. So invariably your bands play there, and you get a lot of similar bands coming through and a lot of people from, I guess a lot of the staff and stuff all drink here [at the Old Bar] and become friends here and vice versa and stuff like that. So, it is quite the sense of community [and] scene in that you just sort of drift from bar to bar and run into the same people. So, it's only natural that you go from one place to another where your interests lie.
> (interview, Joel Morrison, 2015)

The Tote is an institution in the narrative of Melbourne's live music scene. This is observed in its role as a headline venue for musicians and is also reflected in the general fondness found in the personal accounts of its patrons, as discussed in the following section.

The Tote

The Old Bar is lucky in comparison to many of its contemporaries. Other local venues such as the Tote have faced closure, as they struggle against increasing operation costs and mounting noise complaints. During my interview with Andre Fazio, he commented on the emotional cost of venue closures, discussing the obstacles that venue owners and music scene participants have come to expect due to gentrification:

> I think people get into it because they have a love for it but then it's such a flawed thing, live music, especially in this city just because there's so many adversities. There's the constant threat of being shut down, people moving in next door and redeveloping the place and suddenly there's a noise complaint. It just seems like there's a constant struggle from that side and it seems like, as soon as you fall in love with somewhere, there's something just around the corner waiting to tear it down, and that can be really tough for people.
> (interview, Andre Fazio, 2015)

Fazio considers the emotional investment that regulars and staff place in a venue; its symbolic value – a sense of 'falling in love' with the space – and the threat of that being taken away by environmental and economic conditions beyond their control. For those that participate in them, the music scenes that inhabit small venues are almost familial and provide a support network for participants.

However, these scenes do not remain static, and place-based factors such as gentrification can have a profound effect on a venue's sense of identity.

The Tote has been heavily affected by disparate actors operating outside of the local live music scene. The events that led to the Tote's closure were a product of conflicting interests in Melbourne's live music ecosystem, and the effects of these events are symbolic of the Tote's position in this ecosystem. The Tote was already in a precarious financial situation due to a combination of pre-existing factors, some of these management-related, others environmental. The liquor licensing laws brought into effect in Victoria at the time – late 2009/early 2010 – in response to alcohol-related violence at late-night 'high-risk' venues required extra security guards to be posted at venues that had a late-night licence and hosted live music. The extra costs incurred by these types of venues due to this legislation meant that a variety of venues across Victoria were placed in financial strife. As a result, given its already precarious financial position, the Tote was forced to close. This is a demonstrable case of outsider policymakers having a substantial effect on the live music ecosystem, despite not being involved in related local music scenes, either directly or indirectly. However, due to advocacy groups such as SLAM and political action that occurred as a result, the Tote later reopened, albeit under new management. The venue's current owners have capitalized on this conflict and eventual triumph, releasing a run of merchandise with the slogan 'This is the Tote. Never say die!' emblazoned on it to celebrate '30 years of rock'n'roll, 1981–2011', an interesting example of cultural capital transformed into economic capital and the co-option of symbolic value for financial gain.

The Tote proclaims itself to be 'The Home of ROCK' in Melbourne (http://thetotehotel.com/, 2019) and has featured in multiple documentaries, most notably *Persecution Blues: The Battle for the Tote* (van den Dungen 2011), which chronicles the controversy around its abrupt closing and eventual re-opening under new ownership. At the time, this controversy was at the centre of a discussion around live music culture and liquor licensing laws that caused several venues to close in 2010, including the Tote. These laws have since been relaxed, but the outpouring of support for the Tote that occurred at the time has solidified the venue's status in Melbourne's live music scene.

'Snoop' Mitchell, general manager of the Tote, reflected on how gentrification – exemplified in rising rental prices and changing demographics – has affected the Tote's clientele:

There's the community who was kind of here or the people who were always around when I first moved here, when I came here in the late 90s ... musos who lived nearby because Collingwood was a poorer area, like a cheaper area where people could live. But now the nature of real estate is that it's too expensive for these people to still live around here really. It seems like the only ones that do work or used to work here. So, it's a different crew. So they've now moved further out, they're now older, they're in their mid-thirties and forties now and have started families.

(interview, 'Snoop' Mitchell, 2015)

Mitchell's account resonates with typical notions of gentrification and the intersection this has with lifestyle and ageing (see Bennett 2013, 2018; Bennett & Hodkinson 2020).

The Tote is an interesting case study, as it has been active for long enough to see multiple generations of live music participants engaging with the venue and subsequently aging out of the lifestyle associated with its live music scene. That is not to say that differing age groups are not well represented in live music audiences, but that the heavy drinking, loud volumes and more excessive physical fan activity often associated with live music venues usually attract patrons aged in their twenties and thirties (Bennett 2018, p. 52). These observations reflect broader research on music scene participation, aging audiences and small live music venues (Bennett 2018, p. 49).

The Tote has been a fixture of Melbourne's inner north for well over thirty years (http://thetotehotel.com/about/, 2017). The legacy of the Tote is a masterclass in myth making and thus performing at the Tote holds a certain amount of cultural capital. Not only this, but the venue has been heavily impacted by policymakers and developers, social agents who are far removed from the day-to-day management of the space and its surrounding scene yet still have a profound effect on its sustainability as a live music venue. It is considered by many of my interview participants to be the 'big sister' to the Old Bar and is the next tier up from the Old Bar in terms of size, status and heritage. The Tote is therefore a good example of a venue uniquely positioned in the live music ecosystem of Melbourne's inner north.

A key finding of my research was the way my interviewees associated different types of cultural capital with the Tote. The interviewees both respected the Tote for its contribution to the scene, but also expressed scepticism about the 'heritagization' of the venue space and wariness of the parochial nature of those that subscribe to its rockist[9] narrative.[10] Prominent local musician Georgia McDonald of Camp Cope reflected on the status of the Tote in our interview:

> The Tote's great. People were so like, 'What the fuck?' when it got shut down. There's something really, really special about it that it's still going. The Tote, it's a piece of Melbourne's history. It's a really big part of the cultural scene of Collingwood.
>
> (interview, Georgia McDonald, 2015)

This quotation from a young musician who would not have been old enough to have lived through most of the Tote's history as a venue reaffirms the status that the venue has in Melbourne, maintained through vernacular culture and a kind of unofficial heritagizing (Strong & Whiting 2018). Further, the Tote's history of struggle is a prime indicator of its cultural capital. The fact that it survived this period of disruption leant the venue an 'underdog'[11] quality that resonates with presumed 'Australian values' (Bode 2006). This cemented the Tote's place in Melbourne's live music ecosystem as a middle-tier venue that caters to a specific clientele and hosts bands with complementary levels of cultural capital to the venue itself. However, in 2021 this cultural capital was contested, as the management of the venue space became mired in an industrial dispute that brought the broader venue space into disrepute.

During ongoing difficulties brought on by the COVID-19 pandemic, it was revealed (for a second time since 2013) that the Tote's management had not been fulfilling their legal obligation to contribute to nominated staff superannuation accounts.[12] This was reported by the Australian public broadcaster (the ABC)[13] across multiple articles originally published on 9–10 August 2021 (Marozzi 2021a, 2021b). This reporting resulted in a significant community backlash within the Melbourne music scene, a backlash that has seen the venue lose

---

[9] 'Rockism ... is treating rock as normative. In the rockist view, rock is the standard state of popular music: the kind to which everything else is compared, explicitly or implicitly' (Wolk 2006). Rockism is also often equated with working-class masculinities (Frere-Jones 2003; Sanneh 2004; Wolk 2006), particularly in an Australian context. The term was coined by Pete Wylie, a musician who organized the wittily titled 'Race against Rockism' campaign in 1981 to mock rock purists (Morley 2006).

[10] In the documentary *Persecution Blues* (van den Dungen 2011), supporters of the Tote can be seen wearing T-shirts emblazoned with the statement 'ROCKIST' in plain black and white.

[11] In the Australian cultural context, it is generally considered decent to support the expected loser of a competition or wager, otherwise known as 'the underdog'.

[12] Australian employers are obliged to contribute a certain percentage of wages to staff superannuation accounts. The scheme is designed as a compulsory, involuntary retirement savings and investment scheme for Australian workers.

[13] The ABC (Australian Broadcasting Corporation) is the country's publicly owned media entity, like the BBC in the UK.

significant symbolic and cultural capital within those communities that make up Melbourne's broader live music ecosystem.

Although the Tote has since announced that the superannuation arrears have been paid and are up to date (Perring 2021), the immediate aftermath of the public dispute was a community boycott and divestment in the space, as musicians and patrons turned away from a previously well-loved institution. While the Tote has operated under the management of multiple individuals and groups over the span of its life as a dedicated live music venue, and the actual venue space will likely remain as such, there is no doubt these industrial issues harmed its perceived value as a small venue. Having survived multiple external threats from developers, onerous liquor licensing legislation and other institutional forces, the so-called Battle for the Tote (van den Dungen 2011) could be brought to an unceremonious end by the workers, musicians and patrons that initially imbued it with symbolic and cultural capital. Regardless of the outcome of this recent dispute and its lasting impact, the Tote serves as a unique case study in how local small live music venues serve their communities, and ultimately depend on them for legitimation.

'The local': A place of belonging

The Old Bar and the Tote are representative of a broad swathe of live music pubs and small venues in Australia, known collectively by those who patronize them as 'the local'. A sense of belonging often motivates music scene participants to regularly engage with and participate in live music culture. That this engagement takes place in small venues reinforces notions of familiarity, consistency and 'the local' as a space of reliable social interaction. Regular Old Bar patron Jo Gardiner spoke to this in our interview:

> If we didn't know anyone here, we'd probably still come [to the Old Bar] but might not stick around as long or might not just come down here on a whim on a Tuesday night and know that you'll see someone. It is very 'Cheers-y' in that way, but that's the handy thing about living behind a pub: it's your definite local and it really is the old-school local.
>
> (interview, Jo Gardiner, 2015)

Describing the Old Bar as a 'local' aligns it with 'the peculiar character of the live music pub as quintessential Australian cultural infrastructure' (Gallan & Gibson 2013, p. 174). This framing of the Old Bar as an 'old-school local' also refers to the Anglo-Australian institution of 'the local pub' (Gallan & Gibson 2013). Venue manager Dan McKay elaborated further on the topic of small venues as 'local pubs':

> Amongst the community these places are legendary, they're temples of sorts. It's a place where you can always feel comfortable, and that's what anyone really wants from their local. And the Tote and the Old Bar are people's locals ... it's where all your mates are, it's where all the bands that you like play, and people that have a passion for watching live music.
>
> (interview, Dan McKay, 2015)

In Australia, the 'live music pub' caters to a specific sociocultural niche and the act of going to the pub is a ritual of everyday Australian life that adheres to dominant narratives of mateship and social lubrication (Bode 2006). Pubs resonate with the working-class values that Anglo-Australian cultural identity is (stereotypically) aligned with and have long been known as meeting places for such identities and the formation of a sense of belonging among them. Pubs are therefore gendered spaces, where masculine norms prevail (Kirkby 2003), but also where such norms can be challenged within the context of niche spaces of cultural production, such as alternative live music venues (Lindsay 2006, pp. 48–50).

In this context, small live music venues represent an intersection of traditional Australian pub culture and emerging local music scenes that cannot be replicated in larger arena venues, as these venues do not allow for the same kinds of intimate cultural experiences and expressions of community that pubs afford. This intersection reflects notions of the everyday, the cultural capital associated with small-scale music-making activities, and 'the local pub'. Musician and bartender Chris Drane spoke to this point, referring to the Old Bar and similar venues as 'social clubs':

> Well, it's more of a social club ... before people had mobile phones and stuff, you'd go to the pub and if nobody knew where you were, they'd call the pub and see if you were there. There's more of that vibe at some of those pubs.
>
> (interview, Chris Drane, 2015)

There is an emphasis here on offline interaction, wherein the physical presence of participants in a specific time and space is at the centre of understanding the scene. This is noteworthy in the current age of cultural production and consumption, as online communities and social media have a large influence on music scenes. In contrast, space, place and the body are central to engagement with small venues, live music events and the local music scenes that are articulated around them:

> it's almost like venues have replaced community halls, churches and other social clubs like dances you'd have in the 1950s. People will now go to somewhere like a pub that they know their friends might be at [knowing that] the people that go there, they're probably going to get along with.
>
> (interview, Bek Duke, music industry professional, 2015)

The analogy of a community hall or church – traditional places of worship and social gathering – emphasizes sociality in an offline space where participants are physically present and engage as a group. Participants further emphasized the sense of belonging often found in these venues:

> Pretty much no one except my parents that I know go to church, so you don't have that congregation where you all feel like part of a community. Live music venues are people's churches, they are their sporting teams basically, so you feel like you are part of something. No one likes to be a total loner, so that's our social aspect. That's where we go.
>
> (interview, Bek Duke, 2015)

The notion of collective participation is significant, as are the memories and experiences generated from such affinities. These affinities lead to commonly held associations, contributing to the vernacular cultural history of these spaces. Of course, this history is also informed by the musical cultures that occupy small venues.

Connections between specific venues and certain bands or genres are common in local music scenes. Peter Garett, lead singer of Australian rock band Midnight Oil and later federal Arts Minister (2007–10), emphasized this in 1984: 'Every Australian band comes from a different pub, and it's there they define what they are about. Every band remembers that pub, and it's more than sentimental value; it's something much stronger' (Walker 2012, p. 18).

Local bands have strong connections to the venues in which they start out. These venues hold a specific place in the history of each band and inform their broader cultural identity. In this context, 'social space' (Bourdieu 2000; Reed-Danahay 2015) and 'place' (Connell & Gibson 2003; Massey 1994) are one and the same, both giving form to the spatial component of a cultural field, the local music scene. The idea of 'the local pub' has influenced Australian music history since the 1980s heyday of 'pub rock', and the impact of venues on the musical practices of Australia's live acts can be observed in the genre's name. Further to this, Australian live music practices are inherently localized (Walker 2012) and, although the live music landscape has endured immeasurable change since the era of 'pub rock', such localization persists in the practices of the country's live acts. As groups of musicians participating in local music scenes – scenes that are sustained by social connection in which venues serve both a valuable and circumscribing function – it is natural that bands gravitate towards certain venues, constructing and maintaining these as ritualized spaces of socialization and performance. The identity of a defined place is simultaneously constructed while also informing the practices of those making music in said place.

Finally, Australia's live music scene is heavily associated with alcohol, and this is both historically noteworthy in terms of the pub rock of the country's musical past (as discussed above) and problematic given the link between alcohol and potentially violent behaviour. Here, place and identity are often framed in a negative light and the moral panic around alcohol-fuelled violence has led to an incorrect assumption that a combination of live music and alcohol is responsible for violent behaviour (Homan 2011b). This moral panic continues to impact licensed live music venues on a regular basis (Homan 2010, 2014; Shaw 2010a, 2010b), as the case of the Tote so clearly demonstrates. Despite these associations, the significance of local music scenes and the role of place in shaping notions of identity should not be discounted. Such scenes have distinct benefits for those that engage with them, such as a sense of community, belonging and a mutual network of support. As local sound engineer and musician Lara Soulio stated:

> Everyone helps each other out. There seems to be this knowledge, like if someone's in trouble or needs a place to crash or if someone needs help booking a show, everyone kind of knows what everyone's situation is. Or at least that's what I find from working at Old Bar. And there's a general element of care … whenever something is going on that I can't get done, if I tell someone, it's always that group of people that are first to help.
>
> (interview, Lara Soulio, 2015)

Here Soulio described a support network that stems from the Old Bar, referring to the relationships and social situations that make up the scene. Such knowledge comes only with immersion and a particular sense of habitus, reinforcing both the culture of participation and its benefits, and the somewhat closed nature of the scene. Much of this is shaped by the built environment of the bricks-and-mortar venue spaces themselves.

The venue space

I have separated my analysis of the venue spaces themselves into two sections focusing on 'the front bar' and 'the band room' as distinct sites. These are discussed with specific reference to my fieldwork interviews, drawing on descriptions of each venue's front bar and band room. My discussion of the front bar centres on the role of staff, patrons and the atmosphere or 'vibe' in terms of spatial and social concerns. This is juxtaposed against the performative aspects of the band room and the role that musicians, audience members and other participants play in this space.

Participants identified a spatial differentiation between each venue's front bar – primarily an area synonymous with drinking, socializing and leisure activities (such as playing pool, billiards or darts) – and the dedicated performance space of the 'band room'. The front bar is associated with a social atmosphere. Old Bar manager and musician Dan McKay discussed the 'front bar vibe' in reference to the social interactions between musicians, patrons and bartenders:

> I'll still recommend bands that I see here, like we generally tell the owners who's a good band, and we tell other people. If people come and go, 'See any good bands?', because they might not go out that much and we see bands all the time, and I'll go, 'Oh the Infants are good, Palm Springs is good, Batpiss you've got to see, Flour [as well]', you know, stuff like that. And that goes with that community thing … like everyone knows everyone and everyone's talking about their mates' bands or that sort of front bar vibe.
>
> (interview, Dan McKay, 2015)

The front bar is a place to network and socialize with other musicians and fans, a social space wherein sociality and spatiality are co-constructed. The front bar is also aligned with a social environment where 'everyone knows everyone'. In this context, the bartender is an authority on the local music scene as they 'see bands all the time'. Patrons ask the bartender for recommendations as they are entrenched in the everyday goings on of the scene and carry a certain amount of cultural capital with them. This is exchanged for economic capital, as the bartender serves both drinks and tacit knowledge.

In most venues the front bar is spatially separated from the band room. Live music enthusiast and creative industries professional Claire Portek described a night at the Tote during which her partner and herself spent most of their time in the front bar:

> There was a band that was great but we turned up and they were already sold out and so we just hung out in the front bar and when people came in to get drinks in between bands we got to chat to people, chat to our mates. It's still a good place to hang even if there's not bands on.
>
> (interview, Claire Portek, 2015)

Portek made it clear that the front bar is a social space removed from the band room. The live music experience is still the primary point of attraction and, although they were not able to participate, Portek and her partner were able to socialize with those participants who were.

The front bar of a live music venue is a social space beholden to but not necessarily defined by the live music experience, a space for interaction, networking and the sharing of common interests. Portek made a clear distinction between the Tote's front bar and band room (back bar):

> It's kind of front bar or back bar, it's a great place to see bands. More than likely, depending on who you're going to see, you will know a bunch of people in the crowd. It's a great place to piss on afterwards, it's around the corner from my house.
>
> (interview, Claire Portek, 2015)

The front bar also hosts bands, usually on weekday or Sunday afternoons. However, it remains primarily a drinking space, particularly at the peak times of Friday and Saturday nights. The main band room of the Tote (see Figure 4) is only open to the public during musical performances. The same applies to the upstairs band room. As both band rooms are dedicated performance spaces their primary function is hosting bands, whereas the front bar is only used as a performance space occasionally.

In contrast, the Old Bar's front bar is located next to its band room (see Figure 5), so that the sound and crowd spills into the front bar area. This arrangement of spaces is due to the Old Bar's small size and narrow layout. A few of my interview participants responded specifically to the dialectic that occurs between the front bar and band room of certain venues. Musician Chris Drane gave a detailed description:

> I go into the Old Bar and there's a casual vibe and you might not even be there to see a specific band, but you end up finding a band that you really like that night.

Whereas you go to Howler,[14] you buy a ticket, and you're there for a very specific purpose. Same with The Curtin.[15] Although the Curtin's got a good front bar, it's just not my local or whatever. The Corner[16] I used to frequent more, as just a punter to go and hang out, but that's changed a lot over the years as well. It's much more, I don't want to say segregated, but this is the crew that goes upstairs to the beer garden, this is the crew who drinks in the front bar, and this is the crew who goes to watch the bands. Very specific distinctions between them. But I'll often go to the Public Bar and just sit at the bar all day.[17] I can hear what the band is like, and I might not necessarily want to go and see them, so I won't be involved in that aspect. There are different bars with different vibes.

(interview, Chris Drane, 2015)

Space matters. How music scene participants move through venue spaces changes their perception of each venue and the live music experience as a whole. Drane made it clear that those venues that lack a clear boundary between the front bar and band room have a more relaxed, informal vibe. Venues with dedicated band rooms are inherently more formalized. The distinction between the front bar and band room creates a divide between an informal social space and a space for the consumption of live music.

The front bar

The 'front bar' is located close to the entrance of a venue, in easy sight and reach of anyone entering. It is the first point of call for patrons and its placement in a venue is significant because of this. It is also the primary point of sale and therefore serves a crucial financial purpose. The 'front bar culture' of a venue

---

[14] Howler is a medium-sized live music venue in Melbourne's northern suburb of Brunswick, which features a very clear separation between the band room and front bar, in terms of the music, atmosphere and clientele.
[15] The Curtin Hotel is a medium-sized venue in Melbourne's inner suburb of Carlton wherein the front bar and dining room make up the ground floor, with the band room located upstairs.
[16] The Corner Hotel is a larger, dedicated live music venue with a medium-sized band room (800 capacity) that features touring international and popular Australian headline acts. The Corner operates almost as three separate businesses, with the band room containing multiple bars and stages and the 'front bar' encompassing the rest of the ground floor (featuring pool tables and games areas), while the upstairs beer garden also has a separate bar and kitchen serving food and hosting corporate events and parties.
[17] The Public Bar was a small live music venue in North Melbourne previously owned and operated by the owners of the Old Bar. The band room at the Public Bar is separated from the front bar by the bar area itself, demarcating these spaces quite clearly. However, this division is only spatial, as those in the front bar can still see into the band room and hear the band performing if they are seated in the front bar.

makes an important contribution to its character and aesthetic, and is distinct from the live music experience of the band room. As Claire Portek explained:

> Well, [the front bar is] an area that's a little bit away from the music, not everyone wants to go and see all three bands and stand in the band room for those three bands. It's much more of a place you can talk and a place you can have conversations with friends … You get to chat in a way that you can't when you're in the middle of the band room.
>
> (interview, Claire Portek, 2015)

The front bar is essential to the vernacular culture of small venues, acting as a space next to the music, where patrons can relax, socialize and play. A sense of scene is established in the exchanges that occur around the bar, enacting Straw's 'purposeless sociability' (2001, p. 250). This differs from the social dynamic of the band room, which is inherently more rigid and fixed.

The interviewees often referred to the front bar of a venue as being 'like a club house' (interview, Andre Fazio, 2015): spaces pervaded by a sense of familiarity, belonging and sociality. Regulars, staff and musicians responded similarly, stating '[y]ou know everyone there, it's like *Cheers*. Everyone knows your name' (interview, Katie Drane, 2015). References to the popular American situation comedy *Cheers* were common, with interviewees citing similarities between the Old Bar and the show's central premise of a bar populated by a group of eccentric regulars (interviews with Andre Fazio, Chris Drane, Katie Drane, Jo Gardiner and Joel Morrison, 2015). Like the show, locals meet to drink, relax and socialize, but also to engage with live music. However, this sense of comfort and sociality is entirely dependent on each participant's habitus – field congruence, and their distinct cultural and social capital.

As a social space, the front bar of the Old Bar has been closely curated by the owners and other venue staff. Owner and band booker Joel Morrison stated that the owners intentionally fostered the familiarity, community and social cohesion inherent in the social space of the Old Bar, inclining the venue towards those with complementary habitus:

> It makes it more of a social gathering and people tend to look out for the place a little bit more than they would maybe in a bigger place, because they feel removed from something that's happening … That's the thing as well, cultivating a place where everyone feels comfortable and safe and wanting to be here and feeling a little bit of ownership. We like our patrons to feel like this is their place as well as the staff's, so that they will look after it and we'll look after them … Because

we've both [Joel and co-owner Liam Matthews] been patrons of bars involved in the music scene, we noticed before what we wanted from bars, what worked for us and what seemed to work for everyone. So, we came with those ideas firmly entrenched that this is the type of venue we want to make. We wanted it to be like *Cheers* but with bands.

(interview, Joel Morrison, 2015)

Maintaining a sense of social responsibility among participants is beneficial for the venue in that it promotes mutual respect. This strengthens an idea of the venue as a distinct social space. A feeling of common ground permeates the Old Bar, as participants bond over their experience of the venue, the musical performances and other identifying traits. This contributes to the venue's vernacular culture (see Gallan 2012; Gallan & Gibson 2013; Rahnema 1997; Shorthose 2004) and cultural capital, as music scenes organize tastes or affinities as itineraries across venue spaces (Straw 2001, p. 254). Small live music venues therefore facilitate distinct music scenes that bleed into neighbouring venues, bars and house parties, reifying the tastes and affinities that make up their vernacular culture across the cultural field and social space of the local scene.

The front bar is a focal point for sociality. This is particularly apparent at the Old Bar (see Figure 5), due to the small size and spatial confines of the bar:

[The Old Bar] is smaller and everyone's sort of jammed in, especially on a busy night, [and] there's only minimal places to sit and you end up talking to just everyone. So, it's quite a more sort of forced social interaction. Which works as well and is good for the venue because everyone ends up knowing at least half the crowd by the end of the night, and then if someone fucks up someone will tell the staff before the staff find out, a lot of the time. So that's good to know.

(interview, Joel Morrison, 2015)

A tightknit social situation benefits both the staff and patrons, as patrons can police each other, leaving staff free to administer the space. The front bar integrates the social experience of the bar into the total experience of the venue and is a microcosm of the larger social interface of the venue.

The small size of the Old Bar has an impact on the venue's culture, as '[it is] a size that lends itself to being more homely and welcoming ... that front bar sort of aspect is all sitting around the front bar, having a chat on a quiet night' (interview, Claire Portek, 2015). Portek posits the social environment of the Old Bar as an intimate one, facilitated by the smaller setting of the front bar itself. Small venues such as the Old Bar facilitate personal encounters between strangers, encouraging socializing and informal networking more readily than larger venues due to their intimate setting and lack of anonymity (Holt 2014, p. 24). Portek also stated that the owners of the Old Bar deliberately encourage the social atmosphere of the bar, stating: 'I think it's partially created by and fostered by the owners ... I think it's a conscious thing. I think it's also the size, it's a smaller venue' (interview, Claire Portek, 2015).

Small venues such as The Old Bar encourage a consistent clientele. This is partly due to their localized nature, their ease of access in terms of cost and other factors (e.g. accessibility, geographic centrality, proximity to public transport), as well as the social nature of the front bar itself. Participants become more familiar with the venue, its staff and other musical acts, and thus feel welcomed and likely to return. This emphasizes the intersection between the venue space as a cultural field and a social space, wherein sociality and spatiality inform one another and habitus – field congruence is reliant not only on an alignment between habitus and the field, but also the social space itself.

Myth making around live music scenes is fundamental to their existence. Narratives, cultural memory and 'everyday' vernacular culture play a role in this myth making. These are perpetuated in a local context among social actors that become more familiar and at ease as their engagement with the scene progresses, inclining the field towards their habitus and vice versa (Butler 1999). This 'feedback loop' of participation, interaction and satisfaction is unique to the small venue experience, as it reinforces a culture of participation that is difficult to sense in the anonymous environment of larger concert venues.

The common experiences shared between participants in music scenes include an emphasis on the 'local' aspects of the space (both in terms of the performers and the nature of the venue itself) and a lack of barriers (whether social, cultural or physical). However, each space, scene and associated field has its own idiosyncrasies to be navigated. Small venues provide a sense of space and place for participants, a crucial factor for their success and a defining characteristic of the live music ecosystem. Front bar culture plays an integral role in facilitating interactions and the generation of social capital between musicians, which also contributes to a sense of scene.

Along with their role as points of consumption, front bars are sites of social exchange. Bands are formed, relationships are sparked and friendships are cemented. Dan McKay outlined the relevance of front bar culture to musicians:

> Someone once said that they wanted to do a website that was basically like Frontbar.com which is like, 'I'm looking for a drummer', go to Frontbar.com,

which is sort of how I guess like the Tote and the Old Bar work. It's like, 'I'm looking for a drummer', I'm like, 'Oh fuck, there's this dude I saw the other night in this band, he was awesome' … that's the appeal, just being connected in that way, it's easy.

(interview, Dan McKay, 2015)

McKay described the ease with which musicians are able to form alliances in the setting of the front bar. This was echoed by music industry worker Bek Duke:

The Old Bar and the Tote especially, they have a front bar and that's a social point for people. It's a meeting place. So, it's not just the band room but it's a part of the venue that people can just hang out and socialize. Whether they go in to see the band or not doesn't matter, it's a meeting point.

(interview, Bek Duke, 2015)

The front bar provides the conditions in which social encounters occur more readily. Common ground, familiarity and a shared sense of habitus contribute to both the narrative of these musicians' lives and the live music scene as a whole.

Familiarity was a dominant theme throughout my fieldwork. Bec Reato stressed familiarity in terms of her ability to feel welcomed in a venue:

It's the music, it's the posters on the walls and it's the staff behind the bar that are always choosing what is playing in the room, and you can ask them about it, and you talk about it, and you can sit up at the bar. Sitting up at the bar is a really important thing, I reckon … at the Old Bar there's not really anywhere, apart from the beer garden, to sit, unless you're sitting up at the bar on a quiet night.

(interview, Bec Reato, 2015)

Reato emphasized the significance of the front bar, specifically her relationship with the bar's staff. Music photographer and former bartender Elisa Bryant Jones described the Old Bar as 'a second lounge room' (interview, Elisa Bryant Jones, 2015). Jo Gardiner also described her connection to the Old Bar and the Tote in deeply personal terms:

I remember – when you could smoke inside – sitting at the bar of the Tote with a beer on a Tuesday afternoon when it was tight-arse Tuesdays and just playing pool in the front bar. It just felt like home, like completely felt like home, and that's what it's like here [at the Old Bar] as well. Sitting at this table in the beer garden of the Old Bar or just sitting at the bar, I could play Uno in [the bar] and no-one bats an eyelid or they're just happy for it to happen. So yeah, it is like a lounge room because we pretty much treat it like one.

(interview, Jo Gardiner, 2015)

Gardiner emphasized the relaxed nature of these venues. Her attitude towards the space hinges on her ability to make herself feel 'at home'. This emphasizes the intersection between the venue as a field, its materiality and its social space. Musician Sarah 'Thomo' Thompson also spoke of the casual nature of my case study venues:

> Yeah, definitely spend a bit of time at the Tote as well. The same as the Old Bar, friends that work behind the bar helps and you can go in there if you're just on your way home and you're like 'I feel like a beer'. You don't have to call anyone; you can just stop in at either of those [venues] and someone you know will be there … So, you can just stop and have a quick beer and then head on your way again.
> (interview, Sarah Thompson, 2015)

The informality of the front bar as an accessible social space that is connected to but does not necessarily centre on the live music experience adds to the feeling of these venues as places to meet for a casual drink, share mutual interests and discuss music and the local scene. Participants add to the social fabric of these venues, giving the music scenes that inhabit them a sense of place. The personal histories, shared memories and events that occur in a venue culminate in a collective knowledge of the space, an embodied cultural capital. This process is what turns an average bar into a beloved space of community practice.

Both Joel Morrison and 'Snoop' Mitchell discussed a sense of collective ownership over each venue, which Mitchell linked to the role of the front bar as a social space:

> I think if neither venue had a front bar, then we wouldn't have the feeling that's around this place, so there wouldn't be this sense of people feeling an ownership for the Tote or wanting to come back here on a regular basis if the front bar wasn't there. I think that helps foster that sense of community, because drinking in the same space as people, even if you've never met them before, seeing the same people, you're going to talk to that person.
> (interview, 'Snoop' Mitchell, 2015)

Mitchell compared the front bar to the band room, stating that the venue would be 'kind of just weird' without the front bar (interview, 'Snoop' Mitchell, 2015). He stated that the Tote's front bar helps to 'foster that sense of community' (interview). This inclines the field of the venue towards its participants' habitus and emphasizes the importance of a public space (i.e. the front bar) where people can congregate and socialize. As Morrison stated, '[the] front bar helps a lot [in] having a social scene … There's somewhere to just sit down and have a drink and a chat instead of just watching the bands' (interview, Joel Morrison, 2015). The front bar is a meeting place for scene participants. It is therefore an inherently public space, which lends itself to an open, informal and multifaceted dialogue that contributes to the culture of small live music venues and the continued generation of social capital. Despite this, habitus, and social and cultural capital influence who can participate and how they participate, as not everyone can access these spaces. Much of a live music venue's front bar 'vibe' is influenced by its relationship with the corresponding band room.

The band room

Band rooms are performance spaces and provide a stage for musical practices that involve a variety of interactions unique to live performance. They are also spaces where audiences engage with and participate in live performances. Further, the role of the audience – how they respond to and interact with the performer – shapes notions of the venue space and its position in the live music ecosystem.

A venue's band room is a space of performance, celebration, consumption, reverence and revelry. Many of my interviewees framed it as a discrete space of its own, separate from what occurs throughout the rest of the venue:

> I went the Tote the other night and I was in the front bar talking to people and I was like, 'Oh, I just want there to be a band on so I don't have to talk to anyone.' And then went into the band room. I knew a lot of people in the front bar, there [was] a lot going on and it was really, really social. But then once [the band] Nation Blue started playing, I just got to stand and watch and not actually be switched on, because during the day, part of my job is being really chatty and full on, really social.
>
> (interview, Bec Reato, 2015)

Reato positioned the band room of the Tote as a space of meditation, wherein she can enjoy the bands without social pressure. However, this experience becomes muddied if we situate it in the spatial environment of the Old Bar, which offers little separation between the front bar and band room. As the Old Bar's band room is situated immediately next to the venue's front bar (see Figure 5), there is a spatial overlap between these two areas. We must therefore consider both, framing the discourse in holistic terms that takes in all aspects of the venue space and considers how decisions pertaining to the operation of the band room indirectly affect the venue as a social space.

Bands explain that the intimate setting of the Old Bar makes it a space that is exciting to play:

> It's much more intimate. There can be some big bands that play, like say when the Meanies play here it's absolutely intense. They never play shows this small anymore on a stage this small … So it's good for bands to come back to little grassroots rooms and just play right there and face the crowd. All those things help make it reputable and a great gig.
>
> (interview, Joel Morrison, 2015)

The informal nature of the Old Bar removes much of the spectacle of performance. The stage is relatively low, with musicians only a few feet higher than the audience. On busy nights sightlines are limited, adding to the intimate feel of the band room. Audiences and performers occupy a similar social space at the Old Bar, heightening the authenticity of the musical experience. As Shuker states:

> For many critics, fans and musicians, there is a perceived hierarchy of live performances, with a marked tendency to equate the audiences' physical proximity to the actual 'performance' and intimacy with the performer(s) with a more authentic and satisfying musical experience.
>
> (2022, p. 210)

Intimacy is emphasized in spaces like the Old Bar. However, this sits in contrast to the Tote, where the stage is higher and large stacks of speakers give an imposing feeling to the stage.

The Old Bar's owner Liam Matthews discussed the appeal of having a band room that spills into the front bar:

> I'd say a quarter of the people that are here every Friday night have just paid the entry fee to come in to be here and they either sit out the back or they discover new bands or something like that, which is something that I've always loved about this place, and I love it being all inclusive, not having a separated band room. The bands get to maybe win a few people over and it just creates a whole environment here.
>
> (interview, Liam Matthews, 2015)

Although the Old Bar's front bar is slightly separated from its band room via a brick archway, the two spaces are effectively the same, and one must walk through the band room to access the venue's other spaces. Nick Finch, a long-time manager at the Old Bar and prominent musician, described the layout of the venue:

It's that perfect size, you know, the stage isn't too high, so you can play a gig you can have 30 people in there and have a really good vibe, and the band feeds off the energy of the audience … There are no tables in there, there's nowhere to fucking sit if you go to the Old Bar because they want to keep the band room focused on bands, without having tables all over the place.

(interview, Nick Finch, 2015)

Here, spatiality informs sociality, which in turn shapes the field and habitus of those that engage with the space. This was reflected in my interviews with owners Liam Matthews and Joel Morrison. While the bands serve as the focus, the small size of the band room means that the 'vibe' is intimate and relaxed. This contrasts with the Tote, which is larger, more spread out, and features a main band room that is separate from the rest of the venue. This separation affects perceptions of the live music experience, for both musicians and the audience.

Rich Stanley, former booking agent of the Tote and member of former Brisbane band the Onyas, discussed the status and cultural capital associated with the Tote:

If a band could headline at the Tote on a Friday night, I think they would be like, 'We've made it.' I have to remember that … it particularly came into mind when Wet Lips[18] had a thing on, they were putting a bunch of their girl bands on upstairs on a Friday night, and I had a gig fall through downstairs and so about a month out, instead of me trying to scramble a half decent gig a month out, I said to them, 'Do you just want to move downstairs, add a couple of extra bands and see how you go?' … it was the biggest fucking deal for all of them and I hadn't realized that.

(interview, Rich Stanley, 2015)

Stanley identified and emphasized the cultural capital connected to the Tote's main band room. A well-equipped space in terms of production values, the Tote's band room also holds a certain amount of status and cultural capital due to the venue's iconic history. This history has been affirmed in media narratives, vernacular culture and personal accounts:

The Tote, because of the history it's had and has still got, it's a big thing for bands to play their first gig. You might have played 10 or 15 gigs around town, but when you play your first gig at the Tote, it's still a big thing … There's just a

---

[18] Wet Lips are a local punk trio.

certain feeling about it. A feeling of there's substance to what you're doing ... It's kind of a graduation almost.

(interview, 'Snoop' Mitchell, 2015)

This emphasizes the cultural capital associated with the Tote and the venue's status in the live music ecosystem of Melbourne.

Small venues and everyday life

Definitions of 'the everyday' relate to both time, place and space. The term refers to those events that take place every day, week, month or year and occur in a local setting that is accessible to those engaging with them regularly (Hesmondhalgh 2002, p. 125). We perceive the everyday as commonplace and perpetual. Everyday events are part of daily life and can be valued as much as they are taken for granted. This makes such events routine and part of the larger process of 'getting through the day'. The 'everyday' is often mundane, as 'events that happen every night or every week, even every month and every year, are part of mundane, ordinary living, and might serve to remind us of lived experience "beyond" structures of power' (Hesmondhalgh 2002, p. 126). In the abstract, the local small venue gig is one of many ordinary experiences that make up everyday engagement with music.

Small gigs – those that take place in local, small venues, whether formal or informal – are part of the everyday life of music scenes and can be viewed as either novel entertainment for those engaging with them occasionally, or a 'way of life' for those more entrenched in the scene. Tia DeNora (2000) has written extensively on everyday engagement with music, with an emphasis on affect. Building on DeNora, Prior argues that an adequate understanding of music in everyday life 'means shifting the level of examination from a general sociology of music to a specific sociology of people doing things with music; from the idea of constraining social structures to the constitutive effects of musical meanings' (Prior 2013, p. 189). As 'people doing things with music', small venue gigs give scenes coherence and the means to construct and maintain collective identities.

Small venue performances have often been overlooked in studies of popular music. Local small gigs lack the spectacle of the live concert and are too often bound up with notions of amateurism. However, since the early 1990s local music scenes and the small gigs that populate them have received further attention in scholarly studies of popular music. The impetus for this new research was articulated by David Hesmondhalgh in 2002:

> what we need to focus on in providing a more adequate conception of ordinary experiences of music than in existing audience studies is not merely the idea of the everyday, but time and space ... there has been too much attention to spectacular and supposedly rebellious uses of popular music, at the expense of the mundane and the banal.
>
> (2002, p. 127)

This appeal seems to have been largely answered given the numerous publications and research projects on local small live music events published in the following years (Behr et al. 2014, 2016b; Bennett & Peterson 2004; Bennett & Rogers 2016a, 2016b; Cohen 2007; Gallan 2012; Gallan & Gibson 2013; Gibson & Homan 2004; Holt 2014; Rogers 2008). Such research has served to elucidate the importance of small venues and local gigs. These small venues act as performance spaces for emerging artists and musicians while the gigs provide an opportunity for audiences to engage with live music on an everyday level.

The impact of space and place on the sustainability of music scenes cannot be understated. Many internationally recognized scenes initially revolved around a handful of venues operating in a specific place (Kronenburg 2013, pp. 4–5). Identifiable musical styles, sounds and genres have found their birthplace in the music scenes of specific cities:

> The performance of popular music endows places with special identities that create an international image for their host cities – the US cities of Nashville, Detroit and Seattle are, respectively, synonymous with Country, Motown, and Grunge. Elsewhere in the world, Tamworth is styled the Country Music capital of Australia, Cologne the birthplace of Krautrock (in Germany known as Kosmische Musik, cosmic music), and Ibiza the centre for Dance and House (sometimes known as Balearic Beat).
>
> (Kronenburg 2011, p. 139)

The venues of these cities serve as incubators for distinctive musical styles, mixing in the melting pot of each scene and the live music ecosystem that serves to create them. These musical styles are intrinsically tied to place. The small gigs that contributed to their birth are organized and performed by working musicians, each looking for their next opportunity to work a live room. The network of venues and social actors – the live music ecosystem – facilitates an identifiable music scene that eventually becomes recognized, either locally, nationally or internationally. Without the opportunity for participants to organize, socialize and perform, many of these scenes and their associated musical styles may not have come to fruition. It is evident then that place, space and everyday engagement with live music is integral to the formation of live music scenes.

As discussed above, place, space, scene and the live music ecosystem all inform the production of live music events (Brennan et al. 2016), and each serve as the focus of my analysis as they relate to the small venue experience and the diverse ways in which it can be valued. However, my interest is not in the authenticity of performance as a cultural form or even the music itself. Rather, the focus of this book is the activities that form around live music, the scenes and live music ecosystem, and the generation and mobilization of non-economic forms of capital that contribute to their sustainability, as discussed further in Chapter 4.

Space, taste and class

Small venues are inherently imbued with meanings that go beyond the live music experience, facilitating a transient community that centres on engagement: the live music scene. Music scenes are fluid and ephemeral, and their relationship with time and space can be framed in a similar way to Doreen Massey's (2005, p. 55) definition of these terms as distinct yet co-implicated arenas of temporality and interrelation. Transience and change are implicit in place-based music scenes, as scenes flow between space and across time. They are, like localities, 'the intersection of social activities and social relations and, crucially, activities and relations which are necessarily, by definition, dynamic, changing' (Massey 1994, p. 136). The transience inherent in music scenes shapes our understanding of venue spaces. Scenes reify dynamic processes of sociality that recreate the social experience of live music venues anew night after night within a specific horizon of possibility.

The changing trends in fashion and genre that define local music scenes are further influenced by global developments in international music cultures but are also reified in the concrete actions and processes that make up the live music ecosystem, all of which are influenced by taste, culture and changing perceptions of these. Individual taste is implicated in discussions of music scenes, as participants classify their level of engagement and interest through participation. This aligns with Bourdieu's understanding of taste as a marker of classification:

> Taste is a practical mastery of distributions which makes it possible to sense or intuit what is likely (or unlikely) to befall – and therefore to befit – an individual occupying a given position in social space ... the social agents whom the sociologist classifies are producers not only of classifiable acts but also of acts of classification which are themselves classified.
>
> (Bourdieu 1984, pp. 466–7)

Participants position themselves in the social space of a music scene via the way that they engage with venue spaces, what venues they choose to visit, and how regularly they visit them. The positioning of participants in the social space of a live music scene is also closely related to each participant's habitus.

Habitus accounts for both a participants' position in the spatial setting of the venue, their role in the music scene that the venue houses and their movements in and throughout the geographical boundaries that make up a local scene, as well as the social space of the scene itself. This is because 'habitus refers frequently to spatial positioning, both in physical settings and in social life more generally ... Social space is therefore about both positions in geographic space and in the more abstract arena of social positioning' (Reed-Danahay 2015, pp. 81–2). The social space of music scenes is therefore represented in physical space. Music scenes tend to be concentrated in hip, urban neighbourhoods synonymous with niche spaces of cultural production such as small live music venues. Musicians and other participants often live close to these venues and hence their position in social space is aligned with physical space. This socio-spatial positioning is further influenced by their sense of habitus. Therefore, habitus becomes intersectional with space and place in discussions of music scenes, intersecting with physical space to mark out the status of scene participants in social space. This reflects an anti-essentialist notion of identity: space as 'the intersections and interactions of concrete social relations and social processes in a situation of co-presence' (Massey 1994, p. 138). This definition of space as intersectional fits with both the concept of 'scene' and Bourdieusian notions of capital and habitus. Social and cultural capital play a significant role in an individual's positioning in social space, as does the live music event itself, as the everyday nature of small gigs allows a level of access that appeals to participants rich in these capitals. Therefore, space, habitus and alternative forms of capital all play significant roles in the articulation of music scenes.

The small gig further differs from 'the live concert', in that gigs are of the 'everyday'. This is due to their ubiquity, their high rate of incidence in cities and their low operational costs. Large concerts require considerable planning, logistics, expertise, dedicated or highly adaptive performance spaces equipped with quality audio-visual technology, plenty of staff and a revolving door of professional musicians. The venues that local gigs take place in are often more informal and accessible than large performance spaces (Whiting & Carter 2016), the level of production is generally lower, and the musicians are usually either amateurs, hobbyists or semi-professionals who hold down day jobs outside of musical performance (Rogers 2008). The relationship between the musicians and audience also differs, as any clear distinction between the two groups is blurred (Rogers 2012). Therefore, the accessibility and 'everyday' nature of small gigs is the key sociocultural difference between them and larger concert events.

In addition to this, due to the financial struggles that beset small live music venues (such as the Tote and the Old Bar) and in the Australian context discussed here, the 'live music pub' is aligned with cultural narratives of 'the underdog'. This narrative takes many forms and continues to be reified in the re-telling of Oz rock history and Australian pub rock's working-class roots (Walker 2012). The 'live music pub' has thus been re-framed in terms of the Anglo-Australian notion of the 'Aussie battler'[19] (Bode 2006). This was expressed in the discourse surrounding the venue in the local press and media at the time of the Tote's closing (Donovan 2010a–2010h; Donovan & Roberts 2010).

The working-class coding of small live music pubs in Australia is demonstrated in the vernacular of my case study venues and their regular patrons. Although much of the live music audience is middle class in background, many participants adopt working-class vernaculars and dispositions when engaging with these spaces. This reflects a socially mobile habitus and the ability to 'perform' class that has resulted in accusations of 'class tourism', also seen in other realms of cultural consumption associated with working-class identities such as the real-ale festivals of Northern England (Spracklen, Laurencic & Kenyon 2013). Such anxieties around class reflect broader distinctions between 'mainstream'

---

[19] 'Aussie battler' is an Australian colloquialism for 'ordinary' individuals triumphing over adversity. In this context, adversity often comprises low pay, environmental hardships and lack of recognition, historically aligning the 'Aussie battler' with white, working-class identities.

(i.e. middle class) and 'alternative' nightlife spaces and the desire to keep these distinct and separate,[20] as working-class identities are seen as more authentic in 'alternative' spaces such as the Old Bar and the Tote and are aligned with 'rockism' more broadly.

Place, social space and identity

Place strongly influences the social process of participating in and engaging with music scenes. The geographical context and socio-historical setting of the Old Bar and the Tote contributes to their status in the local live music ecosystem, with place also influencing how scene participants engage with these spaces. A distinct and identifiable local music scene that is shared across these two venues can be observed, one that overlaps and inhabits much of the same social space. Place, social space and cultural capital are interconnected in a web of exchange and identity formation. Social space is used to identify an individual's position in an artistic field; their status, degree of influence and structural relations to economic and cultural resources as '[o]ne's "objective relation" to another is one's proximity to them in social space' (Bottero & Crossley 2011, p. 101). Here, social space and place intersect, articulating the same understandings of meaning and identity through cultural consumption and production associated with place. A place-based live music scene thus serves as a prime example of an artistic field. Further, social relationships are integral to the construction of social space and are demonstrated in the ongoing production and mobilization of social capital (Bottero & Crossley 2011, p. 102).

The music scene discussed within this chapter is concentrated in the inner-northern Melbourne suburbs of Fitzroy and Collingwood. This scene was observed as sharing many of the same participants – and therefore much of the same social space – by my interviewees:

---

[20] In their research on Wollongong's Oxford Tavern, Gallan and Gibson position participation in the Oxford's music scene as an 'alternative' choice, with participants 'imagining and constructing "otherness" in relation to the restrictive cultural norms of the commercial mainstream' (2013, p. 179). Such a choice sits comfortably with the assumption that participation in Australian live music scenes revolves heavily around 'the local pub' and an associated drinking culture. In this sense, '[p]ubs embody the broad contradictions of Australian society and are important sites of vernacular cultural expression' (Gallan & Gibson 2013, p. 177), despite anxieties around keeping live music pubs working class and an overall resistance to middle-class gentrification and 'mainstream' nightlife.

> It seems to be, like, you see the same heads at the same things, especially around the Old Bar and the Tote. There are people that I see there whenever I go to those places or if I'm in that area. I don't think it's necessarily on purpose either; I think it just works out that way. People go where they're comfortable.
>
> (interview, Jarrod Brown, 2015)

Habitus plays an important role in facilitating access to certain spaces. Each venue is coded with distinctive forms of cultural capital and caters for specific demographics. The Old Bar and the Tote exist on a similar spectrum of cultural capital, habitus and social space, making them more accessible to participants that share these characteristics, a topic I will discuss further in Chapter 4. Furthermore, the Tote is often compared to the Old Bar not as a business rival, but as the next step up in the local live music ecosystem. This coexistence is key to the sustainability of the live music ecosystem.

Throughout this chapter I have defined 'space' and 'place' as both geographical and sociocultural formations that intersect to inform an idea of the local music scene of Melbourne's inner north as a defined social space specific to a delineated area, as well as the social interactions that take place within and between this area and my case study venues. This is important as it emphasizes the spatiality inherent in discussions of local music scenes and the role that shared social space plays in facilitating the common associations that make scenes identifiable as social formations. This spatiality and the materiality of the venue spaces themselves is discussed further in the following chapter, which examines the relationship between capital, value and cultural intermediaries as they relate to small live music venues specifically.

Part Three

Precarity

4

Capital, value and cultural intermediaries

This chapter utilizes Bourdieu's theories of capital to explain the types of cultural production and sociality facilitated by small venues, and how these are converted from 'tacit knowledges' (Lobato 2006; O'Connor 2004) that are embodied, shared and inscribed in practice, into more identifiable forms of social and cultural capital (e.g. social connections and specific knowledges), and finally their mobilization towards economic opportunities. Making specific use of Pierre Bourdieu's theories of capital (1984, 1986), habitus and field,[1] I explicate the role of small live music venues as producers of social and cultural value. The aim of this chapter is to make clear the kinds of cultural work that small live music venues do, and the forms of sociality that they encourage.

Social and cultural value[2] are conceptualized here according to definitions provided by cultural economics, cultural policy and urban planning scholars (Belfiore 2012, 2015; van der Hoeven & Hitters 2019), along with several live music scholars who have deployed these concepts further (Behr, Brennan & Cloonan 2016a; Behr et al. 2014). As I argue, the social and cultural value of live music are formally embodied within Bourdieusian forms of capital. Such forms of value are intrinsic to niche spaces of cultural production and signify their importance as sites of sociality. To demonstrate this, I utilize Bourdieu's theories of capital, which have been updated, criticized and amended by scholars from

---

[1] A field is a 'space of objective relations between positions defined by their rank in the distribution of competing powers or species of capital' (Bourdieu & Wacquant 1992, p. 113). Fields are social and cultural spaces that are organized around identifiable modes of interaction and practice, such as the classroom, the sporting field or the live music venue (Edgerton & Roberts 2014, p. 195).

[2] In their excellent review of the academic and grey literature on the social and cultural value of live music, Arno van der Hoeven and Erik Hitters define the social value of live music as 'the contribution of live music to the social relationships between people, a sense of belonging and collective identity' (2019, p. 266), and cultural value as that which deals with 'the artistic qualities of live music, the symbolic meanings expressed through the performance of an artist, and creativity as reflected in a rich diversity of genres and artistic experimentation' (p. 266).

across a range of disciplines (Hennion 2007; Jensen 2006; Moore 2005; Prior 2013; Wright 2015), to explain the types of cultural production and sociality facilitated by small venues. These concepts are modified to fit more modern notions of cultural production and consumption specific to niche spaces of cultural production such as small live music venues.

This chapter will discuss how various cultural intermediaries, such as venue booking agents, mobilize alternative forms of capital (e.g. social, cultural, symbolic) and exchange these for revenue. As its primary example, this chapter posits that venue booking agents mobilize the intrinsic value (i.e. use value) of their venues, drawing on the cultural and symbolic capital of the venue spaces themselves, the combined capital (and labour) of others working in these spaces and their own social and cultural capital to do so. These hybrid forms of capital take on an instrumental value (i.e. exchange value), which is traded for economic capital. This is significant, as such processes serve both to legitimate the status of small venues in local music scenes and to attract the revenue and economic capital that allows niche spaces of cultural production to remain financially sustainable. However, the emphasis throughout this process remains on intrinsic forms of value, which are the true source of small venues' revenue and capital, economic or otherwise.

This chapter will outline, define and critique various Bourdieusian concepts such as cultural, social and symbolic capital, habitus and field, discussing their impact on small venue spaces and their significance in discussions of small venues as sites of social and cultural value. Using Bourdieusian notions of capital, I posit that booking agents and other cultural intermediaries convert venues' intrinsic value into instrumental value. This conversion is exercised through a booking agent's curation of the venue space, their relationships with musicians and artist managers and their ability to promote an air of sociality in and around small venue spaces. The primary argument of this penultimate chapter is that small venues contribute to live music cultures in nuanced, informal ways that remain vital despite their elusiveness. This chapter determines that financial precarity is endemic within the small live music sector, but that such precarity is a by-product of niche, cultural capital–oriented spaces that view economic capital as a dull necessity for sustaining cultural production (Scott 2017).

It is important to note that, although this chapter focuses on transactions of capital, these value forms are always hybridized and entangled in collective understandings, as the notion of cultural value 'accrues in aggregate rather than in a set of individually ascribable experiential transactions' (Behr et al. 2016a,

p. 409). This aligns with Bourdieu's (1993) theorization of the field of cultural production, in that it delimits what is 'culturally valuable' to the field in which it is valued. Following this, an ongoing quandary of this chapter is the relationship between intrinsic and instrumental value, and what this relationship means for niche spaces of cultural production such as small venues that must walk the line between exploiting both.

Capital and value

Local music scenes are built on complex systems of sociality, cultural and social capital, and habitus. It is from this perspective that I have approached the music scenes and live music ecosystems that encompass my field of research: not in terms of what they are defined by – musical genres, cultural signifiers and so on – but more by how they are constructed through human interactions and exchange as they occur within the specificities of the spaces which they inhabit, demonstrated most visibly and regularly in small live music venues.

This chapter makes specific use of Pierre Bourdieu's theoretical apparatus to investigate, analyse and explain the value of small live music venues. One significant point of tension regarding Bourdieu is the apparent rigidity of his conceptual apparatus (Prior 2013, p. 185), deemed too structuralist in nature to account for the nuances of modern cultural consumption. Cultural studies scholars and sociologists have criticized Bourdieu's structuralism as being unable to adequately account for everyday practices of music consumption (DeNora 2000; Hennion 2007), as it '[n]eglects the ways our lives are intimately entwined with music, including how it surprises us or modulates our tastes and emotions' (Prior 2013, p. 182). Alternatively, theorists such as Antoine Hennion (2015) and David Wright (2015) propose a return to a phenomenological understanding of taste, rejecting notions of habitus and field – with their predispositions and 'classified classifiers' (Bourdieu 1984, p. 6) – and emphasizing the empirical and personal world of the senses, along with feeling and affect (Highmore 2016, p. 161).

Although these criticisms of Bourdieu are justified, I argue that understandings of taste such as those proposed by DeNora (2000), Hennion (2015) and Wright (2015) are not mutually exclusive of Bourdieu and his assertion that engagement with culture is an inherently classed and classified act. Rather than focusing on how processes of distinction delineate class and other social categories

(Hennion 2015; Prior 2013; Wright 2015), I am more interested in how processes of distinction are operationalized and converted into economic forms within decidedly *niche* spaces of cultural production, such as small venues. The emphasis here is on the production and reproduction of culture rather than its consumption (Straw 2010). Importantly, Bourdieu's theories of capital allow us to appraise niche spaces of cultural production in both instrumental and intrinsic terms. These concepts facilitate an understanding of how these venues convert their social and cultural capital into economic capital, drawing on a 'currency of cool' – cultural capital – and a network of participants – social capital – to build a mutually beneficial community of practice that contributes to the financial sustainability of small venue spaces. This question of conversion is central to Bourdieu's concept of capital, as 'capital is only capital to the extent that it can be converted into other types of capital' (Jensen 2006, p. 268). For these reasons, much can still be drawn from Bourdieu's understanding of certain value forms, as their various articulations are integral to the functioning of marginal spaces of cultural production.

Cultural capital

Cultural capital is knowledge specific to a cultural field (Bourdieu 1984, p. 4), such as local music scenes, and utilized within this field towards various ends. For example, knowing which bands draw a crowd is a form of cultural capital that has the potential to be exchanged for economic capital. Alternatively, the social connections necessary to book said bands can be conceptualized as social capital.

The concept of cultural capital was formally defined by Bourdieu (1984) and relates specifically to types of '"cultural competences," which can be embodied (internalized and intangible), objectified (cultural products), and institutionalized (officially accredited)' (Bourdieu 1997, cited in Edgerton & Roberts 2014, p. 195). The cultural capital gained from engaging with live music facilitates access to certain spaces and social networks: the live music 'scene' (Snell & Hodgetts 2007, p. 438). Cultural capital performs a large role in scenes, giving them a set of markers to group themselves around. However, these can be renegotiated and adapted depending on context, as participants need not be committed to only one scene and may participate in several. Further, examples of cultural capital 'such as dressing a certain way, frequenting a bar and dancing are central to community maintenance and the reaffirmation of shared identities' (Snell & Hodgetts 2007, p. 430).

Subcultural capital

Fundamental to local music scenes and the small live music venues that house them are distinct forms of cultural capital that could otherwise be defined as 'subcultural capital' (Thornton 1996). However, I make a strong distinction between cultural and subcultural forms of capital. Much like cultural capital, 'subcultural capital' can be objectified in the form of fashionable haircuts and record collections or embodied by those 'in the know' using current slang (Thornton 1996, p. 11). However, the concept of subcultural capital has been strongly critiqued, with scholars suggesting the term needs to be updated in line with criticisms of subcultural theory more broadly (Bennett 2011; Bloustien & Peters 2011; Jensen 2006; Threadgold 2015).

An extension of the work of the BCCCS and Bourdieu's (1984) theory of cultural capital, Sarah Thornton's use of subcultural capital has come under criticism alongside broader critiques of 'subculture' as an accurate descriptor of cultural practice. Jensen (2006), for example, notes that Thornton's definition of subcultural capital lacks intersectionality. He calls for a more nuanced understanding of subcultures and subcultural capital, stating that

> the relation between the subculture and its surroundings is best understood by focusing on what is appreciated within the subculture (i.e., subcultural capital) and at the same time analytically situating the subculture in terms of class, gender, ethnicity and 'race'.
>
> (Jensen 2006, p. 257)

However, this reliance on 'subculture' as a descriptor of social practice is problematic, as the term itself has largely fallen out of favour (Muggleton & Weinzierl 2003). Although it is useful to consider culture as a hierarchy, with a variety of codes and signs embedded in each layer (Jensen 2006, p. 263), to accept the concept of subcultural capital is to give credence to that of subcultures and their continued proliferation, an assumption that has been criticized throughout the literature since the 1990s (Weinzierl & Muggleton 2003, p. 4), as discussed in Chapter 1.

Further, Jensen's argument relies on a presumption that subcultures are socially autonomous. While critiquing Thornton's use of subcultural capital, he simultaneously defends the term, stating: 'The notion of subcultural capital could help us ... through potentially grasping the relative autonomy of subcultures without defocusing social structure' (2006, p. 260). Jensen's solution is to take an intersectional approach, accounting for the various social pressures and power structures that are ever-present in and around subcultures by 'relating the types of subcultural capital "found" in various subcultures to intersections between the social position, gender, ethnicity and "race" of the participants in the subculture' (Jensen 2006, p. 263). However, as outlined in Chapter 1, the idea of subcultures as socially autonomous is widely disputed.

While maintaining that the term is still useful, subcultural capital becomes problematic when the lines between it and cultural capital are blurred. This is because subcultural capital is only significant within 'alternative' fields of cultural production, whereas 'things should only be thought of as a Bourdieu[s]ian form of cultural capital if it can be utilised for success in "legitimate" fields' (Threadgold 2015, p. 54). Viewing niche spaces of cultural production as subcultural and analysing them in terms of subcultural capital misrepresent them as being somehow removed from, subordinated by, or otherwise opposed to hegemony (Weinzierl & Muggleton 2003, p. 7). For such reasons, and in shared agreement with the increasing body of literature that problematizes the term 'subculture' (Bennett 1999b; Kahn-Harris 2000; Muggleton & Weinzierl 2003; Stahl 2003b), I resist the use of the term 'subcultural capital' for the purposes of this chapter.

Social capital

Bourdieu (1997) defines social capital as 'social obligations' or 'connections' (Edgerton & Roberts 2014, pp. 194–5). Social capital is particularly potent in the live music industry, as it relies heavily on face-to-face networking and personal relationships (Crewe & Beaverstock 1998). The informal nature of the music industry 'blurs the business–social divide' (Watson 2008, p. 18), flattening the significance of social and business relationships. This is consistent with the experience of cultural and creative industry workers in general (Pratt 2000, p. 431), as such careers depend on the complex interplay of individual traits, personal relationships, diverse forms of 'support' and a multitude of other social, economic and cultural factors (Threadgold 2015, p. 57). Motives beyond the live music experience – such as interactions external to the production and performance of live music (e.g. social congress) – are a key component of music scenes. This emphasizes the role of live music as a mediated practice where mutual interest in the performance provides an opportunity for relationship building, through which participants may accumulate and exchange social capital.

Although relevant within an industry context where connections are key to making career and economic advances, I define social capital in the Bourdieusian sense, as a network of mutual support and opportunities at work in a specific cultural field, such as a local music scene. However, such a field is not removed from the broader music industries. The distinction I make is that the exchange value of Bourdieusian social capital is not limited to economic capital, as social capital can be exchanged for other types of capital.

Symbolic capital

Bourdieu (1984, p. 291) equates symbolic capital with authority, notability and fame, often coupling it with economic capital and other signifiers of power and success. Symbolic capital is distinct from cultural capital as it holds value across many fields, or the broader 'field of power', which is structured by two competing principles: 'the distribution of economic capital and the distribution of cultural capital' (Edgerton & Roberts 2014, p. 195). Symbolic capital can be framed as the meta-capital (Jensen 2006, p. 268), that which is most easily converted into economic capital. Certain musicians and industry figures hold symbolic capital as key players within the music industry.

Habitus, the 'scene' and embodied cultural capital

Habitus is inherently tied to notions of cultural, social and symbolic capital, and is influenced and shaped by a large swathe of factors, articulated in multiple, multifaceted ways (Bourdieu 1984, pp. 470–1). Habitus also serves to reproduce and re-inscribe in individuals the divisions that already occur across class, gender, ethnicities and society. As '[h]abitus is rooted in family upbringing (socialization within the family) and conditioned by one's position in the social structure' (Edgerton & Roberts 2014, p. 195), it is subconscious and entrenched and operates on a level beyond self-control and personal agency (Bourdieu 1984, p. 466). It is so deeply ingrained in an individual that it is difficult to unpack, as it is often made up of a complex web of interrelated factors and characteristics. This impacts individuals' ability to generate, mobilize and convert capital. However, some elements of the habitus can be altered and adapted, particularly through the accumulation of alternative forms of capital (Scott 2012).

An understanding of the embodiment of cultural capital is integral to any discussion of habitus. The way that habitus and cultural capital intersect with the performance of identity is where Bourdieu and prominent gender studies theorist Judith Butler (1999) agree, as both view the body as culturally constructed and reproduced through the notion of 'practice'. Therefore, like gender, embodied cultural capital can be viewed as another type of cultural construction, ascribed to the body through the performance of taste. However, for Bourdieu, it is through the habitus that tastes are ritually installed and memorized in the body, manifesting themselves as physical dispositions: the bodily 'hexis' (Prior 2013).

Participation in local music scenes results in the formation of the scenes themselves, as the habitus of scene participants constructs the field of the scene as they encounter it. Participants are the scene, in that the collective interaction of their habitus forms the field and its social space. This aligns with Butler's (1999, p. 119) interpretation of field and habitus as performative and mutually co-constituted. In positioning the subject – their habitus and body – as formative in the construction of the field, Butler reaffirms an understanding of music scenes as fields in the Bourdieusian sense while simultaneously suggesting that such fields are the product of an ongoing exchange of capital and the constant interaction of various co-constituted habitus through participation and engagement: 'the habitus is formed, but it is also formative … Strictly speaking, the habitus produces or generates dispositions as well as their transposability' (Butler 1999, p. 116).

By subjecting participants to the demands of live music scenes, the participants' habitus constructs the field of the scene by adapting to the impositions of that field that are simultaneously constituted in the dispositions of the habitus that it engages with. Local music scenes are therefore the mutual co-creation of field and habitus in a delimited social space. However, such interactions sometimes result in a lack of congruence between the habitus of a potential scene participant and the social space of a particular venue. Not all can 'incline' or adapt to local music scenes and small venue spaces, resulting in exclusions and social barriers.

Space limits how participants move. This experience of space also relates to one's habitus, capital and position in social space. We can extend this understanding of social space to a participant's interaction with the venue itself and their habitus in this space, as '[t]he economic and social conditions which [capital] presuppose … are very closely linked to the different possible positions in social space and, consequently, bound up with the systems of dispositions (habitus) characteristic of the different classes and class fractions' (Bourdieu 1984, pp. 5–6).

An intertwining of social and cultural capital is common in niche fields of cultural production (Throsby 1999, p. 5; Zweigenhaft 1993), such as local music scenes. Further, participation in music scenes takes multiple forms and can be articulated in nonverbal and embodied ways (Driver & Bennett 2015). The tacit, embodied knowledge demonstrated in knowing how and when to dance or 'mosh' to a song is itself a kind of cultural capital, reaffirming and building on a participant's habitus. Different types of dancing suit different types of music and this embodied knowledge is gained only through engagement and participation. However, there are many forms of cultural capital other than the embodied that are taken for granted and largely invisible in the fields in which they are valued. This is what makes measuring them such a challenge.

It is important to determine cultural capital more in the distinctions it marks out than the status it bestows, as this status is subjective and often only meaningful in the fields to which it is born. In this context, taste is used 'to establish and mark differences by a process of distinction which is not (or not necessarily) a distinct knowledge' (Bourdieu 1984, p. 466). Therefore, taste cultures often lack reflexivity and, in many cases, a reflexive approach would harm the illusion of an innate sense of taste. The booking agent of a live music venue must know the scene intrinsically or they would potentially lose the perceived authority that they hold: 'The crucial factor is that knowledge about music and style cannot appear to have been acquired through the mainstream media or other outlets of the culture industry' (Moore 2005, pp. 232–3).

Taste cultures are knowledge cultures, as one must be familiar with the various codes and signs that are particular to each field. Such understandings of the articulation of power in the fields of cultural production proposed by Bourdieu are relatively transferable to modern music-making activities.[3] In cultural studies generally and popular music studies specifically, Bourdieu's theory of cultural capital is often deployed in reference to highly valued knowledge, symbols, associations and tastes of a cultural field (Threadgold 2015, p. 53). Cultural capital is useful in demonstrating that symbolic knowledge and taste not only imbue a music scene with meaning, such as in the case of aesthetic and musical markers (e.g. fashion, instrumentation, genre), but are

---

[3] Although *Distinction* (Bourdieu 1984) was written as a critique of the French upper class, Bourdieu's concepts and theories are applicable to local music scenes and the cultures of engagement that surround them. Hence, they have been adapted and applied to various taste cultures and music scenes, such as those explored in Sarah Thornton's *Club Cultures* (1996) and other work in Australia by Steve Threadgold (2015) and Pam Nilan (Threadgold & Nilan 2009).

also representative of status. As Prior states, 'consumers no longer restrict their tastes to elite forms of art ... but participate in a heterogeneous range of cultural practices and receive some degree of prestige from doing so' (2013, p. 187). This 'prestige' could otherwise be framed as cultural or even symbolic capital, as opposed to subcultural capital, which becomes less relevant in an age of cultural omnivorousness due to the limits of its application. However, 'cultural capital is a concept that is meant to help understand not just how a field works, but how fields are hierarchical and how some fields are more important than others' (Threadgold 2015, p. 53).

Like most spaces that hinge on social interactions and exchanges of 'insider' knowledge, music scenes and the live music venues that house them are semi-hierarchical spaces wherein the lines between cultural capital and harder forms of capital are often blurred. Pecking orders emerge within these spaces, based on the individual cultural and social capital of bands, booking agents and other scene participants. Further, venues embody history and tradition, and provide social hubs for music scenes, suggesting that the concept of 'culture' carries with it a notion of 'value' (Throsby 1999, p. 6), and that some venues might therefore be more valuable than others. However, not everyone can convert soft social and cultural capital to harder economic capital, as 'the ability to transform subcultural to cultural and then economic capital requires tactics and negotiations that need reflexivity' (Threadgold 2015, p. 53). Only those with a considerable amount of status in the scene can leverage such status into economic advantages. Venue-booking agents are a good example of this (Gallan 2012). Like booking agents, independent label owners, music publicists and rock journalists are other examples of professional and semi-professional music industry careers. Their conversion of social and cultural capital is an essential part of their professional activities, effectively transforming these into a career (Threadgold 2015, p. 54). Such niche professional pathways hinge on the ability to convert key contacts and knowledge of the scene into a viable occupation. Contacts, networks and the social skills needed to capitalize on such networks can also be understood as 'social capital', as defined previously.

To summarize, Bourdieu's theories of capital facilitate an understanding of how niche spaces of cultural production convert their social and cultural capital into economic capital. Yet, this conversion presupposes other, intangible forms of value. The role of the venue booking agent is integral to this process.

The booking agent

A major concern in any account of live music ecosystems is the disparate yet interdependent social actors that affect and influence the sustainability of live music scenes and the venues that house them. In this section I analyse the role of venue-booking agents, entrenched insiders who have a profound influence over the social space of each venue. This influence is mobilized via their power and associated types of capital across the curation and coordination of a venue's nightly or regular line-ups.

The role of a venue's booking agent is one of a curator, tastemaker and businessperson. They trade in social and cultural capital to co-ordinate the 'live music event' (Behr et al. 2016b; Frith 2012) and generate a flow of revenue into the venue space. Their tastes influence the space, and they are hired based on their pre-existing cultural capital and the social capital they maintain throughout the local music scene. Booking agents are also gatekeepers, 'intermediaries [who] use cultural knowledge to influence consumer behaviour and control "taste" and "style", occupying authoritative positions between production and consumption spheres' (Gallan 2012, p. 39). However, they must also balance their own carefully cultivated cultural capital and the symbolic capital of the venue space with the financial necessities associated with running a capitalist enterprise. The role of the booking agent is therefore pivotal to the venue's status in the local music scene and its financial sustainability, priorities that are often intertwined.

The role of the booking agent is usually either a professional or semi-professional one. Booking agents are either hired by the venue as in-house employees, outsourced from professional concert promoters or are owners or part owners in the venue business. The duties of the booking agent are to liaise with musicians, their management or tour promoters (also often called 'booking agents' who advocate on behalf of bands and musicians rather than venues) to coordinate the live music event. This organizational work happens weeks, months or sometimes even years before the live music event and is heavily reliant on tacit knowledge of the music industries and strong networks built over years working within these industries. Cultural and social capital come heavily into play here, as the various actors involved with booking, coordinating and publicizing the live music event draw on their inherent understanding of the 'live gig' and its various moving parts to ensure it is a success. Specifically, the booking agent makes decisions around which bands play on which night of the week, along with which bands or musicians are selected to support or open for a headlining act. This group of bands or musicians – those that are consecutively booked at a venue on the same night, or across a similar period – is referred to as the 'line-up'.

Venue-booking agents also handle decisions around performance fees and monetary guarantees on behalf of the venue, and therefore have significant influence over the allocation of economic capital. Many booking agents are 'known' in local music scenes, as part of their job requires wielding a significant amount of social, cultural, symbolic and ultimately economic capital. They engage with both local and translocal music scenes while further liaising with outside agents more commonly associated with the live music ecosystem, interacting with multiple, disparate yet interdependent actors to ensure the live music event goes ahead (Behr et al. 2016b).

Booking agents curate venue spaces to align with the field of the local music scene, and the needs and social space of the venue as a small business and social hub. Their tastes influence the space, yet they are hired on the basis of their pre-existing cultural capital, the habitus they bring to the role and the social capital they maintain throughout the local music scene. The role of the booking agent is therefore pivotal to the venue's status in the live music ecosystem, as their curatorship has a significant impact on the venue's success and ongoing financial sustainability.

Booking agents act as arbiters of taste and cultural capital. They have great influence over venue spaces as 'cultural fields'. In this context, '[f]ields overlap and exist at various levels, with smaller fields (e.g. family) nested in larger fields (e.g. educational field, economic field)' (Edgerton & Roberts 2014, p. 195). Within the context of the case study venues explored throughout Chapter 3, we can consider the local music scenes of Melbourne's inner north as one of many fields or focus on each venue and the discrete social spaces therein.

The status of booking agents in the live music ecosystem is derived from the interrelation of their habitus with the capital they mobilize in the field of the local music scene(s) (Edgerton & Roberts 2014, p. 195). Booking agents hold positions of considerable social, cultural and symbolic capital among music scene participants. Their gatekeeping practices delineate a sense of scene around the venue space, encouraging participants to invest meaning in the venue's inherent field and the social pathways that constitute it (Gallan 2012, p. 36). Booking agents negotiate the terms of the venue as a field and therefore which participants the field inclines towards.

It is worth considering Simon Frith's materialist approach to live music here, which asks that if 'live music takes as its basis that a music event is constructed through a complex of socio-historical economic and ideological forces, just like a music work', then 'from a sociological perspective there has to be some sort of agreement among all the social actors involved in a musical event as to what the event entails (in terms of behaviour) and means' (Frith 2012). The booking agent is fundamental to this event in that they curate, organize and ensure that the event goes ahead. Although they are not always the catalyst, they are instrumental.

Venue-booking agents are essential to the live music ecosystem and hold an influential position within it, as well as surrounding scenes. Each has a specific function in the broader live music ecosystem and the status of each venue in this ecosystem. They are also responsible for a microcosm of the ecosystem as represented in the venue's 'field'. This microcosm relies on the interdependence between staff, musicians, other venue workers and the surrounding live music scene. Thus, successful curation of the venue space by each booking agent impacts the live music ecosystem directly.

Booking agents are also pivotal in developing a sense of inclusivity (and often exclusivity), self-sufficiency and vibrancy in the venue spaces that they administer 'by generating and then consistently implementing a strict philosophy on what music and which bands perform' (Gallan 2012, p. 35). Throughout his research, Gallan (2012) states that local bands who held strong connections – social capital – with the Oxford Tavern were often favoured over better known or more lucrative bands. Thus, the role of the booking agent hinges on social and cultural capital, which is heavily influenced by habitus. This strongly affects the venue as a cultural field, coding and influencing the space.

In an interview Joel Morrison, the booking agent of the Old Bar, outlined the ways in which he navigates the cultural field of his venue space:

> It's also wrapped up in being the venue owner as well as the band booker, where you've got to create allegiances ... Like where a band will make it feel like their own home and then if they get bigger then they can always come back and it's like a grassroots, building from the bottom sort of thing. And if they feel a bit of ownership of the venue then they're always going to help you out later down the track when they're a lot bigger.
>
> (interview, Joel Morrison, 2015)

Morrison's role as a venue owner informs his practice as a booking agent, and his role as a booking agent further informs his practice as a musician (interview,

Joel Morrison, 2015). The cultural field of the venue is first and foremost in his decision-making processes, as is instilling a sense of ownership over the venue in the bands that frequent the venue space, emphasizing the co-constitution of their habitus in the field of the venue. This contributes to the idea of a venue-specific field and affirms the venue's place in the live music ecosystem, as the booking agent's power over the space aligns the venue with a certain aesthetic and network of bands/musicians.

Many of the musicians interviewed throughout my fieldwork discussed the role of small venues in creating a social space for them. Nick Finch discussed the importance of the Old Bar in providing his former band Graveyard Train with a hub in Melbourne's inner north during the early 2010s:

> I think at the time in Collingwood and Fitzroy there was, I mean it's kind of a musical hub, especially at that time, when Graveyard Train was starting, there was a real kind of, old country scene thing happening. It seemed to focus on the Old Bar, like all the old country bands were playing at the Old Bar. We were just one of those bands. I guess Joel [Morrison], the band booker, really kind of picked up on that scene and it just seemed like the Old Bar was the kind of epicentre of that kind of folk country, old country thing that was happening five years ago in Melbourne.
>
> (interview, Nick Finch, 2015)

Morrison's ability to create a 'hub' for these bands is indicative of the role of booking agents in the live music ecosystem. By giving musicians space to perform and hone their craft, he allowed these acts to become integrated into the venue culture and local music scene around it.

Many of the bands that have come through the Old Bar have gone on to have successful careers in the Australian music industry, a testament to the Old Bar as a platform for emerging acts and a launching pad towards bigger stages. Former bar manager and musician Adam Curley echoed this point:

> I do probably associate a few bands with the Old Bar ... There seems to have been a time when [the owners] were nurturing a group of Melbourne bands who have since gone on to be a bit too big to play at the Old Bar.
>
> (interview Adam Curley, 2015)

This nurturing was a deliberate decision on the part of the venue's owners and its booking agent Joel Morrison, resulting in the establishment of a distinct scene that revolved around the venue for a moment in time and place. Much of this was premised on Morrison's social and cultural capital and his ability to mobilize these in curating live music events.

The individual cultural capital held by each booking agent is integral to their curation of the venue space. Each agent has distinct tastes and a pre-existing knowledge of the local music scene that informs their booking policies. Each venue is therefore a reflection of its booking agent's own tastes and cultural capital, moderated by a need to get people through the door, that is, the conversion of social and cultural capital into economic capital. This can be seen in the way specific booking agents' tastes seem to fit with each venue space:

> I think it's dominated by whoever's booking it, I guess. The venue chooses that booker based on what they've already had working for them. Rich [Stanley] booking the Tote isn't a coincidence. They figure his taste suits that venue. George [Hyde] booking the Spotted Mallard,[4] he can get some sort of gypsy band one night and then a loud surf rock band the next night. It depends on the venue.
>
> (interview, Chris Drane, 2015)

The cultural capital of each booking agent suffuses the venue space, imbuing it with an aesthetic and shaping its position in the scene and its status in the live music ecosystem. This is indicative of how the ecosystem and scene intersect.

The booking agent's habitus influences the venue space in a particular way. This influences the venue's position in the live music ecosystem, attracting certain scenes and their participants. This is habitus–field congruence on a mass scale. However, what scene does not account for is how the built environment of the venue, its location in the cityscape and social actors that are removed from the scene (e.g. developers, the police, policymakers, bureaucrats) affect its ongoing sustainability. This is the advantage of using live music ecology as a conceptual framework.

The tacit knowledge of promoters informs each venue space. Rich Stanley, former booking agent of the Tote, made a point of dismissing 'careerist' bands, emphasizing his disinterest in a specific brand of professionalism:

> I think it's important to keep it organized but informal and friendly. I really have an aversion to bands who start off as if they want to be big bands, like careerist professional bands … It's like you know they suck, you know they're going to be awful, and it doesn't really matter what they sound like, you know they just want Triple J[5] airplay or something like that and you just have to avoid that shit. The

---

[4] The Spotted Mallard is a live music and dining venue in Brunswick, featuring a seated show and a wide variety of musical genres.
[5] Triple J is an Australian national radio station and public youth broadcaster.

other way you can screen bands is if they send you BandCamp and SoundCloud links they're probably going to be cool, but if they send you ReverbNation links just delete it.

(interview, Rich Stanley, 2015)

Stanley ascribes cultural capital to certain websites that he deems more authentic. He also asserts a distinction between bands that are self-managed DIY ventures and those that have a manager, making clear that such a position is linked to careerist ambitions and an overt desire for economic capital.

Assumed notions of authenticity influence the way Stanley conducts himself as a booking agent. His role is premised on his ability to manufacture an 'authentic' cultural experience (Grazian 2004, pp. 138–9) with the assistance of others. Stanley's curation of the space is delimited by what he assumes to be authentic, which is directly related to his habitus and cultural capital. We can therefore frame each venue's status as largely, but not wholly, a product of the booking agent's habitus and symbolic capital as well as their habitus–field congruence manifested through curation of the space. Further, their social and cultural capital is repeatedly called upon to book, organize and finalize live music events, assuring the venue's status.

In this context, Stanley privileges cultural capital over a desire for economic capital. Those bands that prioritize credibility, artistic integrity and authenticity in the form of DIY practices and autonomy are given precedence over 'careerist' bands. Further to this, it is useful to consider the live music ecosystem in terms of the relationship between economic, cultural and social capital. In the live music ecosystem of Melbourne's inner north, cultural capital is often more valuable than economic capital. Certainly, it is more abundant, and with a general scarcity of economic capital across the local music sector, it is also more easily traded. Social capital is also a large contributor to the everyday functioning of the live music ecosystem and may be exchanged for economic capital when the latter is particularly scarce.

Although there is clearly an element of performance here, Stanley's distinction and the gatekeeping that maintains it are in line with the aesthetic and cultural field that he was attempting to curate at the Tote at the time of our interview, demarcating it as a decidedly *niche* space of cultural production. This curation contributes to ongoing processes of myth making that surround the Tote, which have consistently positioned it as an 'alternative' nightlife space (Gallan 2015; Hesmondhalgh & Meier 2015) within the music scene(s) of Melbourne's inner north. Such myth making assists the Tote to carve out its own distinct niche in the live music market, increasing its popularity in spite – or perhaps because – of its booking agent's disinterest.

Booking agents correspond with and coordinate a vast number of diverse social actors to ensure that a gig goes ahead:

> There'll be a band I'm not really that interested in, but I really like the person, and that's where the social side of it's more important ... It comes back to that cultural thing we were talking about, if I think they're well intentioned and I like the way they go about their footy[6] I'm into it. And that's really one of my main driving things is I want to find people like that and help them do what they want to do.
>
> (interview, Rich Stanley, 2015)

The emphasis on 'good intentions' demonstrates the role that social capital plays in the ongoing sustainability of the live music ecosystem. Stanley prefers to work with bands that 'go about their footy' in a way in which he likes, emphasizing mutual respect. The importance of social capital was echoed by Lara Soulio:

> I think because the owners and the bookers do go to the bands and go to other venues ... They know the bands they're booking. Everyone's sort of involved in some way, whether it's art or music or building something for the bar. People are multi-skilled, and it is a community because of that, and therefore it becomes a social environment.
>
> (interview, Lara Soulio, 2015)

These interviewees emphasized engagement with the scene and the way such engagement feeds into the live music ecosystem is a by-product of interdependence between disparate social agents. Without this, the venues would not be able to sustain themselves, as the kind of competition-based business practices inherent in neoliberal capitalist economics would undermine the live music ecosystem that this culture relies on. A mutually beneficial community arises out of this, wherein venues and scene participants support each other across the ecosystem. This aligns closely with earlier definitions of music scenes, with the exception that the live music ecosystem takes the actions of those agents operating outside of the scene and the material concerns of live music venues into account, as well as how these interdependent factors contribute to an ongoing live music culture.

The pursuit of profit is often expressed as a secondary objective by most booking agents and small venue owners, who see themselves as curators of cultural space and facilitators of the types of sociality required for such spaces to thrive. This

---

[6] 'Go about their footy' is a local colloquialism for 'going about their business', relating to how they conduct themselves personally.

initial 'input' value is contrasted against the much reported 'output' or 'impact' of instrumental value[7] (Belfiore 2012, 2015), a metric that has dominated cultural policy discussions for decades, especially in Australia (Carter 2015; Deloitte Access Economics 2011; Ernst & Young 2011; Newton & Coyle-Hayward 2018). Belfiore criticizes instrumentalism as 'the way in which the attribution of value to the outcome of aesthetic encounters has become part of the technocratic machinery of cultural policy-making' (2015, p. 97). Yet despite the economic contribution of the live music sector, the economic capital (i.e. profit) that small venues generate is often quite marginal,[8] rendering the day-to-day operation of small live music venues a precarious financial operation (Whiting 2019, p. 126). As van der Hoeven and Hitters state, 'such venues are in a vulnerable position due to their small scale and independence from larger chains. Rising rents following on from gentrification and increased costs associated with soundproofing or security measures weigh heavily on their budgets' (2019, p. 268). In this context, the doxa of 'defensive instrumentalism'[9] (Belfiore 2012, 2015) has left small-scale niche spaces of cultural production in an increasingly precarious position. The consumer spending that occurs around and is attracted by live music as a specific benefit worthy of investment is irrelevant to the small venue owner struggling to make ends meet. A new conceptualization of the contribution that small live music venues make to the arts, culture and society beyond that of defensive instrumentalism and its associated 'impact' value is therefore necessary. However, disentangling these value forms is complicated and requires further problematizing.

Financial precarity, musical labour and small venue cultures

The live music sector is a financially risky industry in which to operate. Both the labour of musical performance and the capital needed to fund such performances are subject to factors beyond that of a usual exchange. Musical performance as labour is bound up with notions of self-actualization, creativity, musical

---

[7] Instrumental value as it relates to the live music sector and the arts in general emphasizes economic impact – the 'impact value' – over other benefits (Belfiore 2015, p. 97).
[8] This is supported by previous research on small live music venues conducted in the UK (Behr et al. 2014; Music Venue Trust 2015; Parkinson et al. 2015; Webster et al. 2018).
[9] Belfiore (2015, p. 101) argues that the type of instrumentalism perpetuated in arts and cultural policy has taken on an increasingly defensive bent. Yet this defensive strategy has done little to justify public spending on the arts, and the continued emphasis on impact value has not taken the sector to a place of financial stability. Despite this, the dominance of an economic frame for the discussion of value remains unchallenged (Belfiore 2015, p. 102).

comradery, sociality, physicality and many other affective experiences that are often prioritized above the pursuit of an income. Likewise, consumption of live music is driven by feelings of affect and is an emotionally driven impulse wherein consumers do not act 'rationally'. For promoters, booking agents and venue owners, predicting this interplay between the labour of musical performance and what audiences are willing to exchange for such performances is largely informed by tacit knowledges, habitus and 'a feel for the game'. Some factors are easier to predict than others, and most decisions are based on precedent, but in such an affective space outcomes are unpredictable. Complicating this further, small live music venues are often caught in a tricky position, trying to balance their promotion of niche musical acts with making ends meet as a small business. In Australia, small venues are not treated as dissimilar to most other small businesses, and therefore do not receive state or community support beyond that of a small business or bar. This is despite small venues taking an approach to their business that does not always prioritize profit making. Indeed, other forms of capital and value are often prioritized above profit.

Small venues rely on complex systems of social and cultural capital and their continued exchange. Booking agents trade their social capital to book popular bands, which brings in economic capital. This speaks to the nature of capital: 'accumulated labour ... which, when appropriated on a private, i.e., exclusive, basis by agents or groups of agents, enables them to appropriate social energy in the form of reified or living labour' (Bourdieu 1997, p. 46). These social agents include scene participants, and the capital that they mobilize is embodied in their knowledge of local music scenes, objectified in the concert tickets they purchase, or otherwise played out through social connections. Further, social and cultural capital take an investment of either time, labour or money to acquire, are inscribed in a variety of tangible and intangible ways and can be reproduced in different contexts towards multiple ends (Bourdieu 1997, p. 46). The cultural capital of local music scenes – inscribed and embodied in an insider knowledge of that scene or objectified in such things as band merchandise – often only has exchange value in the same field of practice in which it is generated. Likewise, social capital gained through participation in music scenes is often specific to that field of participation and lacks the same conversion value outside of said scene/field. However, such forms of capital can still be converted into economic and symbolic capital within these fields, which can then be useful elsewhere. This is how the social and cultural value of small venue spaces is converted into economic value.

Small venue spaces offer an insight into how cultural fields are represented in both social and material spaces. In my analysis, I observe small live music venues as social spaces and commercial businesses that mobilize social and cultural capital to generate economic capital. These venues rely on local music scenes for this conversion, as these scenes constitute a network of social actors that regularly participate in the venue culture and live music events hosted therein, exchanging their economic capital for the opportunity to participate in said scene. Small venues therefore mobilize social and cultural capital to bring economic capital (i.e. revenue) into the venue space. This is significant as economic capital is often otherwise scarce in local music scenes and other niche spaces of cultural production. However, it is in this social and cultural value that the worth of these venues truly lies, as spaces that provide music scenes with vital performance sites and meeting places as well as acting as the grassroots foundation of live music ecosystems fundamental to the sustainability of a live music culture.

Conclusion

This book has reconsidered and cast a narrow but deep focus on the role of small live music venues within the music industries, the cultural economy and society at large. To do this effectively, it has challenged, revised and critiqued established understandings of popular music cultures and the conceptual apparatus necessary to elucidate the ways in which these cultures are organized, such as 'scenes', 'subcultures' and 'the live music ecology'. I have offered the 'live music ecosystem' as an alternative to the recently conceptualized 'live music ecology' and have juxtaposed this altered term against the longer standing concept of 'scene'. The live music ecosystem is a complementary but distinct descriptor for the social organization of musical activities and the interdependencies between social actors within and outside of musical scenes, the bricks-and-mortar venue spaces themselves, and the co-efficiencies that exist between venue spaces of different size and scale. This book therefore offers a new contribution to the literature on the social organization of cultural production specific to live and popular music, which is further clarified and summarized below.

Scenes and the live music ecosystem

Popular and academic understandings of music scenes have been fundamental to conceptualizing how informal cultural and music-making activities are organized in the current post-subcultural context. While still identifiable as coherent sociocultural formations, music scenes allow for a plurality of popular music cultures and the ad-hoc participation in these cultures of most participants. Scenes have thus served as a useful way for describing cultural participation that accounts for the cultural omnivorousness of participants in popular music in late modernity, emerging as the dominant term for discussing music making and engagement in the post-subcultural context.

Cultural consumption and production in late modernity, specifically that of popular and live music, has gone through several significant disruptions and changes since the early 2000s. Importantly, live music has gained precedence as a primary source of income for many performers and musicians, often above the sale of merchandise and records. Consumption of live music and participation in live music events has also increased alongside the rise of the so-called experience economy (Pine & Gilmore 2013). Music scenes have been a helpful way of framing engagement with popular music cultures across these multiple changes and developments happening throughout the music industries and broader cultural economy.

Scene is also helpful in describing how participants engage with multiple and varied cultural contexts across spatial and temporal boundaries, without adhering to one too strongly or with a level of commitment that might demonstrate a lasting or significant shift in a participant's cultural consumption or social life. Of course, participants engage in specific scenes more intensely than others, but these scenes are not as rigid or all-encompassing as prescribed by previous notions of subcultures. However, what scenes do not account for are the built environments and material infrastructures – the bricks-and-mortar venue spaces – and the policy settings and officials that govern the administration and regulation of these spaces, spaces which are necessary for the cultural events that they host. Nor do scenes adequately include those social actors outside the scene whose power nevertheless shapes and impacts such scenes on a daily level.

The 'live music ecology' emerged as a way of accounting for these extra-scenic elements, providing a new way of conceptualizing live music production that accounts for resources, capital, precedent and the political economy. However, although I believe 'live music ecology' is an important conceptual distinction that provides an entry point for new ways of thinking about live music cultures and materiality, I have updated and adjusted the term to 'live music ecosystem' to fit existing policy settings and governmental frameworks (Homan 2016; Martin 2017; New South Wales Parliament 2018; Rozbicka et al. 2022). I also offer 'live music ecosystem' as a point of difference in that ecology refers to the study of ecosystems, whereas ecosystem refers to those combined and interdependent structures that suggest mutual aid and modes of competitive collaboration.

Beyond this semantic distinction, what I have proposed throughout this book is an integrated understanding of how music scenes and live music ecosystems function and intersect. This is fundamental to an appropriate theorization of the role of small live music venues within these systems. While small venues serve as staging grounds for scenes and the kinds of sociality that lead to new musical projects, cultural innovations and the establishing of bonds between music and cultural workers – as well as the performance and facilitation of nascent and developing musical projects – they remain built spaces subject to zoning requirements, liquor licensing, rent, pressures associated with gentrification and other place-based factors. Such preconditions and cultural and policy settings are administered and overseen by a variety of social actors who often have very little to do with music scenes themselves. Further, venues and other music industry firms rely on a network of interdependence to function as feasible ventures. These extra-scenic elements – those outside the regular scope of music scenes and their participants but highly influential in terms of their material and economic constraints on scenes, and upon which scenes are predicated – need to be taken into consideration in tandem with both local scenes, but also within a broader field of power. The live music ecosystem is therefore a useful substratum within the broader cultural economy (and the political economy beyond that) for theorizing the factors impacting music scenes, scene participants and the venues that play host to these.

Such factors of political economy were brought to the fore throughout the COVID-19 pandemic. For example, the role of government in both disrupting and sustaining live music venues, and the arts and cultural industries in general, was particularly apparent during the pandemic. Government support packages, both general and specific, were essential in preventing most live music venues from collapsing amidst state-imposed lockdowns and other public health restrictions. In Australia, many music industry operators were excluded from the federal government's large-scale private sector support package JobKeeper, particularly those on short-term, casual or invoice-based contracts. However, as small-to-medium businesses, live music venues qualified for the program, and were thrown a lifeline throughout the first year of the pandemic in Australia (March 2020–March 2021).

Following the end of JobKeeper in March 2021, state governments intervened to support the sector, through such programs as COVID-19 disaster payments – made available to workers and businesses in Victoria (State Government of Victoria 2022) – live music support and project support programs in South Australia (Music Development Office 2022), and the performing arts COVID support package in New South Wales (NSW Government 2022). In 2021, the Victorian government announced that it would be offering COVID-19 event insurance for the 2022 calendar year via the

Victorian Managed Insurance Authority (VMIA 2022), providing the state's events industry with confidence to plan events into the future: 'This insurance provides cover for creative, business, sporting and community events in Victoria that have to be cancelled (or have to run at reduced capacity) because of a State or Federal Government restriction due to the COVID-19 pandemic' (VMIA 2022).

Clearly, Australian state governments have played large roles in assisting the live music and events sectors throughout the uncertainty of the COVID-19 pandemic. However, much of this support was necessitated by health restrictions and lockdowns imposed by those same governments, which limited the ability of events and venues to function, as well as a general lack of leadership from the federal government around cultural policy and live events throughout the pandemic (Banks & O'Connor 2021; Pacella, Luckman & O'Connor 2021a). For better or worse, the role of governments had a significant impact on the live music sector and cultural economy throughout this time, and any discussion of live music venues and the music industry in general must take this role into account. The live music ecosystem offers a conceptual framework for understanding the impact of governments which previous descriptors of musical cultures and practices (e.g. scenes, subcultures, fields, art worlds) do not.

To summarize, 'scenes' and 'live music ecosystems' coexist and are layered atop one another as complementary yet distinct descriptors of socio-musical practice and the flows of capital and labour specific to live music production. Each term serves to elucidate a separate area of consideration that is relevant to the other but does not replace it. Such a distinction might seem arbitrary, but it plays an important role in delineating the social and cultural function of small venues, and how these are influenced by factors within their sphere of influence but also well outside of it. It also re-centres the role of policy in creating amenable conditions for live music cultures to thrive and acknowledges that adjustments to systemic features and infrastructure (e.g. public transport, trading hours, capacity restrictions) will have an impact on the ability of live music scenes to function. It provides a marriage of concepts and a broader social theory that considers the 'insiders' and their specific modes of organization, celebration and production/consumption, but also the 'outsiders' and the complex interrelationships and interdependencies between these groups and other social actors in between. To explain these interdependencies more accurately, along with the tangible and tacit flows of labour and capital that provide them with power and agency, a further theoretical intervention is proposed, specifically the relevance and significance of alternative forms of capital within small venue spaces.

Capital, value and small venue spaces

Music scenes need cultural spaces around which to congregate. Small venues are ideal for the kinds of informal social gatherings and engagement with niche musical cultures that scenes thrive on, simultaneously providing the venue with a steady stream of revenue through the sale of tickets, food and alcohol. As explored throughout this book and specifically in Chapter 4, Bourdieu's theoretical apparatus allows us to further appreciate this cultivation of space. It demonstrates how small venues walk the line between various systems of power, not by partitioning them, but by disguising their engagement with one – the project of remaining a financially sustainable business – within their mastery of another – as a decidedly niche space of cultural production, blurring the distinction between intrinsic and instrumental forms of value and bringing any binary understanding of these value forms into question.

This is done by a process of drawing on, transacting and exchanging distinct articulations of capital relevant to cultural fields of production; capital that is premised on value forms inherent within small venues and the social actors that give them meaning. Such social actors include a constellation of participants working in and around local music scenes: musicians, sound engineers, hospitality staff, creative industries professionals, live music enthusiasts and more. These participants make up a community that is both 'lived' and 'imagined', with the physical and symbolic walls of each venue forming a nexus of social space, emphasizing the role of space and sociality in these scenes. Their participation and interaction with these venues contributes to their public, collective identity and its broader social and cultural value, which is embodied within them.

In addition to their value as performance sites for musicians, these venues also hold intrinsic cultural value. Their materiality, sense of space and the surrounding place in which they find their context are imbued with objectified cultural capital (Bourdieu 1997, p. 50). This includes the posters on their walls, the iconography of the venue's visual aesthetic, the atmosphere of the venue space itself and the ambiance that permeates these spaces and their neighbourhoods with a distinctive identity and character. In this context, cultural capital does not necessarily have to be possessed by a social agent but can instead be embedded in material objects, objectified not only as economic capital 'momentarily imprisoned' (Massey 1994, p. 136), but as cultural capital tied up in the spatial fix of buildings and other objects. The staff, owners, musicians, patrons and curators of small venues play a large role in imbuing venue spaces with this objectified cultural capital, which can otherwise be determined as a type of cultural value.

The social space of music scenes intersects with the materiality of live music ecosystems, and small venues are prime examples of this intersection, embodying the social and cultural value of live music in their spatial coding and utility as social hubs and performance sites for musicians and music scene participants. Further, the value of this kind of objectified cultural capital is inherent in its conversion, which can only occur through an expression of agency. This value, a combination of a sort of 'currency of cool' – cultural capital – and a network of participants – social capital – affirms small venues as the foundation of a city's live music ecosystem but is also what these venues exchange for economic capital to remain profitable and financially sustainable.

Conversions of social and cultural value/capital into economic capital are what sustain small live music venues, which emphasizes that they operate outside of traditional value chains. By prioritizing live music over more financially lucrative business models, small venues demonstrate a disinterest in economic capital. However, this disinterest and the social and cultural capital generated by their alignment with an original music culture has its own social and cultural value: value that is 'soaked up' by the venue spaces and drawn upon to attract revenue and economic capital. Although this is not necessarily typical of all small venues, it is symbolic of their general position as niche spaces of cultural production.

The specific knowledges held by venue workers and the way that these are used to bring people into these spaces – to consume (music, food, alcohol, etc.) but also to engage with music-making practices and other music scene participants – contributes to feelings of belonging and facilitates sociality that could lead to further creative opportunities. These are significant for intrinsic reasons beyond their exchange value. Yet the commitment of small live music venues to the creation of social and cultural value often seems at odds with their role as a small business. Such a commitment is common among small-scale cultural capital – oriented producers, who cast economic capital as a simple necessity for sustaining cultural production (Scott 2017, p. 72). Further, as decidedly niche spaces of cultural production, the disinterest in economic capital that serves as a point of distinction for small live music venues contributes to their cultural capital, which ironically is exchanged for economic capital by way of their niche appeal.

Social and cultural capital are key components of any live music ecosystem, as promoters and musicians regularly trade in these to ensure the planning and success of the live music event. However, such a business model is also ripe for exploitation due to the unequal distribution of social, cultural and economic capital between agents, musicians and promoters. In fact, concert promotion has previously been described as 'a mess of contradictions – a contract-based business without contracts, an exploitative business based on face-to-face goodwill, a highly regulated business which often seems close to chaotic (and criminal)' (Frith 2010, pp. 2–3). As an ontological framework, the live music ecology makes such contradictions, corruptions and power imbalances salient and aims to reconcile them in a framework that considers each while also holding a view of the bigger picture. Building on this, the live music ecosystem places an emphasis on live music above other forms of music media (e.g. recorded music, video clips, house/canned music), and therefore the venues, social actors and live music culture that dictate the live music event.

Small venues and live music events accommodate local music scenes, providing them with social space. Their value as social hubs for music scenes and as important 'stepping-stone' performance sites for budding musicians contributes to the crucial role small venues serve as the foundation of a city's live music ecosystem (Behr et al. 2014; Webster et al. 2018; Whiting 2019). This demonstrates that small venues have determinable use value that precedes the accumulation of economic capital – yet is central to this process of accumulation. As we begin the work of rebuilding our cultural sector following the COVID-19 pandemic, such an understanding of the complexities among and between value forms is worth considering as we move out of the shadow of defensive instrumentalism that has dominated arts and creative industries policy for the better part of the last thirty years (Belfiore 2012, 2015).

Summary

Throughout this book, I have considered small live music venues from a variety of disciplinary and theoretical perspectives. These include how they are positioned within broader systems of social, cultural and economic organization, their role within urban and other built environments, and the impact of historical precedents, policy settings and contexts, demonstrated by a variety of case studies. The influence of place and space on these venues has also been considered, as has the influence of these venues on places and spaces. Finally, I have discussed how intangible and tangible flows of labour and capital are deployed by creative workers and administered by various cultural intermediaries to create value forms specific to live music as experienced within these spaces.

The discussion of small venues and their relationship with socio-musical concepts of identity, social organization, policy settings, economic impact, and cultural production and consumption featured in Chapter 1 introduced two conceptual interventions that recast established ideas within popular music studies. First, 'subculture' is not a particularly useful or relevant term in discussions of modern popular music cultures and venues,[1] as such spaces and cultures are by their nature porous and do not represent coherent or consistent identity formations. Nor are they 'sub' in that they do not represent a recognizable subversion or resistance to dominant or hegemonic cultural forms in a way that positions them as radical, opposed to or somehow removed from said dominant culture. This is not to say that subcultures do not exist, but that they are not inherently musical cultures nor are music cultures inherently subcultural, and in fact many modern music cultures are resistant to such rigid forms of identity construction as those traditionally represented by subcultures. 'Scene' is therefore a more useful and accurate term for the kinds of sociocultural activities that occur in and around musical activities and events, although it does not provide the full picture, as was also established in Chapter 1.

This second intervention in popular music studies relates to a definition of the 'live music ecosystem' as distinct from the concept of 'live music ecology'. Although much merit and worth lies in the remit of 'live music ecology' as a conceptual project aimed at expanding the scope of musical activities to encompass the built environment and physical settings of venue spaces, along with the influence of social agents removed from music scenes, and the networks of interdependence between co-located music spaces that each rely on for their financial sustainability, the 'live music ecosystem' is ultimately a more useful and convenient term. This is because 'live music ecology' refers to the study of live music 'ecosystems', whereas 'live music ecosystems' are those established networks of infrastructure that are fixed to place and observable within a city, state or town. The 'live music ecology' might then be thought of as the epistemology through which to document 'live music ecosystems'.

Chapter 2 provided important historical context for a discussion of the live music venue as an urban phenomenon which has shaped and been shaped

---

[1] Following this, 'subcultural capital' (Thornton 1996) – a popular term among scene studies used to describe a distinct form of cultural capital specific to subcultures – also becomes irrelevant. For if subcultures do not describe actual systems of cultural production and fields of power, what is described by 'subcultural capital' is simply cultural capital specific to niches spaces of cultural production and consumption. This does not make it distinct from cultural capital, just more difficultly or tangentially transferable into economic capital.

by significant scenes and cities throughout the history of popular music and continues to play an active role in the musical cultures of diverse locales that have previously been hostile or otherwise indifferent to such spaces. Building on the theoretical framework developed in Chapter 1, Chapter 2 grounded this framework in specific places and built environments, demonstrating the connections between policy settings, historical precedents and social movements that have shaped these places and their impact on the musical cultures and grassroots venue spaces of such cities. It is important to acknowledge the deep connection that cultural spaces have with place and that the specificities of place, which are interminably multiple and diverse, inherently shape cultural spaces such as small venues.

A discussion of place, space and small venues continued in Chapter 3. However, whereas Chapter 2 considered the broader perspective of live music and the city, Chapter 3 focused on the forms of sociality and cultural production that occur in venue spaces themselves, and how their physical limitations and layouts impact experiences of these spaces. It unpacked the role of intra-venue spaces (such as the front bar and the band room) in shaping the projected and perceived identities of venue spaces (which are themselves distinct), and the connections and interdependencies between small venues in a live music ecosystem. This chapter centred on ethnographies of two small venues in Melbourne, Australia to explore what is specific and unique about small live music venues, the kinds of cultural production they facilitate, the sociality they encourage, the scenes they give space to and the tensions inherent in attempting to make niche spaces of cultural production profitable.

Profit, capital and value were explored further in Chapter 4, which considered how various cultural intermediaries mobilize diverse resources such as tangible and intangible forms of capital – as well as the creative and manual labour of musicians and venue staff – to turn these niche spaces into profitable enterprises. The role of the venue booking agent was used as a case study to tease out these ideas further, and Bourdieusian concepts such as cultural, social and symbolic capital, as well as habitus, field and disinterest assisted in making clear the kinds of tacit and intangible cultural value small venues hold, and how this is mobilized to retain economic capital. In utilizing Bourdieu's theories of capital, habitus and field in tandem with scene and live music ecology, I have been able to illustrate how small venues mobilize and convert non-economic value forms into revenue, and to unpack the power relations demonstrated in interactions between scene participants, small venue workers and the venue spaces themselves, all while explicating the role these small venues play within live music ecosystems. However, this mobilization and conversion is not necessarily an end in itself, as also discussed in Chapter 4. The deployment of Bourdieu's theoretical apparatus here, as well as my critique and updating of his key ideas, allowed for a depth of discussion regarding the social and cultural value of small venues and other niche spaces of cultural production that got to the very crux of the argument. Further, it demonstrated the significant labour cultural intermediaries perform in negotiating for small venues as ongoing cultural enterprises that must consistently advocate for their own existence through market, community and public mechanisms.

Chapter 4 also raised questions about how venues might be better supported by communities and the state, not just as for-profit small businesses but as valuable cultural institutions. These are questions for future research that need to be seriously considered if the live music sector is to be adequately revived following the COVID-19 pandemic. Small venues and other SMEs within the music industries were arguably the hardest hit by lockdowns and government restrictions, and federal and state relief packages have now set a precedent for the direct financial support of such firms. This raises important questions about the role of governments in supporting popular arts and culture more broadly, as the vast state interventions in global economies that accompanied the pandemic have signalled an end to the neoliberal era, reaffirming the role of states in leading initiatives within the cultural sector rather than simply encouraging market mechanisms.

Recommendations

Small live music venues play a vital role in facilitating the proliferation of diverse musical cultures, act as important social hubs for local music scenes and are the grassroots foundation of regional and urban live music ecosystems fundamental to a thriving cultural economy. This is a significant social and cultural contribution that cannot be reduced by economic rationalism to a mechanism of cost versus benefit, nor can it be ignored as just another positive externality of small enterprise. The impact that these spaces have on the lives and well-being of musicians and other cultural workers, not to mention their ability to pursue a career in these industries, goes beyond that of normal hospitality spaces or even other cultural institutions where audience consumption is prioritized over social and cultural production, such as theatres, cinemas or larger concert venues. Such spaces do not facilitate a comparable atmosphere of sociality, community or belonging, and do not often provide a platform for emerging cultural forms in the same way that small venues do. Yet small venues are still viewed primarily as for-profit small businesses that are exposed to similar levels of risk as other hospitality or retail spaces. A reconsideration of the research and policy contexts that frame and impact the ability of small venues to operate as valuable cultural institutions is therefore necessary.

Such a reconsideration must begin with an acknowledgement of the substantial contribution small live music venues make to music cultures and the broader cultural economy that is framed outside of and removed from economic rationalism and its blunt instrumentalism, but also considers the live music ecosystem and the role of small venues within it. An acknowledgment such as this – one that accounts for the social and cultural value of small venues and not just their material, economic value – may provide further opportunities for state and community support for small venues to be explored and considered. Such support might include wage subsidy schemes, state-backed insurance policies, agent-of-change principles and/or government-supported loans. At a macroeconomic level, basic income, job guarantees and the inclusion of arts and cultural spaces within policies of universal basic services and public value would also serve to better support the live music sector.

There are many improvements to be gained from such a reframing. Not only would it provide small venues with security of tenure, but this sense of stability would also flow through the rest of the live music ecosystem, providing musicians with further reliable opportunities to hone their craft, technicians and staff with job security and improved employment outcomes, and the ability for promoters and booking agents to engage with the work of hosting live events more confidently. Such 'cultural producer confidence' would ensure a thriving live music ecosystem, musical culture and broader cultural economy. By guaranteeing stability for grassroots spaces of cultural production such as small venues so that they can continue the important work of facilitating music scenes, live music ecosystems and the broader music industries will have a solid foundation to build their endeavours upon.

Throughout this process, state and community support should also improve the material conditions facilitated by small venues, holding such spaces to the same standard as other objects of public investment, and placing pressure on venues to improve working and labour conditions, an issue that has plagued many small venues and hospitality businesses. This support, of course, must avoid rewarding venues for doing the wrong thing, and therefore should be conditional on ensuring working conditions are consistent with award rates and other Union-negotiated wages. In fact, the first condition for any public support should be making sure that such basic conditions are met, and that they have been so for a period prior to support being offered. Such prerequisites would assist in ending the cycle of wage theft and other forms of exploitation endemic in many hospitality venues and might also allow a 'seat at the table' for Unions so that they may play a more significant role in negotiating wages and conditions for venue staff, workers and the musicians themselves.

Further, as many musicians and music industries workers retain part-time employment in venues, state and community support for small venues will assist in supporting musicians onstage and off, ensuring that they have access to stable employment adjacent to their cultural practice while also providing them with reliable performance opportunities. The flow-on effect of direct and continued public support for small live music venues and their workforce would bolster other parts of the live music ecosystem, both in terms of musicians' and cultural workers' livelihoods, but also in relation to the live music ecosystem's ability to function as interdependent networks of spaces and firms. Such widespread and large-scale state support for SMEs and other small institutions within the cultural and creative industries has few relevant precedents, and until recently did not have a strong example to follow. However, the policy mechanisms used to offset the economic damage done by the COVID-19 pandemic and associated government restrictions has shifted the political goalposts around cultural policy and introduced new and direct means for funding the arts and cultural sectors that were previously dismissed by politicians and policymakers.

In Australia, a country that has often been reluctant to provide direct support for arts and culture – let alone support for popular culture and the music industries – a precedent has now emerged for sustained intervention in the music industries and broader cultural economy. Although targeted federal support remains rare and many contractors and artists remain excluded from national funding arrangements, the JobKeeper wage subsidy scheme kept many SMEs within the cultural and creative industries (such as small venues) afloat throughout much of the COVID-19 pandemic. Following the end of this scheme in March 2021, further support was offered to businesses and workers impacted by continuing lockdowns and restrictions in the form of disaster relief payments. In those states not heavily affected by lockdowns (such as South Australia), support was offered in the form of live music support programs and other relief packages. Although taxpayer support for other sectors in Australia has been larger, more targeted and provided on more clearly political grounds – such as support for the construction, mining and fossil fuel industries (Pacella et al. 2021a, 2021b) – while many artists and arts workers were excluded, perhaps intentionally, from the JobKeeper wage subsidy scheme (Pledger 2020), there is now a strong precedent for state and federal support for the live music sector, previously a pipedream.

Around the world, similar interventions have been made and other larger initiatives have begun to be tested. In 2022 Ireland began to pilot a guaranteed basic income scheme for artists and arts workers as part of its economic recovery plan. Although this scheme is ostensibly designed to ameliorate the impacts of COVID-19 on the sector, it goes some way towards addressing other systemic issues within the arts and events sectors, as artistic and creative employment is characterized by low, precarious and often seasonal income (Falvey 2021; Reddan 2022). Wales is also considering a general universal basic income scheme (Morris 2022), which would undoubtedly have benefits for artists and cultural sector workers. The French model, 'Intermittents du Spectacle' – an unemployment insurance stipend for workers that have seasonal or intermittent patterns of work, otherwise described as 'bulimic work patterns' (Luckman et al. 2020, p. 5) – was originally proposed to cover contract workers and technicians in the film industry and has served as an incredibly reliable cultural policy in guaranteeing artists, musicians and other cultural workers regular income (Bisker 2012). Guaranteed income and employment schemes have flow-on effects for the rest of the music and cultural sector, as income security means that artists and other workers stay in the sector for longer and are less likely to exit due to a lack of opportunities. This contributes to an expanding pool of expertise, talent and skills which begets more experienced music and cultural industries workers, growing the sector.

As a result of the COVID-19 pandemic, wage subsidies, state-funded cultural work and basic incomes for artists are now mainstream initiatives and have many precedents. These are not radical policies and would benefit small venues too, as a healthy public appetite for live music events generated by the proliferation of producer-consumers (i.e. scene participants who are both musicians and audience members) would encourage a wider variety and diversity of performance spaces. The re-entrance of the state as a market leader rather than simply a facilitator of private enterprise also introduces the possibility of state and community-owned venues, venues that would not need to be reliant on volunteer labour for management and staff (as current community-run not-for-profits often are), nor subject to the volatile winds and uncertainties of the market (such as in the case of for-profit, commercial spaces). As publicly run performance spaces with the affordances and resources to pay all staff and performers proper wages and conditions, community-owned and managed venues might better steel themselves against the diversity of problems plagued by privately owned small venues discussed throughout Chapters 2, 3 and 4.

Unfortunately, following the COVID-19 pandemic some Australian city councils and state governments are looking backwards to the same tired creative industries – led strategies for urban revitalization to solve the problem of widespread vacancies in their CBDs (Shaw 2020), strategies that have been widely debunked, even by their original theorists (Florida 2017). However, established scholars in the field have been quick to remind us that government-led rather than market-led solutions will return better investments in the cultural life of cities (Shaw 2021). Small venues have a lot to gain from such investment strategies, and security of tenure along with the assured ability to provide quality working conditions for creative and hospitality workers should be a priority. As Kate Shaw (2021) states, the way to guarantee the vibrancy of a city's cultural life is quite simple: 'Plenty of space and cheap rent'. Governments must intervene to ensure that these prerequisites remain possibilities, as many other vibrant cultural cities are reliant on community and state support to remain sustainable. For example, in response to Berlin's recent gentrification:

> Cultural entrepreneurs are responding by buying their venues, often with institutional assistance, before the land becomes too expensive. Housing activists are building their own co-ops, and artists are campaigning effectively for more social housing, rent caps and freezes and renationalisation of private housing companies. Most of these initiatives are aided by considerable financial or government support, with cultural producers and entrepreneurs recognised and respected members of civil society.
>
> (Shaw 2021)

This last point is significant and highlights another benefit of continued state support for small venues and other niche cultural institutions.

When communities and governments come together to support and fund cultural initiatives, these initiatives begin to be seen and considered as more legitimate by the public and body politic. Not only this, but governments and political parties vying for government are then required to articulate their cultural policies so that electorates can vote on them. This increases the standing and reputation of arts and culture in the public's eye long term. Such a legitimating effect means that the electorate must consider cultural policy, and therefore the cultural and creative industries that it governs, more closely. By encouraging cultural policy, publics are required to engage with culture and the arts as an integrated component of civil democracy. Cultural policy that engages with small live music venues might enhance their standing in communities as valuable spaces of engagement, participation, belonging and celebration. However, a reconsideration of the role of small live music venues in the social and cultural life of communities, as well as their position in the cultural economy, should not overlook the fact that such venues are not without their problems.

Problems and future research

Different venues host different scenes, but few small venues are completely exclusive in terms of what musical cultures they play host to, although most venues certainly do specialize. While genre-specific clubs and venues remain popular for those musical styles with more mainstream appeal, the ongoing impacts of gentrification on land value in urban and inner-suburban neighbourhoods as well as the general financial precarity of running a niche cultural institution have meant that most small live music venues simply cannot afford to maintain rigid cultural barriers. Instead, small venues narrowcast to a diversity of audiences across multiple scenes. However, what they have and continue to maintain is their niche appeal.

Small venues are implicitly demarcated cultural spaces. They are niche, and their appeal is inclusive of those that might feel otherwise alienated by mainstream musical cultures or the dominant night-time economy. However, this sense of inclusion often comes at the cost of excluding others. Indeed, the exclusion of certain cultural, ethnic or socio-economic identities from small venues in favour of an 'in-group' of participants has been explored most rigorously in dance music and club culture studies (Measham & Hadfield 2009). Such work asserts that the informal processes that govern niche spaces of cultural production – contributing to feelings of belonging to some – are responsible for the alienation and social and spatial exclusion of others. The question then is, 'How do niche cultural spaces remain socially accessible whilst retaining what makes them distinct, unique, and ultimately financially sustainable?'

The interaction between the habitus of individuals and the cultural field of a small venue is important to consider, as not all individuals feel welcome in these spaces. Those excluded might be of an otherwise already-catered-for demographic and will have no trouble finding multiple entertainment options and cultural experiences that appeal to their tastes and sensibilities – their habitus – within the mainstream night-time and cultural economy. However, small venues also exclude otherwise marginalized identities as a side effect of their nature as niche spaces of cultural production. This is difficult to counter, as the niche appeal of small venues also underpins their cultural and social value, demonstrating a compounding of issues relating to access.

The demarcation of small venues as cultural spaces, and what this means for the types of music cultures, scenes and identities that can thrive and those that are side-lined, is a research area that requires further exploration. The reproduction of exclusions inherent in music cultures is a process that should be mitigated, and venues can play an active role in this mitigation. Such work will require an awareness of the types of capital – economic, social, cultural and symbolic – that venues trade in, and an understanding that not all participants have equal access to such capital. Such an understanding and awareness should also consider where each venue sits in relation to other venues, the local live music ecosystem and the broader cultural field. This future work might also assist venues in addressing certain questions regarding what communities each are serving, how they might better serve these communities – in terms of improving ease of access, not only physically but also socially and culturally – and what local communities they are not serving that they could possibly engage with more fully. A realistic way that such issues could be addressed is through public support for those venues that are better placed to cater to marginalized communities that also considers the complexities and interdependencies of various live music ecosystems within a city, state or country.

Along with the marginalization of certain identities and the imposition of social boundaries, new parents, children and the elderly are also broadly excluded from small venue spaces, as factors such as loud volumes, late opening hours and licensing laws restrict access, and discourage all-ages audiences. These are not factors that are strictly limiting, but present certain complexities in terms of access. For example, parents are unable to bring their children to many live music events as these venues are often premised on loud volumes and late performance times, even on weeknights. However, venues often host child-friendly performances on weekend afternoons, with an emphasis on quieter volumes and child-appropriate acts. Further, physically disabled and wheelchair-bound patrons have severely limited access to these spaces. Most small venues lack adequate wheelchair facilities, as they are often spaces adapted from previous uses and lack the funding to upgrade their facilities to be fully accessible, due to broader issues of financial precarity.[2] This raises questions of what kinds of bodies can access these spaces (young, energetic, able-bodied, etc.).

Other important areas for future research into small live music venues include:

- social barriers to participation
- exclusion of marginalized identities
- a perceived appeal to certain cultural groups that ultimately serves hegemony

As this book only serves as an introduction to the topic of small live music venues, focusing on themes of precarity and vibrancy, it is limited in its ability to address these broader issues, and the specificities of access and inclusion within live music scenes, ecosystems and the cultural economy. However, there is much established, ongoing and emerging work on the topic of place-based music scenes, small venues and their exclusions,[3] and I would direct the reader to this literature for further reading.

Final thoughts

Music venues need to be considered in context relative to the scenes they play host to and the ecosystems they are embedded in. Small venues play a vital role within these ecosystems, as their localized nature and informal atmospheres are desired for socializing among music scene participants. An understanding of the role and status of each venue within the live music ecosystem will help venue owners, staff, musicians, policymakers, promoters, publicists and other social actors working in and around music scenes to appreciate the strengths and weaknesses of each venue, which will in turn provide a base knowledge through which to support the local live music ecosystem, possibly through the provision of public support for those venues that address a gap in each ecosystem.

---

[2] This is another area of need where public support might be of use.
[3] See, e.g. Ålander (2020), Gallan (2012), Griffin (2012), Hill and Megson (2020), McDowell (2017), O'Meara and Tretter (2013), Richardson (2014), Sharp (2019), Sharp and Threadgold (2019), White (2006).

The intimate and immediate nature of small venue spaces allows for a co-mingling between audience and performer, the type of sociality important for dynamic and thriving music scenes. These spaces are where many bands and artists perform their first shows, making public creative pursuits that might have only occupied the bedroom, garage or rehearsal space up until that point. For this reason, they are incredibly important spaces for musicians not just as stepping-stones towards larger stages, but as formative spaces that are significant in the narratives of their lives and their careers.

Throughout this book, I have discussed the cultural work of small venues, what they do and how they do it, their priorities, their alignments and their unique position within the cultural landscape of cities and towns. This 'work' is coloured by the music scenes that they play host to and their place within the live music ecosystem of their suburb, their city and their state. As community and commercial spaces that host musical cultures, small venues are pivotal in bringing various scenes and their participants into contact with one another. The sociality that they facilitate is fundamental to the networks and relationships that are needed for music scenes to flourish. This sociality feeds into their role as performance spaces for emerging cultural forms and new musical futures, as musicians and other cultural workers meet and discuss their craft in the same spaces where they hone and refine it. However, none of this should be taken for granted, as small venues remain threatened spaces of cultural production. Many lack long-term security of tenure and are exposed to more risk than other place-based cultural establishments that might own their premises outright (i.e. freehold), receive state funding support or are operated in trust, as a non-commercial entity or charity. This dilemma of institutional precarity, endemic within many quarters of the creative and cultural industries but felt acutely by small live music venues, positions them as unique institutions.

References

ABC 2021, 'Brain drain undergoing "big reversal" in SA as net interstate migration hits 30-year high', *ABC News*, 5 May, viewed 19 July 2022, <https://www.abc.net.au/news/2021-05-05/interstate-migration-helping-reverse-brain-drain-in-sa/100116514>.

Adelaide Fringe 2020, *Annual Review 2020*, Adelaide Fringe, Adelaide, viewed 19 July 2022, <https://2016-assets-adelaidefringe-com-au.s3.amazonaws.com/production/2020/07/01/16/38/28/ca917095-98c4-43de-85bb-a5d2c26f405d/2020_AnnualReview_Digital_03.pdf>.

Age, The 2006, 'Here's cheers after 20 years', *The Age*, 21 March, viewed 19 July 2022, <https://www.theage.com.au/lifestyle/heres-cheers-after-20-years-20060321-ge1yv8.html>.

Ålander, J 2020, '"It's about togetherness": The creation of culturally diverse music venues in Sweden', *Nätverket Kulturforskning i Uppsala*, vol. 22, pp. 51–62.

Althusser, L 1969, *For Marx*, Penguin, London.

Althusser, L 1984, *Essays on ideology*, Verso, London.

ARE Entertainment Company 1996, *Submission to the New South Wales Musicians' Union*, 23 May.

Atkinson, R & Bridge, G 2005, 'Introduction', in R Atkinson & G Bridge (eds), *Gentrification in a global context: The new urban colonialism*, Routledge, London, pp. 1–17.

Auslander, P 2008, *Liveness: Performance in a mediatized culture*, Routledge, London.

Auslander, P 2012, 'Digital liveness: A historico-philosophical perspective', *PAJ: A Journal of Performance and Art*, vol. 34, no. 3, pp. 3–11.

Australian Bureau of Statistics (ABS) 2018, *Fitzroy*, Australian Statistical Geography Standard 2016, ABS, Canberra.

Badcock, B 2001, 'Thirty years on: Gentrification and class changeover in Adelaide's inner suburbs, 1966–96', *Urban Studies*, vol. 38, no. 9, pp. 1559–72.

Ballico, C 2016, 'Live music, liquor and the city: An examination of the influence of liquor regulation on place-specific live music activity', *Cities, Communities & Territories (CIDADES, Comunidades e Territórios)*, vol. 32, pp. 103–17.

Ballico, C & Carter, D 2018, 'A state of constant prodding: Live music, precarity and regulation', *Cultural Trends*, vol. 27, no. 3, pp. 203–17.

Banks, J & Cunningham, S 2016, 'Creative destruction in the Australian videogames industry', *Media International Australia*, vol. 160, no. 1, pp. 127–39.

Banks, M & O'Connor, J 2017, 'Inside the whale (and how to get out of there): Moving on from two decades of creative industries research', *European Journal of Cultural Studies*, vol. 20, no. 6, pp. 637–54.

Banks, M & O'Connor, J 2021, '"A plague upon your howling": Art and culture in the viral emergency', *Cultural Trends*, vol. 30, no. 1, pp. 3–18.

Battan, C 2021, 'The brash, exuberant sounds of hyperpop', *The New Yorker*, 9 August, viewed 19 July 2022, <https://www.newyorker.com/magazine/2021/08/09/the-brash-exuberant-sounds-of-hyperpop>.

Baulch, E 2007, *Making scenes: Reggae, punk, and death metal in 1990s Bali*, Duke University Press, Durham, NC.

BDA Committee for Brisbane (BDAC4B) 2018, *Turn it up! – The future of Brisbane's music economy and heritage*, BDAC4B, viewed 19 July 2022, <https://committeeforbrisbane.org.au/wp-content/uploads/2018/09/BDAC4B-Turn-it-Up-Event-Summary-Sept-2018.pdf>.

Becker, HS 1982, *Art worlds*, University of California Press, Berkeley, CA.

Behr, A, Brennan, M & Cloonan, M 2014, *The cultural value of live music from the pub to the stadium: Getting beyond the numbers*, Arts and Humanities Research Council, Swindon, UK.

Behr, A, Brennan, M & Cloonan, M 2016a, 'Cultural value and cultural policy: Some evidence from the world of live music', *International Journal of Cultural Policy*, vol. 22, no. 3, pp. 403–18.

Behr, A, Brennan, M, Cloonan, M, Frith, S & Webster, E 2016b, 'Live concert performance: An ecological approach', *Rock Music Studies*, vol. 3, no. 1, pp. 5–23.

Behr, A, Webster, E, Brennan, M, Cloonan, M & Ansell, J 2020, 'Making live music count: The UK live music census', *Popular Music and Society*, vol. 43, no. 5, pp. 501–22.

Belfiore, E 2012, '"Defensive instrumentalism" and the legacy of New Labour's cultural policies', *Cultural Trends*, vol. 21, no. 2, pp. 103–11.

Belfiore, E 2015, '"Impact", "value" and "bad economics": Making sense of the problem of value in the arts and humanities', *Arts and Humanities in Higher Education*, vol. 14, no. 1, pp. 95–110.

Bennett, A 1997, '"Going down the pub!": The pub rock scene as a resource for the consumption of popular music', *Popular Music*, vol. 16, no. 1, pp. 97–108.

Bennett, A 1999a, 'Rappin' on the Tyne: White hip hop culture in Northeast England – an ethnographic study', *Sociological Review*, vol. 47, no. 1, pp. 1–24.

Bennett, A 1999b, 'Subcultures or neo-tribes? Rethinking the relationship between youth, style, and musical taste', *Sociology*, vol. 33, no. 3, pp. 599–617.

Bennett, A 2001, *Cultures of popular music*, McGraw-Hill Education, New York.

Bennett, A 2002a, 'Music, media and urban mythscapes: A study of the "Canterbury Sound"', *Media, Culture & Society*, vol. 24, no. 1, pp. 87–100.

Bennett, A 2002b, 'Researching youth culture and popular music: A methodological critique', *British Journal of Sociology*, vol. 53, no. 3, pp. 451–66.

Bennett, A 2003, 'The use of "insider" knowledge in ethnographic research on contemporary youth music scenes', in A Bennett, M Cieslik & S Miles (eds), *Researching youth*, Palgrave Macmillan, London, pp. 186–99.

Bennett, A 2004, 'New tales from Canterbury: The making of a virtual music scene', in A Bennett & RA Peterson (eds), *Music scenes: Local, translocal and virtual*, Vanderbilt University Press, Nashville, pp. 205–20.

Bennett, A 2011, 'The post-subcultural turn: Some reflections 10 years on', *Journal of Youth Studies*, vol. 14, no. 5, pp. 493–506.

Bennett, A 2013, *Music, style, and aging: Growing old disgracefully?* Temple University Press, Philadelphia, PA.

Bennett, A (ed.) 2017, *Remembering woodstock*, Routledge, London.

Bennett, A 2018, 'Popular music scenes and aging bodies', *Journal of Aging Studies*, vol. 45, pp. 49–53.

Bennett, A, Green, B, Cashman, D & Lewandowski, N 2020, 'Researching regional and rural music scenes: Toward a critical understanding of an under-theorized issue', *Popular Music and Society*, vol. 43, no. 4, pp. 367–77.

Bennett, A & Hodkinson, P (eds) 2020, *Ageing and youth cultures: Music, style and identity*, Routledge, London.

Bennett, A & Peterson, RA (eds) 2004, *Music scenes: Local, translocal and virtual*, Vanderbilt University Press, Nashville.

Bennett, A & Rogers, I 2014, 'In search of "independent" Brisbane: Music, memory, and cultural heritage', in B Lashua, S Wagg, K Spracklen & MS Yavuz (eds), *Sounds and the city*, Palgrave Macmillan, London, pp. 302–16.

Bennett, A & Rogers, I 2016a, 'In the scattered fields of memory: Unofficial live music venues, intangible heritage, and the recreation of the musical past', *Space and Culture*, vol. 19, no. 4, pp. 490–501.

Bennett, A & Rogers, I 2016b, *Popular music scenes and cultural memory*, Palgrave Macmillan, London.

Bennett, A & Rogers, I 2018, 'The making and remaking of Brisbane and Hobart: Music scenes in Australia's "second-tier" cities', in S Brunt & G Stahl (eds), *Made in Australia and Aotearoa/New Zealand*, Routledge, London, pp. 111–20.

Bennett, A, Stratton, J & Peterson, RA 2008, 'The scenes perspective and the Australian context: Introduction', *Continuum: Journal of Media and Cultural Studies*, vol. 22, no. 5, pp. 593–9.

Bennett, A & Taylor, J 2012, 'Popular music and the aesthetics of ageing', *Popular Music*, vol. 31, no. 2, pp. 231–43.

Bennett, C 2020, 'Challenges facing regional live music venues: A case study of venues in Armidale, NSW', *Popular Music*, vol. 39, no. 3–4, pp. 600–18.

Bennett, T 2020, 'The justification of a music city: Handbooks, intermediaries and value disputes in a global policy assemblage', *City, Culture and Society*, vol. 22, art. 100354.

Bianchini, F 1995, 'Night cultures, night economies', *Planning Practice and Research*, vol. 10, pp. 121–6.

Bisker, E 2012, 'On the dole: France's "Intermittents du Spectacle" system, or you're an artist, so you deserve to get paid', *Fringe Arts*, 2 July, viewed 19 July 2022,

<https://fringearts.com/2012/07/02/on-the-dole-frances-intermittents-du-spectacle-system-or-youre-an-artist-so-you-deserve-to-get-paid/>.

Bloustien, G & Peters, M 2011, *Youth, music and creative cultures: Playing for life*, Palgrave Macmillan, Basingstoke.

Bode, K 2006, 'Aussie battler in crisis? Shifting constructions of White Australian masculinity and national identity', *Critical Race and Whiteness Studies*, vol. 2, no. 1, pp. 1–18.

Bonink, C & Hitters, E 2001. 'Creative industries as milieux of innovation: The Westergasfabriek, Amsterdam', in G Richards (ed.), *Cultural attractions and European tourism*, CABI Publishing, Oxon, pp. 227–40.

Bottero, W & Crossley, N 2011, 'Worlds, fields and networks: Becker, Bourdieu and the structures of social relations', *Cultural Sociology*, vol. 5, no. 1, pp. 99–119.

Bourdieu, P 1984, *Distinction: A social critique of the judgement of taste*, Harvard University Press, Harvard, MA.

Bourdieu, P 1986, 'Forms of capital', in JG Richardson (ed.), *Handbook of theory and research for the sociology of education*, Greenwood, New York, pp. 241–58.

Bourdieu, P 1993, *The field of cultural production: Essays on art and literature*, Columbia University Press, New York.

Bourdieu, P 1997, 'The forms of capital', in AH Halsey, H Lauder, P Brown & AS Wells (eds), *Education: Culture, economy, society*, Oxford University Press, Oxford, pp. 46–58.

Bourdieu, P 2000, *Pascalian meditations*, Stanford University Press, Stanford, CA.

Bourdieu, P 2002, 'Habitus', in J Hillier & E Rooksby (eds), *Habitus: A sense of place*, Ashgate, Burlington, VT, pp. 27–34.

Bourdieu, P & Wacquant, L 1992, *An invitation to reflexive sociology*, University of Chicago Press, Chicago.

Bourdieu, P & Wacquant, L 2013, 'Symbolic capital and social classes', *Journal of Classical Sociology*, vol. 13, no. 2, pp. 292–302.

Brabazon, T 2011, *Popular music: Topics, trends & trajectories*, Sage, London.

Braunstein, P & Doyle, MW 2013, *Imagine nation: The American counterculture of the 1960's and 70's*, Routledge, London.

Brennan, M, Cloonan, M, Behr, A & Webster, E 2016, 'Glossary: Definition of a live music event', *UK Live Music Census*, viewed 1 June 2017, <http://uklivemusiccensus.org/>.

Brown, AR, Spracklen, K, Kahn-Harris, K & Scott, NWR (eds), 2016, *Global metal music and culture: Current directions in metal studies*, Routledge, London.

Browning, B 2002, 'Global dance and globalization: Emerging perspectives', *Dance Research Journal*, vol. 34, no. 2, pp. 12–13.

Brunt, S & Stahl, G 2018, 'Introduction: This is my city: Reimagining popular music Down Under', in S Brunt & G Stahl (eds), *Made in Australia and Aotearoa/New Zealand*, Routledge, London, pp. 1–16.

Buckland, L 2021, *Myponga: South Australia's first pop festival*, Freestyle Publications, Adelaide.

Burke, M & Schmidt, A 2013, 'How should we plan and regulate live music in Australian cities? Learnings from Brisbane', *Australian Planner*, vol. 50, no. 1, pp. 68–78.

Butler, J 1999, 'Performativity's social magic', in R Shusterman (ed.), *Bourdieu: A critical reader*, Blackwell, Oxford, pp. 113–28.

Carah, N, Ferris, J, Goold, L & Regan, S 2019, *Tighter alcohol licensing hasn't killed live music, but it's harder for emerging artists*, University of Queensland, 15 August, viewed 1 June 2022, <https://medicine.uq.edu.au/article/2019/08/tighter-alcohol-licensing-hasnt-killed-live-music-its-harder-emerging-artists>.

Carah, N, Regan, S, Goold, L, Rangiah, L, Miller, P & Ferris, J 2021, 'Original live music venues in hyper-commercialised nightlife precincts: Exploring how venue owners and managers navigate cultural, commercial and regulatory forces', *International Journal of Cultural Policy*, vol. 27, no. 5, pp. 621–35.

Carter, D 2015, *The economic and cultural value of live music in Australia 2014*, National Live Music Office, Sydney.

Clarke, J 1976a, 'The skinheads and the magical recovery of community', in S Hall & T Jefferson (eds), *Resistance through rituals: Youth subculture in post-war Britain*, HarperCollins, London, pp. 99–102.

Clarke, J 1976b, 'Style', in S Hall & T Jefferson (eds), *Resistance through rituals: Youth subculture in post-war Britain*, HarperCollins, London, pp. 175–91.

Clarke, J, Hall, S, Jefferson, T & Roberts, B 1976, 'Subcultures, cultures and class', in S Hall & T Jefferson (eds), *Resistance through rituals: Youth subculture in post-war Britain*, HarperCollins, London, pp. 9–74.

Coaldrake, P & Wanna, J 1988, '"Not like the good old days": The political impact of the Fitzgerald Inquiry into police corruption in Queensland', *Australian Quarterly*, vol. 60, no. 4, pp. 404–14.

Cohen, S 1991, *Rock culture in Liverpool: Popular music in the making*, Clarendon Press, Oxford.

Cohen, S 1993, 'Ethnography and popular music studies', *Popular Music*, vol. 12, no. 2, pp. 123–38.

Cohen, S 2007, *Decline, renewal, and the city in popular music culture: Beyond the Beatles*, Routledge, London.

Cohen, S 2013a, '"From the big dig to the big gig": Live music, urban regeneration, and social change in the European capital of culture 2008', in C Wergin & F Holt (eds), *Musical performance and the changing city: Post-industrial contexts in Europe*, Routledge, New York, pp. 27–51.

Cohen, S 2013b, 'Musical memory, heritage and local identity: Remembering the popular music past in a European capital of culture', *International Journal of Cultural Policy*, vol. 19, no. 5, pp. 576–94.

Connell, J & Gibson, C 2003, *Sound tracks: Popular music, identity and place*, Routledge, London.

Costa, P 2012, 'The importance of gatekeeping processes and reputation building in the sustainability of creative milieus: Evidence from case studies in Lisbon, Barcelona and Sao Paulo', in L Lazzeretti (ed.), *Creative industries and innovation in Europe*, Routledge, London, pp. 304–24.

Creative Victoria 2022, *Victorian Live Music Venues Support Program*, Creative Victoria, viewed 19 July 2022, <https://creative.vic.gov.au/grants-and-support/programs/victorian-live-music-venues-program>.

Crewe, L & Beaverstock, J 1998, 'Fashioning the city: Cultures of consumption in contemporary urban spaces', *Geoforum*, vol. 29, no. 3, pp. 287–308.

Crossley, N, McAndrew, S & Widdop, P (eds) 2014, *Social networks and music worlds*, Routledge, London.

Cunningham, K 2022, '10 Sydney rappers who'll rule 2022', *Red Bull*, 15 February, viewed 3 August 2022, <https://www.redbull.com/au-en/best-sydney-rappers>.

Darchen, S, Willsteed, J & Browning, Y 2022, 'The "music city" paradigm and its policy side: A focus on Brisbane and Melbourne', *Cultural Trends*, advance online publication, DOI: 10.1080/09548963.2022.2062565.

Deer, C 2012, 'Doxa', in MJ Grenfell (ed.), *Pierre Bourdieu: Key concepts*, 2nd edn, Acumen, Durham, pp. 114–25.

Deloitte Access Economics 2011, *The economic, social and cultural contribution of venue-based live music in Victoria*, Arts Victoria, Melbourne.

DeNora, T 2000, *Music in everyday life*, Cambridge University Press, Cambridge.

Devilly, GJ & Srbinovski, A 2019, 'Crisis support services in night-time entertainment districts: Changes in demand following changes in alcohol legislation', *International Journal of Drug Policy*, vol. 65, pp. 56–64.

Dingle, T & O'Hanlon, S 2009, 'From manufacturing zone to lifestyle precinct: Economic restructuring and social change in inner Melbourne, 1971–2001', *Australian Economic History Review*, vol. 49, no. 1, pp. 52–69.

Donovan, P 2010a, 'Clash of the rock titans', *The Sydney Morning Herald*, 23 April.

Donovan, P 2010b, 'Lifting the rug on Tote's secrets', *The Age*, 6 May.

Donovan, P 2010c, 'Nostalgia and anger as lights go down on Tote', *The Age*, 19 January.

Donovan, P 2010d, 'Revamped Tote set to rock again', *The Age*, 10 June.

Donovan, P 2010e, 'Rolling of Collingwood's Tote rocks music fans', *The Age*, 18 January.

Donovan, P 2010f, 'Rule change hope for Tote', *The Age*, 22 January.

Donovan, P 2010g, 'Tote gets a lifeline', *The Age*, 16 April.

Donovan, P 2010h, 'Tote owners upbeat as pub gets new lease of live', *The Age*, 12 April.

Donovan, P & Roberts, J 2010, 'Goodbye to the Tote', *The Age*, 22 January.

Dow, A 2016, 'Non-profit bar Shebeen has not made a donations for almost three years', *The Age*, 17 June, viewed 19 July 2022, <https://www.theage.com.au/national/victoria/nonprofit-bar-sheebeen-has-not-made-a-donation-for-almost-three-years-20160617-gpm04a.html>.

Dowling, J 2012, 'Neighbour discord threatens venues', *The Sydney Morning Herald*, 14 December.
Driver, C & Bennett, A 2015, 'Music scenes, space and the body', *Cultural Sociology*, vol. 9, no. 1, pp. 99–115.
Eccles, D 2022, 'SA jobless rate still highest as national rate drops to 14-year low', *InDaily*, 17 March, viewed 19 July 2022, <https://indaily.com.au/news/2022/03/17/sa-jobless-rate-still-highest-as-national-rate-drops-to-14-year-low/>.
Edgerton, JD & Roberts, LW 2014, 'Cultural capital or habitus? Bourdieu and beyond in the explanation of enduring educational inequality', *Theory and Research in Education*, vol. 12, no. 2, pp. 193–220.
Elbourne, M 2013, *The future of live music in South Australia*, Don Dunstan Foundation, Adelaide.
Ernst & Young 2011, *Economic contribution of the venue-based live music industry in Australia*, APRA/Australia Council, Sydney.
Evans, S 2021, 'South Australia reverses interstate brain drain', *Australian Financial Review*, 15 September, viewed 19 July 2022, <https://www.afr.com/policy/economy/south-australia-reverses-interstate-brain-drain-20210910-p58qmt>.
Falvey, D 2021, '"Once in a generation": Basic income pilot for artists to start in early 2022', *The Irish Times*, 16 December, viewed 19 July 2022, <https://www.irishtimes.com/culture/once-in-a-generation-basic-income-pilot-for-artists-to-start-in-early-2022-1.4756353>.
Fazal, M 2020, 'The trenches of Mount Druitt: OneFour', *The Monthly*, September, viewed 20 July 2022, <https://www.themonthly.com.au/issue/2020/september/1598882400/mahmood-fazal/trenches-mount-druitt-onefour#mtr>.
Finnegan, R 1989, *The hidden musicians: Music-making in an English town*, Cambridge University Press, Cambridge.
Finnegan, R 2007, *The hidden musicians: Music-making in an English town*, 1st Wesleyan edn, Wesleyan University Press, Middletown, CT.
Flew, T 2008, 'Music, cities, and cultural and creative industries policy', in G Bloustien, M Peters & S Luckman (eds), *Sonic synergies: Music, technology, community, identity*, Ashgate, Aldershot, UK, pp. 7–16.
Flew, T, Ching, G, Stafford, A & Tacchi, J 2001, *Music industry development and Brisbane's future as a creative city*, Queensland University of Technology, Brisbane: Creative Industries Research and Applications Centre.
Florida, R 2002, *The rise of the creative class: And how it's transforming work, leisure, community and everyday life*, Basic Books, New York.
Florida, R 2017, *The new urban crisis: Gentrification, housing bubbles, growing inequality, and what we can do about it*, Simon and Schuster, New York.
Foth, M, Kamols, N, Turner, TJ, Kovachevich, A & Hearn, G 2022, 'Brisbane 2032: The promise of the first climate-positive Olympics for regenerative cities', in R Roggema (ed.), *Design for regenerative cities and landscapes: Rebalancing human impact and natural environment*, Springer, Cham, Switzerland, pp. 227–48.

Franklin, A, Lee, B & Rentschler, R 2022, 'The Adelaide Festival and the development of arts in Adelaide', *Journal of Urban Affairs*, vol. 44, no. 4–5, pp. 588–613.

Frere-Jones, S 2003, 'When critics meet pop', *Slate*, 22 August.

Frith, S 1978, *The sociology of rock*, Constable & Robinson, Edinburgh.

Frith, S 2010, 'Analysing live music in the UK: Findings one year into a three-year research project', *IASPM@Journal*, vol. 1, no. 1, pp. 1–3.

Frith, S 2012, 'Live Music 101 #1 – The materialist approach to live music', *Live Music Exchange*, 2 July, viewed 6 June 2017, <http://livemusicexchange.org/blog/live-music-101-1-the-materialistapproach-to-live-music-simon-frith/>.

Fürnkranz, M 2021, 'Fragments of a queer feminist rock and pop history in Vienna', in SK Bridge (ed.), *The Oxford handbook of global popular music* (online edn), Oxford University Press, New York.

Gair, C 2007, *American counterculture*, Edinburgh University Press, Edinburgh.

Gallan, B 2012, 'Gatekeeping night spaces: The role of booking agents in creating "local" live music venues and scenes', *Australian Geographer*, vol. 43, no. 1, pp. 35–50.

Gallan, B 2015, 'Night lives: Heterotopia, youth transitions and cultural infrastructure in the urban night', *Urban Studies*, vol. 52, no. 3, pp. 555–70.

Gallan, B & Gibson, C 2013, 'Mild-mannered bistro by day, eclectic freak-land at night: Memories of an Australian music venue', *Journal of Australian Studies*, vol. 37, no. 2, pp. 174–93.

Galuszka, P & Wyrzykowska, KM 2016, 'Running a record label when records don't sell anymore: Empirical evidence from Poland', *Popular Music*, vol. 35, no. 1, pp. 23–40.

Galuszka, P & Wyrzykowska, KM 2018, 'Rethinking independence: What does "independent record label" mean today?', in E Mazierska, L Gillon & T Rigg (eds), *Popular music in the postdigital age: Politics, economy, culture and technology*, Bloomsbury Academic, New York, pp. 33–50.

Gelder, K & Thornton, S (eds) 1997, *The subcultures reader*, Routledge, London.

Gibson, C 2003, 'Cultures at work: Why "culture" matters in research on the "cultural" industries', *Social & Cultural Geography*, vol. 4, no. 2, pp. 201–15.

Gibson, C 2007, 'Music festivals: Transformations in non-metropolitan places, and in creative work', *Media International Australia*, vol. 123, no. 1, pp. 65–81.

Gibson, C 2008, 'Youthful creativity in regional Australia: Panacea for unemployment and out-migration?', *Geographical Research*, vol. 46, no. 2, pp. 183–95.

Gibson, C & Connell, J 2005, *Music and tourism: On the road again*, Channel View Publications, Clevedon, UK.

Gibson, C & Connell, J 2016, *Music festivals and regional development in Australia*, Routledge, London.

Gibson, C, Grodach, C, Lyons, C, Crosby, A & Brennan-Horley, C 2017, *Made in Marrickville: Enterprise and cluster dynamics at the creative industries – manufacturing interface, Carrington Road precinct*, University of Wollongong, Wollongong.

Gibson, C & Homan, S 2004, 'Urban redevelopment, live music and public space: Cultural performance and the re-making of Marrickville', *International Journal of Cultural Policy*, vol. 10, no. 1, pp. 67–84.

Gill, R & Pratt, A 2008, 'In the social factory? Immaterial labour, precariousness and cultural work', *Theory, Culture & Society*, vol. 25, no. 7–8, pp. 1–30.

Glass, R 2010, 'Aspects of change', in J Brown-Saracino (ed.), *The gentrification debates: A reader*, Routledge, New York, pp. 19–30.

Goshert, JC 2000, '"Punk" after the Pistols: American music, economics, and politics in the 1980s and 1990s', *Popular Music & Society*, vol. 24, no. 1, pp. 85–106.

Gosling, T 2004, '"Not for sale": The underground network of anarcho-punk', in A Bennett & RA Peterson (eds), *Music scenes: Local, translocal and virtual*, Vanderbilt University Press, Nashville, pp. 168–86.

Gough, DJ 2021, 'Who gets to make a living in a cultural capital? Music workers, musical urbanity, and São Paulo's City of Music legislation', *Journal of Global South Studies*, vol. 38, no. 1, pp. 150–67.

Graf, M 2019, *Legend of a musical city: The story of Vienna*, Open Road Media, New York.

Graham, P 2019, *Music, management, marketing, and law: Interviews across the music business value chain*, Springer, Cham, Switzerland.

Gramsci, A 1971, *Selections from the prison notebooks*, International Publishers, New York.

Grazian, D 2004, 'The production of popular music as a confidence game: The case of the Chicago blues', *Qualitative Sociology*, vol. 27, no. 2, pp. 137–58.

Grazian, D 2013, 'Digital underground: Musical spaces and microscenes in the postindustrial city', in F Holt & C Wergin (eds), *Musical performance and the changing city*, Routledge, New York, pp. 141–66.

Griffin, N 2012, 'Gendered performance performing gender in the DIY punk and hardcore music scene', *Journal of International Women's Studies*, vol. 13, no, 2, pp. 66–81.

Grodach, C 2012, 'Before and after the creative city: The politics of urban cultural policy in Austin, Texas', *Journal of Urban Affairs*, vol. 34, no. 1, pp. 81–97.

Grodach, C, O'Connor, J & Gibson, C 2017, 'Manufacturing and cultural production: Towards a progressive policy agenda for the cultural economy', *City, Culture and Society*, vol. 10, pp. 17–25.

Grogan, B 2021, 'Wild, creative, disturbing: Inside China's "hyperpop" music scene', *Sixth Tone*, 5 November, viewed 20 July 2022, <https://www.sixthtone.com/news/1008879/wild%2C-creative%2C-disturbing-inside-chinas-hyperpop-music-scene>.

Gu, X, Domer, N & O'Connor, J 2021, 'The next normal: Chinese indie music in a post-COVID China', *Cultural Trends*, vol. 30, no. 1, pp. 63–74.

Guerra, P 2020, 'Other scenes, other cities and other sounds in the global South: DIY music scenes beyond the creative city', *Journal of Cultural Management and Cultural Policy/Zeitschrift für Kulturmanagement und Kulturpolitik*, vol. 6, no. 1, pp. 55–76.

Guibert, G 2011, 'Forestall control? From quantification as a threat to DIY statistics production as a strategy: The case of the French Federation of Popular Music Venues/Détourner le contrôle? Le cas de la Fédération des lieux de musiques actuelles', *Sociologies pratiques*, vol. 1, pp. 79–92.

Haenfler, R 2004, 'Rethinking subcultural resistance: Core values of the straight edge movement', *Journal of Contemporary Ethnography*, vol. 33, no. 4, pp. 406–36.

Haenfler, R 2006, *Straight edge: Clean-living youth, hardcore punk, and social change*, Rutgers University Press, New Brunswick, NJ.

Haenfler, R 2010, *Goths, gamers, and grrrls: Deviance and youth subcultures*, Oxford University Press, New York.

Haenfler, R 2014, *Subcultures: The basics*, Routledge, New York.

Hall, S & Jefferson, T (eds) 1976, *Resistance through rituals: Youth subculture in post-war Britain*, HarperCollins, London.

Hanifie, S 2017, 'Vacant Adelaide office space very slow to lease, real estate agent warns', *ABC News*, 3 August, viewed 20 July 2022, <https://www.abc.net.au/news/2017-08-03/vacant-adelaide-office-space-slow-to-lease/8771718>.

Hebdige, D 1976, 'The meaning of mod', in S Hall & T Jefferson (eds), *Resistance through rituals: Youth subculture in post-war Britain*, HarperCollins, London, pp. 71–9.

Hebdige, D 1979, *Subculture: The meaning of style*, Routledge, London.

Hennion, A 2007, 'Those things that hold us together: Taste and sociology', *Cultural Sociology*, vol. 1, no. 1, pp. 97–114.

Hennion, A 2015, *The passion for music: A sociology of mediation*, M Rigaud & P Collier (trans.), Ashgate, Farnham, UK.

Hesmondhalgh, D 2002, 'Popular music audiences and everyday life', in D Hesmondhalgh & K Negus (eds), *Popular music studies*, Arnold, London, pp. 117–30.

Hesmondhalgh, D 2005, 'Subcultures, scenes or tribes? None of the above', *Journal of Youth Studies*, vol. 8, no. 1, pp. 21–40.

Hesmondhalgh, D 2006, 'Bourdieu, the media and cultural production', *Media, Culture & Society*, vol. 28, no. 2, pp. 211–31.

Hesmondhalgh, D & Meier, LM 2015, 'Popular music, independence and the concept of the alternative in contemporary capitalism', in J Bennett & N Strange (eds), *Media Independence*, Routledge, New York, pp. 108–30.

Hessler, M & Zimmerman, C 2008, 'Introduction: Creative urban milieus – historical perspectives on culture, economy and the city', in M Hessler & C Zimmerman (eds), *Creative urban milieus: Historical perspectives on culture, economy and the city*, Campus, Frankfurt, pp. 11–38.

Higgins-Desbiolles, F 2018, 'Event tourism and event imposition: A critical case study from Kangaroo Island, South Australia', *Tourism Management*, vol. 64, pp. 73–86.

Highmore, B 2016, 'Taste after Bourdieu', *New Formations*, vol. 87, no. 1, pp. 159–63.

Hill, RL & Megson, M 2020, 'Sexual violence and gender equality in grassroots music venues: How to facilitate change', *IASPM Journal*, vol. 10, no. 1, pp. 3–21.

Hinchliffe, J 2022, "'They brought their politics with them': Will Queensland's newest residents affect the election?', *The Guardian*, 27 March, viewed 20 July 2022, <https://www.theguardian.com/australia-news/2022/mar/27/they-brought-their-politics-with-them-will-queenslands-newest-residents-affect-the-election>.

Hitters, E & Mulder, M 2020, 'Live music ecologies and festivalisation: The role of urban live music policies', *International Journal of Music Business Research*, vol. 9, no. 2, pp. 38–57.

Hitters, E & Richards, G 2002, 'The creation and management of cultural clusters', *Creativity and Innovation Management*, vol. 11, no. 4, pp. 234–47.

Hodgkinson, JA 2004, 'The fanzine discourse over post-rock', in A Bennett & RA Peterson (eds), *Music scenes: Local, translocal, and virtual*, Vanderbilt University Press, Nashville, TN, pp. 221–37.

Hodkinson, P 2002, *Goth: Identity, style and subculture*, Berg, New York.

Hodkinson, P 2004, 'Translocal connections in the goth scene', in A Bennett & RA Peterson (eds), *Music scenes: Local, translocal and virtual*, Vanderbilt University Press, Nashville, TN, pp. 131–48.

Hodkinson, P 2007, 'Gothic music and subculture', in C Spooner & E McEvoy (eds), *The Routledge companion to gothic*, Routledge, Oxon, pp. 260–9.

Holt, F 2010, 'The economy of live music in the digital age', *European Journal of Cultural Studies*, vol. 13, no. 2, pp. 243–61.

Holt, F 2012, 'Have post-Fordist narratives of cool changed the music business? An explorative study of cultural and organisational change in live music clubs', *Live Music Exchange*, 8 November, viewed 20 July 2022, <http://livemusicexchange.org/blog/live-music-clubs-in-new-york-an-explorative-study-of-cultural-and-organisational-change-fabian-holt/>.

Holt, F 2014, 'Rock clubs and gentrification in New York City: The case of the Bowery Presents', *IASPM Journal*, vol. 4, no. 1, pp. 21–41.

Holt, F 2020, *Everyone loves live music: A theory of performance institutions*, University of Chicago Press, Chicago.

Homan, S 2002, 'Cultural industry or social problem? The case of Australian live music', *Media International Australia*, vol. 102, no. 1, pp. 88–100.

Homan, S 2008, 'A portrait of the politician as a young pub rocker: Live music venue reform in Australia', *Popular Music*, vol. 27, no. 2, pp. 243–56.

Homan, S 2010, 'Governmental as anything: Live music and law and order in Melbourne', *Perfect Beat*, vol. 11, no. 2, pp. 103–18.

Homan, S 2011a, '"High risk" music: The live music venue in Melbourne's night-time economy', in J Cattermole, G Smith & S Homan (eds), *Instruments of change: Proceedings of the International Association for the Study of Popular Music (IASPM) Australia-New Zealand 2010 Conference*, IASPM, Melbourne, pp. 41–5.

Homan, S 2011b, '"I Tote and I vote": Australian live music and cultural policy', *Arts Marketing: An International Journal*, vol. 1, no. 2, pp. 96–107.

Homan, S 2014, 'Liveability and creativity: The case for Melbourne music precincts', *City, Culture and Society*, vol. 5, no. 3, pp. 149–55.

Homan, S 2016, 'SLAM: The music city and cultural activism', *Law, Social Justice & Global Development*, vol. 1, no. 1, pp. 1–12.

Homan, S 2019, '"Lockout" laws or "rock out" laws? Governing Sydney's night-time economy and implications for the "music city"', *International Journal of Cultural Policy*, vol. 25, no. 4, pp. 500–14.

Hough, C & Burgemeister, K 2015, 'The acoustic design of "The Triffid" music venue, Brisbane', in *Australian Acoustical Society Annual Conference 2015*, Australian Acoustical Society, Toowong, Qld, pp. 228–37.

Howard, JR 1969, 'The flowering of the hippie movement', *Annals of the American Academy of Political and Social Science*, vol. 382, no. 1, pp. 43–55.

Hunt, M, Gedgaudas, L & Seman, M 2020, *Initial impacts of the COVID-19 crisis on the music industry in Colorado and the Denver Metropolitan Region*, Regional Economic Development Institute, Colorado State University, Denver, CO, viewed 19 October 2020, <https://bit.ly/3sP3VkD>.

Janotti, J Jr & Pereira de Sá, S (eds) 2013, *Cenas musicais [Musical scenes]*, Editora Anadarco, São Paulo, Brazil.

Jayne, M, Holloway, SL & Valentine, G 2006, 'Drunk and disorderly: Alcohol, urban life and public space', *Progress in Human Geography*, vol. 30, no. 4, pp. 451–68.

Jensen, SQ 2006, 'Rethinking subcultural capital', *Young: Nordic Journal of Youth Research*, vol. 14, no. 3, pp. 257–76.

Johansson, O & Bell, TL 2014, 'Touring circuits and the geography of rock music performance', *Popular Music and Society*, vol. 37, no. 3, pp. 313–37.

Kahn-Harris, K 2000, '"Roots"? The relationship between the global and the local within the extreme metal scene', *Popular Music*, vol. 19, no. 1, pp. 13–30.

Kahn-Harris, K 2001, 'Transgression and mundanity: The global extreme metal music scene', PhD thesis, University of London, London.

Kahn-Harris, K 2007, *Extreme metal: Music and culture on the edge*, Berg, Oxford.

Kaitajärvi-Tiekso, J 2018, 'Proud amateurs: Deterritorialized expertise in contemporary Finnish DIY micro-labels', in A Bennett & P Guerra (eds), *DIY cultures and underground music scenes*, Routledge, London, pp. 101–11.

Keogh, B 2013, 'On the limitations of music ecology', *Journal of Music Research Online*, vol. 4, pp. 1–10.

Keogh, B & Collinson, I 2016, '"A place for everything, and everything in its place" – the (ab)uses of music ecology', *MUSICultures*, vol. 43, no. 1, pp. 1–15.

Kibby, MD 2000, 'Home on the page: A virtual place of music community', *Popular Music*, vol. 19, no. 1, pp. 91–100.

Kirkby, D 2003, '"Beer, glorious beer": Gender politics and Australian popular culture', *Journal of Popular Culture*, vol. 37, no. 2, pp. 244–56.

Kornhaber, S 2021, 'Noisy, ugly, and addictive', *The Atlantic*, 14 February, viewed 20 July 2022, <https://www.theatlantic.com/magazine/archive/2021/03/hyperpop/617795/>.

Kronenburg, R 2011, 'Typological trends in contemporary popular music performance venues', *Arts Marketing: An International Journal*, vol. 1, no. 2, pp. 136–44.

Kronenburg, R 2013, *Live architecture: Venues, stages and arenas for popular music*, Routledge, New York.

Kronenburg, R 2019, *This must be the place: An architectural history of popular music performance venues*, Bloomsbury Academic, New York.

Kruse, H 1993, 'Subcultural identity in alternative music culture', *Popular Music*, vol. 12, no. 1, pp. 33–41.

Laing, D 1997, 'Rock anxieties and new music networks', in McRobbie (ed.), *Back to reality? Social experience and cultural studies*, Manchester University Press, New York, pp. 116–32.

Landry, C 2008, *The creative city: A toolkit for urban innovators*, 2nd edn, Routledge, New York.

Landry, C, Greene, L, Matarasso, F & Bianchini, F 1996, *The art of regeneration: Urban renewal through cultural activity*, Comedia, Bournes Green, Stroud.

Lindsay, J 2006, 'A big night out in Melbourne: Drinking as an enactment of class and gender', *Contemporary Drug Problems*, vol. 33, no. 1, pp. 29–61.

Lobato, R 2006, 'Gentrification, cultural policy and live music in Melbourne', *Media International Australia incorporating Culture and Policy*, vol. 120, no. 1, pp. 63–75.

Lonie, J 1978, 'States of the nation: South Australia; A fading bourgeois utopia', *Meanjin*, vol. 37, no. 4, pp. 513–21.

Lovatt, A & O'Connor, J 1995, 'Cities and the night-time economy', *Planning Practice and Research*, vol. 10, no. 2, pp. 127–34.

Luckman, S 2017, 'Cultural policy and creative industries', in V Durrer, T Miller & D O'Brien (eds), *The Routledge handbook of global cultural policy*, Routledge, London, pp. 341–54.

Luckman, S, Anderson, H, Sinha, R, Rentschler, R & Chalklen, C 2020, '"The devil is in the level": Understanding inequality in Australia's film, TV and radio industries', *Media International Australia*, vol. 176, no. 1, pp. 3–18.

Luckman, S, Gibson, C, Willoughby-Smith, J & Brennan-Horley, C 2008, 'Life in a northern (Australian) town: Darwin's mercurial music scene', *Continuum*, vol. 22, no. 5, pp. 623–37.

Lyons, C 2016, *Urban informality: The production of informal landscapes of musical performance in Sydney*, Masters dissertation, University of Sydney, Sydney.

MacKinnon, N 1994, *The British folk scene: Musical performance and social identity*, Open University Press, Buckingham, UK.

Marozzi, M 2021a, 'Long-term hospitality workers victims of unpaid superannuation', *ABC Radio Melbourne*, 10 August, viewed 20 July 2022, <https://www.abc.net.au/news/2021-08-10/hospitality-workers-worried-about-unpaid-superannuation/100349406>.

Marozzi, M 2021b, 'Owners of iconic music venues the Tote, Bar Open fail to pay superannuation a second time', *ABC Radio Melbourne*, 9 August, viewed 20 July

2022, <https://www.abc.net.au/news/2021-08-09/tote-bar-open-not-paying-superannuation-melbourne-music-venues/100348276>.

Marsh, W 2020, 'City of couches: How does Adelaide house its influx of Fringe performers?', *The Adelaide Review*, 12 February, viewed 20 July 2022, <https://www.adelaidereview.com.au/latest/2020/02/12/city-of-couches-adelaide-fringe-accommodation/>.

Martin, D 2017, 'Cultural value and urban governance: A place for Melbourne's music community at the policymaking table', *Perfect Beat*, vol. 18, no. 2, pp. 110–30.

Martin, PJ 2006, '"Musicians" worlds: Music-making as a collaborative activity', *Symbolic Interaction*, vol. 1, pp. 95–107.

Marwick, A 2011, *The sixties: Cultural revolution in Britain, France, Italy, and the United States, c. 1958–c. 1974*, A&C Black, London.

Massey, D 1994, *Space, place and gender*, Polity Press, Cambridge.

Massey, D 2005, *For space*, Sage, London.

McCarthy, G 1996, 'Two and two make one: The collapse of the State Bank of South Australia', *Policy, Organisation and Society*, vol. 11, no. 1, pp. 85–110.

McDowell, L 2017, 'The ideal worker: Inclusion and exclusion in a knowledge-based city: The case of Oxford, UK', in U Gerhard, M Hoelscher & D Wilson (eds), *Inequalities in creative cities*, Palgrave Macmillan, New York, pp. 79–105.

McMillen, A 2011, 'Mess+Noise story: "Lofly Hanger: 2007–2010"', *Mess+Noise*, 19 January, viewed 20 July 2022, <http://andrewmcmillen.com/2011/01/19/messnoise-story-lofly-hangar-2007-2010-january-2011/>.

McRobbie, A 2011, 'Reflections on feminism, immaterial labour and the post-Fordist regime', *New Formations*, vol. 70, no. 70, pp. 60–76.

Measham, F & Hadfield, P 2009, 'Everything starts with an "E": Exclusion, ethnicity and elite formation in contemporary English clubland', *Adicciones*, vol. 21, no. 4, pp. 363–86.

Meusburger, P, Funke, J & Wunder, E (eds) 2009, *Milieus of creativity: An interdisciplinary approach to spatiality of creativity*, Springer Science & Business Media, Berlin.

Middleton, R 1990, *Studying popular music*, McGraw-Hill Education, New York.

Middleton, R & Manuel, P 2010, 'Popular music', *Grove Music Online*, viewed 20 July 2022, <oxfordmusiconline.com/subscriber/article/grove/music/43179#S43179>.

Millward, P, Widdop, P & Halpin, M 2017, 'A "different class"? Homophily and heterophily in the social class networks of Britpop', *Cultural Sociology*, vol. 11, no. 3, pp. 318–36.

Montgomery, J 2004, 'Cultural quarters as mechanisms for urban regeneration part 2: A review of four cultural quarters in the UK, Ireland and Australia', *Planning, Practice and Research*, vol. 19, no. 1, pp. 3–31.

Moor, L & Littler, J 2008, 'Fourth worlds and neo-Fordism: American apparel and the cultural economy of consumer anxiety', *Cultural Studies*, vol. 22, no. 5, pp. 700–23.

Moore, R 2005, 'Alternative to what? Subcultural capital and the commercialization of a music scene', *Deviant Behavior*, vol. 26, no. 3, pp. 229–52.

Morley, D 1992, *Television, audiences and cultural studies*, Routledge, London.

Morley, P 2006, 'Rockism – it's the new rockism', *The Guardian*, 26 May, viewed 21 August 2019, <https://www.theguardian.com/music/2006/may/26/popandrock.coldplay>.

Morris, S 2022, 'Basic income pilot scheme for care leavers to be trialled in Wales', *The Guardian*, 16 February, viewed 20 July 2022, <https://www.theguardian.com/society/2022/feb/15/basic-income-pilot-scheme-for-care-leavers-to-be-trialled-in-wales>.

Moskovitch, G 2016, 'The true story behind the rise & collapse of Shebeen', *Tone Deaf*, 16 June, viewed 20 July 2022, <https://tonedeaf.thebrag.com/the-true-story-behind-the-rise-collapse-of-shebeen/>.

Mosler, SA 2007, 'Heritage politics in Adelaide during the Bannon decade', PhD thesis, University of Adelaide, Adelaide.

Mouillot, F 2018, 'Distribution Ambiances Magnétiques Etcetera and Constellation Records: DIY record labels and the Montreal experimental music scene', PhD thesis, McGill University, Montreal.

Mouillot, F 2021, 'Industrial isolation and cultural self-exile: The formation of an independent music scene in Montreal', in C Ballico (ed.), *Geographically isolated and peripheral music scenes*, Palgrave Macmillan, Singapore, pp. 133–56.

Muggleton, D & Weinzierl, R (eds) 2003, *The post-subcultures reader*, Berg, Oxford.

Mulder, M, Hitters, E & Rutten, P 2021, 'The impact of festivalization on the Dutch live music action field: A thematic analysis', *Creative Industries Journal*, vol. 14, no. 3, pp. 245–68.

Music Development Office 2022, *Artists*, Department for Industry, Innovation and Science, Government of South Australia, viewed 20 July 2022, <http://mdo.sa.gov.au/funding/>.

Music Venue Trust 2015, *Report for City of Edinburgh Council: The challenges for live music in the city*, Music Venue Trust, London, viewed 27 July 2020, <http://musicvenuetrust.com/wp-content/uploads/2016/09/Music-Venue-Trust-Edinburgh-Report.pdf>.

Music Victoria 2014, *How to: Agent of change*, Music Victoria, viewed 19 July 2022, <https://www.musicvictoria.com.au/resource/how-to-agent-of-change/>.

New South Wales Parliament 2018, *The music and arts economy in New South Wales*, Committee No. 6 – Planning and Environment, Sydney, viewed 16 November 2018, <https://www.parliament.nsw.gov.au/lcdocs/inquiries/2471/Final%20report%20website.pdf>.

Newton, D & Coyle-Hayward, R 2018, *Melbourne live music census: 2017 report*, Music Victoria, Melbourne, viewed 20 April 2018, <https://www.musicvictoria.com.au/assets/2018/MLMC-2017-Report-compressed.pdf>.

Nguyen, J 2017, 'Is Melbourne Australia's foremost cultural destination?', *Limelight*, 21 June, viewed 27 June 2022, <https://limelightmagazine.com.au/news/is-melbourne-australias-foremost-cultural-destination/>.

Nilan, P 2006, 'Straight Edge as an Australian youth subculture', in *Sociology for a mobile world: TASA 2006: Annual conference of The Australian Sociological Association, University of Western Australia and Murdoch University, 4–7 December 2006*, Sociological Association of Australia, Hawthorn, Vic.

NSW Government 2022, *NSW Performing Arts COVID Support Package*, NSW Government, viewed 27 June 2022, <https://www.create.nsw.gov.au/funding-and-support/nsw-performing-arts-covid-support-package/>.

Oakley, K 2006, 'Include us out – Economic development and social policy in the creative industries', *Cultural Trends*, vol. 15, no. 4, pp. 255–73.

O'Connor, J 2004, '"A special kind of city knowledge": Innovative clusters, tacit knowledge and the creative city', *Media International Australia*, vol. 112, no. 1, pp. 131–49.

O'Connor, J 2007, *The cultural and creative industries: A review of the literature*, Arts Council England, London.

O'Connor, J 2016, 'After the creative industries: Cultural policy in crisis', *Law, Justice & Global Development*, vol. 1, pp. 1–18.

O'Connor, J 2022, 'Metrics rule in the cultural Hunger Games', *InDaily*, 9 March, viewed 2 July 2022, <https://indaily.com.au/inreview/inreview-commentary/2022/03/09/metrics-rule-in-the-cultural-hunger-games/>.

O'Hanlon, S 2010, *Melbourne remade*, Arcade Publications, Melbourne.

O'Hanlon, S & Sharpe, S 2009, 'Becoming post-industrial: Victoria Street, Fitzroy, c. 1970 to now', *Urban Policy and Research*, vol. 27, no. 3, pp. 289–300.

Olson, M 1998, 'Everybody loves our town: Scenes, spatiality, migrancy', in T Swiss, JM Sloop & A Herman (eds), *Mapping the beat: Contemporary music and contemporary theory*, Basil Blackwell, Oxford, pp. 269–90.

O'Meara, CP & Tretter, EM 2013, 'Sounding Austin: Live music, race, and the selling of a city', in F Holt & C Wergin (eds), *Musical performance and the changing city*, Routledge, New York, pp. 66–90.

Overell, R 2014, *Affective intensities in extreme music scenes: Cases from Australia and Japan*, Palgrave Macmillan, New York.

Pacella, J, Luckman, S & O'Connor, J 2021a, 'Fire, pestilence and the extractive economy: Cultural policy after cultural policy', *Cultural Trends*, vol. 30, no. 1, pp. 40–51.

Pacella, J, Luckman, S & O'Connor, J 2021b, *Keeping creative: Assessing the impact of the Covid-19 emergency on the art and cultural sector & responses to it by governments, cultural agencies and the sector*, CP3 Working Paper #1, University of South Australia, Adelaide, viewed 20 July 2022, <https://www.unisa.edu.au/contentassets/33e97267a93046f1987edca85823e7b1/cp3-working-paper-01.pdf>.

Parkinson, T, Hunter, M, Campanello, K, Dines, M & Smith GD 2015, *Understanding small music venues: A report by the Music Venues Trust*, Music Venues Trust, London.

Paul, A & Sen, J 2020, 'A critical review of liveability approaches and their dimensions', *Geoforum*, vol. 117, pp. 90–2.

Pearson, D 2020, *Rebel music in the triumphant empire: Punk rock in the 1990s United States*, Oxford University Press, Oxford.

Perring, J 2021, *Tote super is all up to date*, The Tote, 28 September, viewed 20 July 2022, <https://thetotehotel.com/tote-super-is-all-up-to-date/>.

Peterson, RA & Bennett, A 2004, 'Introducing music scenes', in A Bennett & RA Peterson (eds), *Music scenes: Local, translocal, and virtual*, Vanderbilt University Press, Nashville, TN, pp. 1–16.

Pine, BJ & Gilmore JH 2013, 'The experience economy: Past, present and future', in J Sundbo & F Sørenson (eds), *Handbook on the experience economy*, Edward Elgar, Cheltenham, pp. 21–44.

Pledger, D 2020, 'The case for a universal basic income: Freeing artists from neoliberalism', *Arts Hub*, 19 June, viewed 20 July 2022, <https://www.artshub.com.au/news/opinions-analysis/the-case-for-a-universal-basic-income-freeing-artists-from-neo-liberalism-260583-2367657/>.

Poon, JP & Lai, CA 2008, 'Why are non-profit performing arts organisations successful in mid-sized US cities?', *Urban Studies*, vol. 45, no. 11, pp. 2273–89.

Potter, A 2021, 'Globalising the local in children's television for the post-network era: How Disney+ and BBC Studios helped Bluey the Australian cattle dog jump the national fence', *International Journal of Cultural Studies*, vol. 24, no. 2, pp. 216–32.

Pratt, AC 2000, 'New media, the new economy and new spaces', *Geoforum*, vol. 31, no. 4, pp. 425–36.

Pratt, AC 2004, 'Creative clusters: Towards the governance of the creative industries production system?', *Media International Australia*, vol. 112, no. 1, pp. 50–66.

Pratt, AC 2009, 'Cultural economy', in R Kitchen & N Thrift (eds), *International encyclopedia of human geography*, Elsevier, Oxford, pp. 407–10.

Pratt, AC 2015, 'Creative industries and development: Culture in development, or the cultures of development?', in C Jones, M Lorenzen & J Sapsed (eds), *The Oxford handbook of creative industries*, Oxford University Press, Oxford, pp. 503–15.

Price, G (dir.) 2021, *Woodstock 99: Peace, love, and rage*, HBO Max.

Prior, N 2013, 'Bourdieu and the sociology of music consumption: A critical assessment of recent developments', *Sociology Compass*, vol. 7, no. 3, pp. 181–93.

Property Council of Australia 2013, *South Australia's youth brain drain: Perception or problem?*, Property Council of Australia, Adelaide, viewed 22 June 2022, <http://www.propertyoz.com.au/sa/library/SAs%20Brain%20Drain%20for%20web_0.pdf>.

QMusic 2022, *Bigsound @ SXSW*, QMusic, viewed 23 June 2022, <https://www.qmusic.com.au/news/bigsound-brunch-sxsw>.

Quader, SB 2022a, 'Being your own aesthetic boss: Practising independence within the central Sydney independent music scene's cultural economy', *Continuum*, vol. 36, no. 1, pp. 135–49.

Quader, SB 2022b, 'How the central Sydney independent musicians use pre-established "online DIY" to sustain their networking during the COVID-19 pandemic', *Journal of International Communication*, vol. 28, no. 1, pp. 90–109.

Quader, SB & Redden, G 2015, 'Approaching the underground: The production of alternatives in the Bangladeshi metal scene', *Cultural Studies*, vol. 29, no. 3, pp. 401–24.

Rahnema, M 1997, 'Afterword: Towards post-development. Searching for signposts, a new language and a new paradigm', in M Rahnema & V Bawtree (eds), *The post-development reader*, Zed Books, London, pp. 377–403.

Reddan, F 2022, '"A welcome step": Ireland's first basic income scheme on the way', *The Irish Times*, 1 March, viewed 20 July 2022, <https://www.irishtimes.com/business/personal-finance/a-welcome-step-ireland-s-first-basic-income-scheme-on-the-way-1.4813429>.

Reed-Danahay, D 2015, 'Social space: Distance, proximity and thresholds of affinity', in V Amit (ed.), *Thinking through sociality: An anthropological interrogation of key concepts*, Berghahn Books, New York, pp. 69–96.

Regan, SB 2019, 'The Brisbane sound', PhD thesis, Queensland University of Technology, Brisbane.

Regev, M 2013, *Pop-rock music: Aesthetic cosmopolitanism in late modernity*, Polity Press, Cambridge.

Reitsamer, R 2011, 'The DIY careers of techno and drum 'n' bass DJs in Vienna', *Dancecult: Journal of Electronic Dance Music Culture*, vol. 3, no. 1, pp. 28–43.

Rex, R 1975, 'The origin of beatnik', *American Speech*, vol. 50, no. 3/4, pp. 329–31.

Richardson, AT 2014, 'Towards a new conceptual framework for attendee engagement in small popular music venues', Master's thesis, University of Oregon, Eugene, OR.

Roberts, R & Whiting, S 2021, 'The impact of COVID-19 on music venues in regional South Australia: A case study', *Perfect Beat*, vol. 21, no. 1, pp. 25–32.

Rochow, K & Stahl, G 2016, 'The scene and the unseen: Mapping the (affective) rhythms of Wellington and Copenhagen', *Imaginations: Journal of Cross-Cultural Image Studies*, vol. 7, no. 2, pp. 124–41.

Rogers, I 2008, '"You've got to go to gigs to get gigs": Indie musicians, eclecticism and the Brisbane scene', *Continuum*, vol. 22, no. 5, pp. 639–49.

Rogers, I 2012, 'Musicians and aspiration: Exploring the rock dream in independent music', PhD thesis, University of Queensland, Brisbane, Qld.

Rogers, I & Whiting, S 2020, '"If there isn't skyscrapers, don't play there!" Rock music scenes, regional touring, and music policy in Australia', *Popular Music and Society*, vol. 43, no. 4, pp. 450–60.

Rose, A 2022, 'Speed address Asian hate crimes on single "Not That Nice", announce new EP', *NME*, 19 May, viewed 3 August 2022, <https://www.nme.com/en_au/news/

music/speed-address-asian-hate-crimes-in-new-single-not-that-nice-announce-new-ep-3228932>.

Rozbicka, P, Behr, A & Hamilton, C 2022, 'Brexit and the UK live music industry', in S Homan (ed.), *The Bloomsbury handbook of popular music policy*, Bloomsbury Academic, New York, pp. 321–32.

Rychter, T 2016, 'Simon Griffiths: "We all wish Shebeen could have achieved more"', *Broadsheet*, 27 June, viewed 20 July 2022, <https://www.broadsheet.com.au/melbourne/food-and-drink/article/simon-griffiths-we-all-wish-shebeen-could-have-achieved-more>.

Sanneh, K 2004, 'The rap against rockism', *The New York Times*, 31 October, viewed 11 November 2017, <https://www.nytimes.com/2004/10/31/arts/music/the-rap-against-rockism.html>.

Sardiello, R 1994, 'Secular rituals in popular culture: A case for Grateful Dead concerts and Dead Head identity', in J Epstein (ed.), *Adolescents and their music: If it's too loud, you're too old*, Garland, New York, pp. 115–39.

Schilt, K 2004, '"Riot grrrl is …": Contestation over meaning in a music scene', in A Bennett & RA Peterson (eds) *Music scenes: Local, translocal and virtual*, Vanderbilt University Press, Nashville, TN, pp. 115–30.

Scott, AJ 2000, *The cultural economy of cities: Essays on the geography of image-producing industries*, Sage, Thousand Oaks, CA.

Scott, M 2012, 'Cultural entrepreneurs, cultural entrepreneurship: Music producers mobilising and converting Bourdieu's alternative capitals', *Poetics*, vol. 40, no. 3, pp. 237–55.

Scott, M 2017, '"Hipster capitalism" in the age of austerity? Polanyi meets Bourdieu's new petite bourgeoisie', *Cultural Sociology*, vol. 11, no. 1, pp. 60–76.

Scott, M & Szili, G 2018, 'Pop-up Polanyi: Cultural entrepreneurs and the "vacancy fix"', *City, Culture and Society*, vol. 14, pp. 22–7.

Shank, B 1988, 'Transgressing the boundaries of a rock 'n'roll community', paper delivered at the First Joint Conference of IASPM-Canada and IASPM-USA, Yale University, 1 October.

Shank, B 1994, *Dissonant identities: The rock'n'roll scene in Austin, Texas*, Wesleyan University Press, Middletown, CT.

Sharp, M 2019, 'Hypervisibility in Australian punk scenes: Queer experiences of spatial logics of gender and sexuality', *Punk & Post-Punk*, vol. 8, no. 3, pp. 363–78.

Sharp, M & Threadgold, S 2019, 'Defiance labour and reflexive complicity: Illusio and gendered marginalisation in DIY punk scenes', *Sociological Review*, vol. 68, no. 3, pp. 606–22.

Shaw, H & Sivam, A 2015, 'A temporary city: Temporary use as a tool for urban design in the creation of convivial urban space', paper delivered at the 7th State of Australian Cities Conference, Gold Coast, 9–11 December.

Shaw, K 2004, 'Local limits to gentrification', in R Atkinson & G Bridge (eds), *Gentrification in a global context*, Routledge, New York, pp. 168–84.

Shaw, K 2005, 'The place of alternative culture and the politics of its protection in Berlin, Amsterdam and Melbourne', *Planning Theory and Practice*, vol. 6, no. 2, pp. 149–69.

Shaw, K 2009, 'The Melbourne indie music scene and the inner city blues', in L Porter & K Shaw (eds), *Whose urban renaissance? An international comparison of urban regeneration strategies*, Routledge, London, pp. 191–201.

Shaw, K 2010a, 'Music venues still threatened as Tote lesson not learnt', *The Age*, 15 April.

Shaw, K 2010b, 'Thinking outside city limits', *The Age*, 13 November, viewed 30 November 2017, <https://www.theage.com.au/national/victoria/thinking-outside-city-limits-20101112-17r90.html>.

Shaw, K 2013, 'Independent creative subcultures and why they matter', *International Journal of Cultural Policy*, vol. 19, no. 3, pp. 333–52.

Shaw, K 2020, 'Empty shops an opportunity for creative revival but planning is key', *The Age*, 22 October, viewed 20 July 2022, <https://www.theage.com.au/national/victoria/empty-shops-an-opportunity-for-creative-revival-but-planning-is-key-20201022-p567im.html>.

Shaw, K 2021, 'Can artists revive dead city centres? Without long-term tenancies it's window dressing', *The Conversation*, 27 October, viewed 20 July 2022, <https://theconversation.com/can-artists-revive-dead-city-centres-without-long-term-tenancies-its-window-dressing-169822>.

Shorthose, J 2004, 'Accounting for independent creativity in the new cultural economy', *Media International Australia*, vol. 112, no. 1, pp. 150–61.

Shuker, R 2013, *Understanding popular music*, Routledge, New York.

Shuker, R 2022, *Popular music culture: The key concepts*, 5th edn, Routledge, New York.

Smyly, BP 2010, '"You went there for the people and went there for the bands": The Sandringham Hotel – 1980 to 1998', PhD thesis, University of Western Sydney, Sydney.

Snell, D & Hodgetts, D 2007, 'Heavy metal, identity and the social negotiation of a community of practice', *Journal of Community and Applied Social Psychology*, vol. 17, no. 6, pp. 430–45.

Spanu, M & Seca, JM 2016, 'Pratiques linguistiques et usages de l'anglais dans les musiques électro-amplifiées en France: Le cas des spectacles à l'international', *French Politics, Culture & Society*, vol. 34, no. 1, pp. 122–42.

Spence, A 2022, 'SA population shrink as "brain drain" resumes', *InDaily*, 23 March, viewed 20 July 2022, <https://indaily.com.au/news/2022/03/23/sa-population-shrinks-as-brain-drain-resumes/>.

Spracklen, K, Laurencic, J & Kenyon, A 2013, '"Mine's a pint of bitter": Performativity, gender, class and representations of authenticity in real ale tourism', *Tourist Studies*, vol. 13, no. 3, pp. 304–21.

Spracklen, K & Spracklen, B 2018, *The evolution of goth culture: The origins and deeds of the new goths*, Emerald Group Publishing, Bingley, UK.

Stafford, A 2006, *Pig city: From the Saints to Savage Garden*, University of Queensland Press, Brisbane.

Stahl, G 2003a, 'Crisis? What crisis? Anglophone musicmaking in Montreal', PhD thesis, McGill University, Montreal.

Stahl, G 2003b, 'Tastefully renovating subcultural theory: Making space for a new model', in D Muggleton & R Weinzierl (eds), *The post-subcultures reader*, Berg, Oxford, pp. 27–40.

Stahl, G 2004, '"It's like Canada reduced": Setting the scene in Montreal', in A Bennett & K Kahn-Harris (eds), *After subculture*, Palgrave Macmillan, New York, pp. 51–64.

Stahl, G 2018, 'Urban melancholy: Tales from Wellington's music scene', in S Brunt & G Stahl (eds), *Made in Australia and Aotearoa/New Zealand*, Routledge, New York, pp. 121–30.

State Government of Victoria 2022, *Financial and other support*, VIC.GOV.AU, viewed 20 July 2022, <https://www.coronavirus.vic.gov.au/financial-and-other-support-coronavirus-covid-19>.

Stauffer, RC 1957, 'Haeckel, Darwin, and ecology', *Quarterly Review of Biology*, vol. 32, no. 2, pp. 138–44.

Stratton, J 2003, 'Whiter rock: The "Australian sound" and the beat boom', *Continuum*, vol. 17, no. 3, pp. 331–46.

Stratton, J 2005, 'Pissed on another planet: The Perth sound of the 1970s and 1980s', *Perfect Beat*, vol. 7, no. 2, pp. 36–60.

Stratton, J 2008, 'The difference of Perth music: A scene in cultural and historical context', *Continuum*, vol. 22, no. 5, pp. 613–22.

Straw, W 1991, 'Systems of articulation, logics of change: Communities and scenes in popular music', *Cultural Studies*, vol. 5, no. 3, pp. 368–88.

Straw, W 2001, 'Scenes and sensibilities', *Public*, no. 22–3, pp. 245–57.

Straw, W 2010, 'Cultural production and the generative matrix: A response to Georgina Born', *Cultural Sociology*, vol. 4, no. 2, pp. 209–16.

Straw, W 2015, 'Some things a scene might be: Postface', *Cultural Studies*, vol. 29, no. 3, pp. 476–85.

Street, J 1993, 'Local differences? Popular music and the local state', *Popular Music*, vol. 12, no. 1, pp. 43–55.

Strong, C & Whiting, S 2018, '"We love the bands and we want to keep them on the walls": Gig posters as heritage-as-praxis in music venues', *Continuum*, vol. 32, no. 2, pp. 151–61.

Svert, P & Caldwell, A 2016, 'Austin, Texas, can show Brisbane the way in music', *The Courier Mail*, 7 May, viewed 20 July 2022, <https://www.couriermail.com.au/goqld/austin-texas-can-show-the-brisbane-the-way-in-music/news-story/d3f9c9add65c07496176c3b0b2f2b8e5>.

Swartz, D 1996, 'Bridging the study of culture and religion: Pierre Bourdieu's political economy of symbolic power', *Sociology of Religion*, vol. 57, no. 1, pp. 71–85.

Tate, JW 2014, 'Paul Keating and leadership: Was the "personal" political?', *Australian Journal of Political Science*, vol. 49, no. 3, pp. 439–54.

Taylor, C 2015, 'Between culture, policy and industry: Modalities of intermediation in the creative economy', *Regional Studies*, vol. 49, no. 3, pp. 362–73.

Taylor, J 2012, 'Scenes and sexualities: Queerly reframing the music scenes perspective', *Continuum*, vol. 26, no. 1, pp. 143–56.

Taylor, N, Miller, P, Coomber, K, Mayshak, R, Zahnow, R, Patafino, B, Burn, M & Ferris, J 2018, 'A mapping review of evaluations of alcohol policy restrictions targeting alcohol-related harm in night-time entertainment precincts', *International Journal of Drug Policy*, vol. 62, pp. 1–13.

Taylor, S 2018, 'A place to play: An historical geographical perspective on live music and poker machines in Australian pubs', *Historic Environment*, vol. 30, no. 2, pp. 112–33.

Taylor, S & Luckman, S 2020, 'Creative aspiration and the betrayal of promise? The experience of new creative workers', in S Taylor & S Luckman (eds), *Pathways into creative working lives*, Palgrave Macmillan, Cham, Switzerland, pp. 1–27.

Terrill, A, Hogarth, D, Clement, A & Francis, R 2015, *The mastering of a music city: Key elements, effective strategies and why it's worth pursuing*, Music Canada, Toronto, viewed 20 July 2022, <https://musiccanada.com/wp-content/uploads/2015/06/The-Mastering-of-a-Music-City.pdf>.

Tesolin, L 2015, 'Northlane bursts out of local shed on to the global stage thanks to success with latest album Node', *The Daily Telegraph*, 6 August, viewed 20 July 2022, <https://www.dailytelegraph.com.au/newslocal/northlane-burst-from-local-shed-to-success/news-story/56a02393db3372eb561dff4ede26e947>.

Thornton, S 1996, *Club cultures: Music, media, and subcultural capital*, Wesleyan University Press, Hanover, NE.

Threadgold, S 2015, '(Sub)cultural capital, DIY careers and transferability: Towards maintaining "reproduction" when using Bourdieu in youth culture research', in S Baker, B Robards & B Buttigieg (eds), *Youth cultures and subcultures: Australian perspectives*, Ashgate, London, pp. 53–64.

Threadgold, S & Nilan, P 2009, 'Reflexivity of contemporary youth, risk and cultural capital', *Current Sociology*, vol. 57, no. 1, pp. 47–68.

Throsby, D 1999, 'Cultural capital', *Journal of Cultural Economics*, vol. 23, pp. 3–12.

Tschmuck, P 2006, *Creativity and innovation in the music industry*, Springer, Dordrecht.

Tschmuck, P, Pearce, PL & Campbell, S (eds) 2013, *Music business and the experience economy: The Australasian case*, Springer, Heidelberg.

van den Dungen, N (dir.) 2011, *Persecution blues: The battle for the Tote*, East Melbourne, Australia: Madman Entertainment.

van der Hoeven, A, Everts, R, Mulder, M, Berkers, P, Hitters, E & Rutten, P 2022, 'Valuing value in urban live music ecologies: Negotiating the impact of live music in the Netherlands', *Journal of Cultural Economy*, vol. 15, no. 2, pp. 216–31.

van der Hoeven, A & Hitters, E 2019, 'The social and cultural values of live music: Sustaining urban live music ecologies', *Cities*, vol. 90, pp. 263–71.

van der Hoeven, A & Hitters, E 2020, 'The spatial value of live music: Performing, (re)developing and narrating urban spaces', *Geoforum*, vol. 117, pp. 154–64.

van der Hoeven, A, Hitters, E, Berkers, P, Mulder, M & Everts, R 2020, 'Theorizing the production and consumption of live music', in E Mazierska, L Gillon & T Rigg (eds), *The future of live music*, Bloomsbury Academic, New York, pp. 19–33.

Victorian Managed Insurance Authority (VMIA) 2022, *Explore COVID-19 event insurance*, VMIA, viewed 20 July 2022, <https://www.vmia.vic.gov.au/event>.

Visit Victoria 2017, *Melbourne: The cultural capital*, Victoria Media Hub, 24 October, viewed 20 July 2022, <https://mediahub.visitvictoria.com/inspiration/melbourne-cultural-capital>.

Waitt, G & Gibson, C 2009, 'Creative small cities: Rethinking the creative economy in place', *Urban Studies*, vol. 46, no. 5–6, pp. 1223–46.

Walker, C 2012, 'History is made at night: Live music in Australia', *Platform Papers*, no. 32.

Wallach, J & Clinton, E 2013, 'History, modernity, and music genre in Indonesia: Introduction to the special issue", *Asian Music*, vol. 44, no. 2, pp. 3–23.

Walmsley, B 2016, 'Deep hanging out in the arts: An anthropological approach to capturing cultural value', *International Journal of Cultural Policy*, vol. 24, no. 2, pp. 272–91.

Ware, I 2013, 'Regulatory frameworks and the cultural legacy of Adelaide's DIY scene with specific focus on the role of Nigel Koop aka "home for the def"', *The Lifted Brow*, vol. 17, pp. 70–1.

Watson, A 2008, 'Global music city: Knowledge and geographical proximity in London's recorded music industry', *Area*, vol. 40, no. 1, pp. 12–23.

Watson, A & Forrest, D 2012, 'The bands culture in Victoria, Australia: Live music benefits career paths, employment and community', *Australian Journal of Music Education*, vol. 2, no. 1, pp. 71–81.

Watson, A & Taylor, C 2014, 'Invisible agents and hidden protagonists: Rethinking creative cities policy', *European Planning Studies*, vol. 22, no. 12, pp. 2429–35.

Webster, E, Brennan, M, Behr, A, Cloonan, M & Ansell, J 2018, *Valuing live music: The UK Live Music Census 2017 report*, Edinburgh, United Kingdom: UK Live Music Census.

Weinzierl, R & Muggleton, D 2003, 'What is "post-subcultural studies" anyway?', in D Muggleton & R Weinzierl (eds), *The post-subcultures reader*, Berg, Oxford, pp. 3–23.

White, R 2006, 'British indie music in the 1990s: Public spheres, media and exclusion', PhD thesis, Goldsmiths, University of London, London.

Whiting, S 2019, '"You're not strangers if you like the same band": Small venues, music scenes, and the live music ecology', PhD thesis, RMIT University, Melbourne.

Whiting, S 2021, 'The value of small live music venues: Alternative forms of capital and niche spaces of cultural production', *Cultural Sociology*, vol. 15, no. 4, pp. 558–78.

Whiting, S, Barnett, T & O'Connor, J 2022, '"Creative city" – R.I.P.?', *M/C Journal*, vol. 25, no. 3.

Whiting, S & Carter, D 2016, 'Access, place, and Australian live music', *M/C Journal*, vol. 19, no. 3.

Whiting, S, Klimentou, P & Rogers, I 2019, '"We're just normal dudes": Hegemonic masculinity, Australian identity, and Parkway Drive', in C Hoad (ed.), *Australian metal music: Identities, scenes, and cultures*, Emerald, Bingley, UK, pp. 55–70.

Williams, R 1976, *Keywords: A vocabulary of culture and society*, Fontana, London.

Willis, P 1972, *Popular music and youth culture groups in Birmingham*, Centre for Contemporary Cultural Studies, University of Birmingham, Birmingham.

Willis, P 1978, *Profane culture*, Routledge and Kegan Paul, London.

Wittel, A 2001, 'Toward a network sociality', *Theory, Culture & Society*, vol. 18, no. 6, pp. 51–76.

Wolk, D 2006, 'Thinking about rockism', *Seattle Weekly*, 9 October.

Wood, RT 2003, 'The straightedge youth sub-culture: Observations on the complexity of sub-cultural identity', *Journal of Youth Studies*, vol. 6, no. 1, pp. 33–52.

Wood, S & Dovey, K 2015, 'Creative multiplicities: Urban morphologies of creative clustering', *Journal of Urban Design*, vol. 20, no. 1, pp. 52–74.

Wright, D 2015, *Understanding cultural taste: Sensation, skill and sensibility*, Palgrave Macmillan, Basingstoke.

Yarra City Arts 2015, *The Old Bar has a New Door*, Yarra City Arts, viewed 11 November 2015, <http://yarracityarts.com.au/2015/02/06/oldbar-new-door/>.

Zacharasiewicz, W 2018, *Transatlantic networks and the perception and representation of Vienna and Austria between the 1920s and 1950s*, Verlag der Österreichischen Akademie der Wissenschaften, Vienna.

Zion, L 1987, 'The impact of the Beatles on pop music in Australia: 1963–66', *Popular Music*, vol. 6, no. 3, pp. 291–311.

Zweigenhaft, RL 1993, 'Accumulation of cultural and social capital: The differing college careers of prep school and public school graduates', *Sociological Spectrum*, vol. 3, no. 3, pp. 365–76.

Index

acoustic (music) 6–7
Adelaide, Australia 19, 59–60, 70, 73, 82–100, 105
aesthetic 8, 32, 36, 43–4, 68, 103, 114, 121, 124–5, 146, 171, 176–180
affect 154, 165, 181
agglomeration 46, 105
alternative
  culture 90, 121–2
  music 32, 38, 68, 78 n. 18, 91, 94, 120, 126–7
amateur (*see hobbyist*)
anonymity 12, 128
art world 23, 54, 186
audience 7, 13–4, 40–1, 48, 103, 111, 113–14, 137, 151–3, 158, 197–8
Austin, Texas 31, 71–2, 99
Australia 13–14, 36–7, 49 n.12, 58–9, 65–9, 104, 138 n. 9, 138 nn. 11–12, 140–2, 158, 159 n. 20, 180–1, 185–6, 194–6
autonomy 29, 91, 167, 178

bands
  emerging (*see also emerging artists*) 5, 75, 132
band room 8, 111, 113, 126–7, 143–6, 151–3, 191
bar (*see small venues*)
basic income 193–5
beer garden 9, 78, 90, 145, 149
belonging 4, 9, 12, 20, 29, 35, 37, 114, 124, 130, 139–42, 146, 163 n. 2, 188, 193, 197
Bennett, Andy 40–1
BIGSOUND 71–2, 75
Birmingham Centre for Contemporary Cultural Studies (BCCCS) 25, 28–30, 167
Bjelke-Petersen, Joh 70–4, 80
blues 6
booking agent 13, 19–20, 133, 164, 171–81, 191, 193

Bourdieu, Pierre 10 n. 2, 17, 19–20, 39, 42, 50, 54, 63, 116, 131–2, 141, 157, 163–72, 181, 187, 191–2
Brisbane, Australia 19, 60, 67–8, 70–81, 98–9
built environment 8, 33, 45, 53, 96, 106, 125, 143, 177, 184, 189–91
businesses 13, 47, 96, 113, 131, 181–2, 192–4
Butler, Judith 170

Canada 13, 37–8
capital
  alternative forms of 11, 16–17, 19, 157, 164, 169, 186
  cultural 16–17, 19, 34, 41, 50, 52, 62 n. 4, 66, 129–30, 132–3, 136–40, 143, 146–7, 151, 153–4, 157, 159–60, 163–78, 181–2, 187–9, 191, 198
  economic 19–20, 50, 101, 131–3, 136, 143, 164–6, 169, 172, 174, 177–8, 180–2, 187–9, 191, 198
  social 11–12, 17, 19, 50, 52, 62 n. 4, 63, 133, 146, 148, 151, 157, 159, 163–6, 168–76, 178–9, 181–2, 188–9, 191, 198
  subcultural 26, 167–8. 172, 190 n. 1
  symbolic 17, 19, 50, 63, 131 n. 6, 133, 139, 164–5, 169, 172–4, 178, 181, 191, 198
capitalism 29, 46
capitalist 12, 52, 58, 73, 101, 173, 179
Chicago School 28
class (socio-economic) 6–7, 25, 28–9, 34, 83–7, 118 n. 3, 120, 124, 140, 156–9, 170
club (nightclub) 4, 8–9, 25, 60, 71, 76, 78, 80, 125
city
  creative 18, 59, 61, 64–5, 72
  music 18–19, 47 n. 11, 57, 59–65, 70–2, 98–9, 103–7

Cohen, Sara 32
communitas 35
community (communities) 5, 9, 11–12, 14, 20, 34, 38–39, 44, 57, 61–63, 70, 100, 101, 102, 105, 138, 140, 141
  marginalized 13, 115, 198
  music 11, 26, 32–34, 36–7, 43, 50, 71, 79, 135, 137, 142–3
  practice 6, 12, 106, 166
cosmopolitan (cosmopolitanism) 32, 44, 70, 103, 117
counterculture 24–5
country (music) 6, 103–4, 155, 176
COVID-19 14, 17, 20, 47 n.10, 71, 87 n.23, 98–100, 116, 132 n. 7, 138, 185–6, 189, 192, 194–6
creative and cultural industries 12, 16, 18, 20, 61, 105–6, 194, 197, 200
creative class 62–3, 121
creative milieu 46
cultural
  consumption 18, 23–4, 27, 29–33, 36, 42, 53, 62, 65, 99–100, 105, 114, 140, 159, 164–6, 184, 190
  economy 13, 15–16, 65, 69, 95, 100, 183–6, 192–4, 197–9
  exchange 20, 43
  geography 43, 64 n. 5
  institutions 20, 90, 119, 122, 192–3, 196–7
  intermediaries 17, 19–20, 59, 160, 163–4, 189, 191–2
  production 5–6, 11–21, 24, 62–3, 65–6, 105, 114, 140, 163–6, 183, 188, 190–3
  small 13, 47, 101, 113, 122, 131, 174, 181, 185, 188, 192–3
  studies 23, 35, 53, 62, 64 n. 5, 165, 171
  worker (*see creative and cultural industries workers*)
culture
  'high' 7
  musical 6, 13, 26, 51, 54, 67, 102, 141, 186, 190–3, 197
cultural sociology 6, 23, 35, 62
curation 9, 13, 20, 81, 130, 164, 173, 175, 177–8
curator 9, 173–4, 179, 187

DeNora, Tia 154, 165
doxa 39, 41, 180
Dunstan, Don 82–3

Elizabeth, Australia 84–6
entry-level
  bands (*see also emerging artists*) 128
  performance spaces 5, 13, 127, 134
Environmental Protection Authority (EPA) 49–50, 49 n. 12
ethnography (ethnographic) 18–20, 27, 33, 111
Europe 13–14, 20, 86
'event'
  everyday 154–5
  live music 3–4, 15–16, 23–24, 26, 45–46, 49, 51, 53–54, 103, 112, 150, 155–58, 173–5, 178, 184, 188–9
  social 45, 109
  spatial 115
exclusion 10, 114–15, 130, 170, 197–9

festivals 3, 24, 66, 100, 103–4
field 10, 19, 34, 34 n. 3, 42, 54, 114–16, 128, 131, 141, 146–8, 150, 153, 159, 163 n. 1, 163–78, 181, 185–6, 191, 198
Finnegan, Ruth 32, 54
Florida, Richard 59, 61–5, 77, 97
folk (music) 6, 32, 79, 103, 176
formal 7, 33, 79, 118, 145, 154, 163
formality. *See* formal
France (French) 13 n. 6, 37, 171 n. 3, 195
Frith, Simon 53, 175
front bar 9, 111, 113, 126–7, 131, 143–52

gatekeeping (gatekeepers) 6, 13, 37, 173–4, 178
genre 6–7, 25–6, 31, 37, 49, 67–9, 79, 101–5, 110, 141–2, 155
gentrification 64, 117–23, 135–37, 197
Gibson, Chris 40–1, 103–4, 159 n. 20
gig 4, 109–10, 112–13, 154–5, 158
globalization 25, 29–30, 32, 42–4, 67, 86
goth 28, 39, 43
Greater London Council (GLC) 65
grunge 38, 75, 109, 121–4, 127, 155

habitus 10, 19, 114–16, 129–30, 133, 142, 146, 148–51, 153, 157–8, 160, 163–5, 169–71, 174–8, 181, 191, 198
hardcore 5, 38, 69 n. 8, 79
hegemony (hegemonic) 13, 24, 26, 28–9, 43, 61, 168, 190, 199
Hennion, Antoine 165
hierarchy
    cultural 7, 167
hobbyist 11, 35, 158
homology 25, 28
hyperpop 39

identity (identities) 12, 13 n. 7, 23, 26–30, 32, 37, 40, 48–9, 53, 62, 103, 109–10, 114–15, 125, 128, 136, 142, 154, 157, 159, 166, 187, 190–1, 197–9
inclusion 10, 32, 114, 197, 199
informal 6, 8, 11–12, 17–18, 20, 27, 33, 35, 74, 76, 78–80, 91–2, 145, 150–2, 158, 164, 168, 177, 183, 187, 197, 199
informality (*see also* informal) 17, 74, 150
infrastructure
    built (*see* hard infrastructure)
    cultural (*see* live music ecosystem)
    digital 47
    hard 10 n. 3, 31, 35, 45, 61, 74, 80
    live music (*see* live music ecosystem)
    physical (*see* hard infrastructure)
    soft 61–2, 61 n. 3
instruments 7
instrumentalization 20, 59, 61–4, 164–6, 180, 187, 189, 193
instrumental value. *See* instrumentalization
intellectual property (IP) 15–16
interdependence 8, 51–3, 58, 175, 179, 185, 190
intimacy (*see also* intimate) 6–7, 10, 19, 40, 44, 111, 134, 152
intimate 4, 7, 10–12, 25, 109, 140, 147–8, 152–3, 200
Ireland 195

jazz 6, 15, 79
JobKeeper 14, 185, 194–5

Kronenburg, Robert 6, 112
Kruse, Holly 32

labour
    creative 6, 16–17, 47–8, 180–1, 191–2
Landry, Charles 59, 61, 61 n. 3, 65
live music
    sector 17, 20–1, 45, 51, 100, 117, 164, 180, 186, 192–3, 195
live music ecology (*see also* live music ecosystem) 10, 17–18, 20, 23–4, 27, 35, 45–8, 52–4, 177, 183–4, 189–91
live music ecosystem, 4, 10, 16, 18, 27, 45–53, 58, 66, 68, 100–1, 115–8, 151, 155–6, 174–9, 183–6, 190–1, 199–200
live music venue
    grassroots 6, 63, 72, 98, 100–1, 106
    large 3, 10, 12, 78, 148
    medium 75, 91, 145 nn. 14–16
    small 4–21, 57–8, 100–2, 105–7, 114, 154, 164, 180–1, 187–200
localism 38, 42–4, 68

mainstream 7, 13, 24–5, 29, 69, 75, 102, 114, 125, 158, 171, 195, 197–8
'making do' 8, 74
managers 20, 48, 124, 132, 164
manufacturing 25, 85–6, 119–20, 124
Massey, Doreen 115, 156
material environment. *See* built environment
materiality 9, 23, 33, 45–6, 49–50, 53–4, 106, 113, 115, 127, 134, 150, 160, 184, 187–8
Melbourne, Australia 8–9, 19, 37, 50, 67–70, 73, 79, 86, 91, 98–9, 111–13, 116–21, 124–5, 127–8, 130–1, 133–9, 154, 159–60, 174, 176, 178, 191
memory 4, 9, 41, 53, 148
merchandise 15–16, 136, 181, 184
metal 25, 68, 69 n. 8, 79, 102 n. 30
metropolitan 36, 84–5, 117
music business studies 35
music industries 9, 11–12, 14, 16, 33, 36, 46–8, 68, 71–2, 89, 105, 169, 173, 183–4, 192–4

musician
    emerging 5, 12, 109, 155
    up-and-coming (*see also* emerging musicians) 5, 11–12, 109

neoliberal 52, 62, 65, 105, 179, 192
network 15, 19, 34, 37–8, 46–8, 53–4, 58, 62, 66–9, 74, 83, 89, 100, 105, 115, 117, 130, 133, 135, 142–3, 155, 166, 169, 172–3, 176, 182. 185, 188, 190, 194, 200
networking 11–12, 66, 144, 148, 168
New Zealand 13, 37
niche
    appeal 11, 13, 24, 58, 75, 102, 114, 188, 197–8
    audience 14, 187
    music 7, 13, 181
    spaces, 5–6, 11–13, 17–21, 27, 43, 80, 82, 98, 100, 105, 114, 119, 140, 157, 163–6, 168, 172, 178, 180, 182, 187–8, 191–2, 197–8 (*see also* small live music venue)
    venues (*see* niche spaces)
nightlife. *See* night-time economy
night-time economy 10, 57–9, 66, 69, 74, 76–7, 81–2, 88–9, 91, 102, 197
not-for-profit 12, 76, 80, 96, 101, 118

patron 41, 48, 57, 75, 113, 117, 126–8, 130, 132–5, 137, 139, 143, 145–7, 158, 187, 199
patronage 14, 132
place
    making 8, 17, 37, 40–1, 102, 107, 115
policy
    makers 33, 46, 49, 51, 54, 66, 72, 106, 121, 136–7, 177, 194, 199
    settings 10 n. 3, 18, 33, 35, 45, 58, 70, 76, 83, 105–6, 184–5, 189–91
popular music
    academic study 23, 35, 42, 111, 171, 190
    culture 23–4, 35, 73, 85, 183–4
post-subcultural 26, 28, 30, 183
precarious (*see also* precarity) 5, 17, 92, 105, 123, 136, 180, 195
precarity 6, 12–15, 20–1, 80, 105, 136, 164, 180, 197–9

profit 5, 12, 14, 21, 53, 64, 76, 80, 89, 105, 117, 131, 132 n. 7, 179–81, 191–3, 196
proximity. *See* intimacy
pub 9, 20, 40, 49, 69, 74, 88, 121, 123, 132, 139–42, 158
pub rock 40, 88, 120, 142, 158
punk 4–5, 25–6, 28, 38–9, 43, 74 n. 15, 79, 94, 109

recording studio 10, 79
record label 14, 38, 51, 65
record store 10, 31
regional, rural and remote 19, 100–1, 104
rehearsal room 31, 121
Renew 59, 95–8
revenue 19–20, 76, 131, 164, 173, 182, 187, 188, 191
rock and roll 6, 8, 136
rockist (rockism) 138, 159

Save Live Australia's Music (SLAM) 59, 117–18, 136
scene (music)
    local, 4–5, 9–12, 17–19, 23–24, 26–44, 48–54, 62, 65, 67–9, 109–10, 114–16, 118, 148, 156–7, 159–60, 165–6, 169–82, 183–9, 199–200
    studies 31, 33, 35–7, 45, 49, 53
    translocal, 31, 35, 37–9, 43–5, 51, 67–9
    virtual 35, 44–5
Shank, Barry 31–2
Shaw, Kate 64–5, 196
SME 47, 105, 192, 194
sociability. *See* sociality
social actors 10 n. 3, 28, 31, 33, 36–40, 45–6, 50–3, 116, 130–1, 148, 155, 173, 175, 177, 179, 182–9, 199
social agents. *See* social actors
social hub 5, 10, 12, 19–20, 128, 172, 174, 188–9, 192
social interaction. *See* socialization
social network analysis 23
sociality 5–7, 9–11, 16–20, 26–7, 30–5, 39, 41, 68, 110–11, 141, 143, 146–8, 153, 156, 163–5, 179, 181, 185, 187–8, 191, 193, 200
socialization (*see also* sociality) 5, 8, 66, 142, 169

sociology 154
space
    adapted 8–9, 50, 57, 73–4, 80, 106, 199
    adopted 9, 112 n. 1
    'alternative' 71, 76, 102, 125–6, 140, 159, 178
    bricks-and-mortar (*see* physical space)
    cultural 5–6, 13, 28, 31, 36, 40, 58–9, 88, 98, 105–6, 179, 187, 191, 193, 197–8
    physical 7, 111–12, 115–16, 157
    social 12, 30, 34, 41, 44, 115–16, 133–4, 141, 143–52, 157, 159–60, 170, 173–4, 176, 182, 187–9
    spatial 8–9, 31, 35, 40–1, 45, 48–9, 82, 91, 94, 116, 141, 143–53, 157, 160, 184, 187–8, 197
spatiality. *See* spatial
stadium (concert) 3–4, 7
stage 7, 16, 75, 77, 127, 152–3
start-up 14
state (government) 13–14, 46, 58, 69, 72–3, 77, 87–8, 90, 97–8, 104, 185–6, 192, 195–6, 200
status 9, 17, 19, 29, 61, 117, 133, 138, 153–4, 157, 159, 164, 171–8, 199
'stepping-stone' 12, 189, 200
Straw, Will 26, 28, 31–2, 35, 39, 42–3, 62, 67
subculture 18, 23–32, 35, 46, 54, 64–5, 110, 167–8, 183–4, 190
sustainability
    cultural 5, 51, 65, 131, 155, 160, 173, 177, 179, 182
    financial 5, 57, 106, 156, 166, 173–4, 190
Sydney, Australia 60, 69–70, 73, 86, 99, 122

tacit knowledge 33, 40, 66, 129, 143, 163, 173, 177, 181
taste 29, 39, 41–2, 85, 147, 156–9, 165, 170–4, 177, 198
tenure 8, 64, 82, 193, 196, 200
Thornton, Sarah 167, 171 n. 3
tradition (musical) 6–7, 32, 111
translocalism 43, 49, 68
Triple J 67, 75, 91, 177

UNESCO 82, 86, 98–9
Unions 88, 194
United Kingdom (UK) 13, 20, 37, 45, 180 n. 8
United States, the (US) 6, 13, 20, 37–8, 155

value
    chain 19–20, 105, 188
    cultural 5, 10, 17, 19–21, 64–6, 98, 101, 116, 122, 163–4, 181–2, 187–8, 191–3
    economic 181, 191, 193
    intangible 27, 172, 191
    intrinsic 20, 164–6, 187
    social 118, 163 n. 2, 198
vaudeville 6
vernacular culture 40–2, 57, 138, 146–8, 153
vibe 4, 7, 120, 143–5, 151, 153
vibrancy 4, 21, 57, 59, 65–6, 81, 105, 196
volunteer 12, 196

White Australia policy 85
Williams, Raymond 11 n. 4
Wright, David 165

youth 7, 24–6, 28–30, 67, 74, 76, 85, 88–91, 125

www.ingramcontent.com/pod-product-compliance
Lightning Source LLC
Chambersburg PA
CBHW052037300426
44117CB00012B/1856